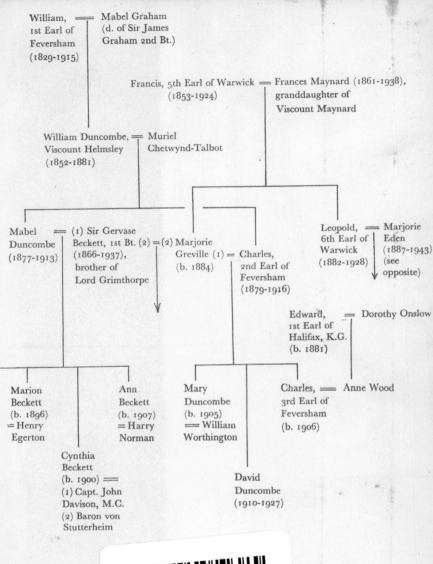

William, === Mabel Graham
1st Earl of   (d. of Sir James
Feversham   Graham 2nd Bt.)
(1829-1915)

Francis, 5th Earl of Warwick === Frances Maynard (1861-1938),
        (1853-1924)   granddaughter of
                                     Viscount Maynard

William Duncombe, === Muriel
Viscount Helmsley   Chetwynd-Talbot
(1852-1881)

Mabel === (1) Sir Gervase (2) === (2) Marjorie   Leopold, === Marjorie
Duncombe   Beckett, 1st Bt.   Greville (1) === Charles,   6th Earl of   Eden
(1877-1913) (1866-1937),   (b. 1884)   2nd Earl of Warwick   (1887-1943)
            brother of   Feversham   (1882-1928)   (see
            Lord Grimthorpe   (1879-1916)   opposite)

                                                    Edward, === Dorothy Onslow
                                                    1st Earl of
                                                    Halifax, K.G.
                                                    (b. 1881)

Marion   Ann   Mary   Charles, === Anne Wood
Beckett   Beckett   Duncombe   3rd Earl of
(b. 1896)   (b. 1907)   (b. 1905)   Feversham
= Henry   = Harry   === William   (b. 1906)
Egerton   Norman   Worthington

        Cynthia
        Beckett
        (b. 1900) ===   David
        (1) Capt. John   Duncombe
        Davison, M.C.   (1910-1927)
        (2) Baron von
        Stutterheim

Sir Anthony Eden and the Author.
Congress of Europe, The Hague, May 1948

RANDOLPH S. CHURCHILL

The Rise and Fall of
SIR ANTHONY EDEN

MACGIBBON & KEE
LONDON
1959

Made and Printed in Great Britain by
The Garden City Press Limited
Letchworth, Hertfordshire

Contents

*Omnium consensu capax
imperii nisi imperasset.*

Preface

ONE week after I had agreed to embark upon this work Colonel Nasser nationalized the Suez Canal. Nineteen weeks were to elapse before Sir Anthony Eden's ill-planned, ill-timed and abortive invasion of Egypt and twenty-five weeks before the regrettable abandonment, through ill-health, of his political career.

The events which supervened in these six months have added considerable interest to the story, but they have inevitably affected the way in which it must be told. When I agreed to write this book Sir Anthony was the most powerful politician in the land. After a long, laborious and successful career he had risen to the eminence of power which he had long desired and for which he had long been marked. What would have been a simple success story with a question mark at the end has become tragedy on an almost classical scale. The fact that Sir Anthony was gravely ill at the time of his fall from power and that he is still far from being restored to full health and vigour naturally accentuates the sense of delicacy with which any author would approach the task of writing about a living character. At the same time, the fact that his political life is ended makes him and his career a part of history.

Now that his work is done, it is possible to take a more detached view of his personality and career than would perhaps have been possible while he was still playing the leading role in the hurly-burly of contemporary politics.

The fact that it was a breakdown in his health which led to Sir Anthony's withdrawal from public life naturally evoked the sympathy of every generous mind, and since this objective appraisal which has been my aim may be thought

by some people in some respects to be of a critical nature
it is only right to state at the outset that it is my firm
conviction that even if Sir Anthony had never been the
victim of ill-health his tenure of power could not have
been prolonged for more than a few weeks. Even before the
Suez misadventure there were many of his colleagues who
felt that he was inadequate to the task and that he would
have to be replaced as quickly and as kindly as possible by
someone with a more robust political stamina.

After Suez this was more than ever true and urgent, and
though it is impossible, even with political hindsight, to
assert what would have been the method by or the moment
at which Sir Anthony would have been removed from
power, there can be little doubt that this would soon have
happened whatever the state of his health.

Writing in the *Evening Standard* of 1 January 1957,
when it was generally supposed that the Prime Minister's
health had been restored by his sojourn in Jamaica, the
author said:

'Throughout the New Year and probably well into 1958,
the country will be paying for the economic consequences of
Sir Anthony Eden. As the bill mounts the Government will
become more and more unpopular; by-elections will go
less and less favourably for the Tory Party.

'Sir Anthony will hang on for some time under the
increasingly vigilant *chaperonage* of Lord Salisbury, Mr.
Butler and Mr. Macmillan.

'This situation will become increasingly irksome to all
concerned.

'As it becomes apparent that the Tories cannot win a
General Election without new leadership, there will be
growing unrest in the party's ranks.

'The feeling will grow that if a change is necessary, the
sooner the better, so that there will be sufficient time for the
Tory Party to acquire a new look and for the country to
have a chance of resuming its economic recovery before a
General Election.

'. . . Granted the foregoing, it seems likely that some method will be found of easing Sir Anthony out of the leadership and into the Lords some time in the spring or early summer. . . .'

The majority of Sir Anthony's colleagues were beginning to lose confidence in him and in his sagacity and administrative powers well before Suez; and during and after the Suez Crisis this diminution of confidence continued at an accelerating rate not only among those—and they were more numerous than generally supposed—who were opposed to the venture, but also among those who were his ardent supporters.

It is easy to be a fair-weather pilot and there are many Toms, Dicks and Harrys who could run a country without misadventure on a calm sea and cooled and aided by favourable breezes. The supreme test of a politician's character is how he behaves in rough weather when he is at the helm. Quite a long time before Suez a number of Sir Anthony's most powerful and perspicacious colleagues had begun to doubt whether he was 'the pilot to weather the storm'.

It is these considerations which have led the author to the belief that it is his duty to persevere in this task. Britain's situation in the world today is on the decline. This process can only be arrested if we brush all false sentimentality aside and try to see the harsh facts of life as they are with no distortion of class or party. It is with this thought constantly in mind that this political and strategic inquisition has been conducted.

Stour, East Bergholt

CHAPTER ONE

Some Assessments

THERE seems to have been something almost inevitable about the political career of Sir Anthony Eden. With the one exception of his resignation from the Chamberlain Government in 1938 his life has been strangely sheltered. Early marked out as a man of promise, he has seldom run risks, but has proceeded up the rungs of the political ladder in a decorous fashion, proving himself serviceable to his superiors and with some spectacular exceptions urbane and courteous to his contemporaries and his juniors.

Elected to Parliament in 1923 at the age of twenty-six he soon became Parliamentary Private Secretary to Sir Austen Chamberlain, who was at that time Foreign Secretary in Mr. Baldwin's Conservative administration. This first political step was to prove decisive in his career. Thereafter, with the exception of a brief spell at the Dominions Office and the War Office in 1939 and 1940, he has been exclusively concerned with the work of the Foreign Office. As Under-Secretary, and later as Minister for League of Nations Affairs, he became, on the dismissal of Sir Samuel Hoare over the Hoare-Laval affair, in 1935, at the early age of thirty-eight, Secretary of State for Foreign Affairs.

Eden had already caught the public imagination. His good looks, his charming smile, his elegant clothes, and his evident attachment to the cause of the League won him golden opinions from the public. Nor were these confined to the Tory Party. Socialists and Liberals were also attracted by the glamour of what appeared to be a new Sir Galahad. It was clear that a new star had been born in the political firmament and he soon far outshone in public favour the mediocrities from whose ranks he had risen.

Mr. Baldwin had won the General Election of 1935 on a policy of firm support of the League of Nations against Mussolini's colonial war in Abyssinia. When his Foreign Secretary, Sir Samuel Hoare, attempted a settlement with M. Laval which smacked of appeasement, Hoare came tumbling down and Eden received his dramatic promotion. This appointment was meant by Baldwin to be a guarantee to the country that the policy of collective security on which the election had been fought and won was to be adhered to in the future. Meanwhile Baldwin resigned, and Neville Chamberlain became Prime Minister. He was alarmed by the growing war clouds which were gathering on the horizon and was firmly convinced that he could negotiate a practical settlement with both Mussolini and Hitler.

He encouraged Eden to begin negotiations in London with the Italian Ambassador, Count Grandi; and when he thought that Eden was making undue difficulties in the conversations he transferred them from the Foreign Office to No. 10 Downing Street. This was the actual issue on which Eden resigned, but there was a background to it which did not become known till many years later. Three weeks before, while Eden was abroad, President Roosevelt had telegraphed to the British Government suggesting that he should take some initiative in calling a conference in Washington which might ease the tensions of Europe. Without consulting the Foreign Secretary, Chamberlain sent a chilly response to this overture. On his return from the Continent Eden persuaded Chamberlain and the Cabinet to send a message of a more friendly character; but by this time the moment had passed. Roosevelt felt rebuffed.

There was therefore already ill-feeling between Chamberlain and Eden when the break came on the Italian question and Chamberlain was quite happy to let Eden go. Eden acquired added lustre through his resignation. For a young man who had just received the second or third highest office in the State to take his career in his hands and seem to throw it away on a matter of principle stirred the heart and mind of the nation. In fact the prime mover in Eden's resignation was his parliamentary Under-Secretary, Lord Cranborne, now Marquess of Salisbury, who indicated that he would resign in any case. This was the final factor in Eden's decision. Of their two resignation speeches in the House, Cranborne's was thought to be the more forceful and effective. But it was naturally Eden, in his superior station, whose laurels were the more gilded in public esteem.

On leaving the Government Eden did not attach himself to the more powerful and growing group of sixty or seventy members whom Mr. Winston Churchill had gathered round him while preaching the cause of collective security and re-armament in the face of the growing menace of Hitler. On the advice of Lord Baldwin (as he had by then become), he joined a small group which was presided over by Captain Sidney Herbert and which included the veteran statesman Mr. Leopold Amery. When a few weeks after he had left the Government Hitler marched into Austria, Eden conspicuously failed to add his views to those of Churchill in protesting against this unlawful act of violence. None the less, when Neville Chamberlain invited Winston Churchill to join the Government on the outbreak of war in 1939, the latter insisted that Eden should also be included. It was in these circumstances that Eden became Secretary of State for the Dominions.

Nine months later when Neville Chamberlain fell and Winston Churchill became Prime Minister, Eden was moved to the War Office; but after a few months the Foreign Secretary, Lord Halifax, was appointed in the place of Lord Lothian as Ambassador to Washington and Eden returned once more to the Foreign Office.

In 1943 when Lord Linlithgow ceased to be Viceroy of India this glittering appointment was offered to Eden and he considered long and carefully before he rejected it. If he had gone to India he would almost certainly have destroyed his chances of becoming Prime Minister. For, by long usage, as Viceroy he would have had to accept a peerage; and today a peerage is an almost insuperable obstacle to the premiership. All who have had the opportunity of studying him at work agree that his outstanding gifts are for diplomatic negotiation. And in the war when a whole host of international conferences replaced the normal workings of diplomacy through Ambassadors, he had ample scope for these talents which he certainly possesses in the highest degree. In his fourteen points President Wilson urged that the world should adopt a system of 'open covenants openly arrived at'. Eden has employed a different technique which he now advertises as his slogan—'open agreements arrived at secretly'. The American State Department have now sensibly accepted this technique.

Eden's talent for diplomacy has grown with use and was certainly never seen to finer advantage than at the conference in 1955 in Geneva about Indo-China which culminated in the cease-fire agreement. The United States Secretary of State, Mr. John Foster Dulles, had flown off in a dudgeon. The Prime Minister of France, M. Laniel, fell in the middle of the conference and for ten anxious days Eden was left to hold the Western Fort alone against the tough and wily tactics of Mr. Molotov and Mr. Chou-En-lai, until with the arrival of the new French Prime Minister, M. Mendes-France, an agreement was concluded. This was an outstanding diplomatic triumph and, if it had not been achieved, the French might have suffered in Indo-China a worse fate than that which befell the British Army at Dunkirk in 1940.

His diplomatic talents were also seen to advantage when he succeeded in enlarging the Brussels Treaty as a substitute for the defunct E.D.C. This won him his Garter.

His arduous and successful negotiations at Geneva were a fine achievement on the part of a man who had only recently recovered from a series of dangerous operations. The year before a most severe abdominal operation in London proved unsuccessful and Eden would almost certainly have died except for the vigorous action taken by his young wife. She found out that there was a surgeon in America, Dr. Cattell, who had performed this new and delicate operation nearly one hundred times. With extraordinary pertinacity and energy, she arranged for Eden to be flown to America and for the operation to be attempted a second time in Boston, this time with triumphant success. He had been in poor health for many years. With his marriage and his operation he seems to have entered upon a new lease of life and has now more robust health than he has had for a very long time.

Eden served with gallantry as a regimental officer in the King's Royal Rifle Corps in the first world war and was awarded the Military Cross. His physical courage and indifference to danger are of a high order. Before the second war a flat was built on the roof of the Foreign Office for the use of Lord Halifax. It was in one of the most exposed situations in London. Eden slept there throughout the blitz and the subsequent aerial bombardment of London. Eden had left Eton to enter the Army, and it was as a man, matured and seasoned by war, that he went to Christ Church, Oxford, soon after he had been demobilized. His contemporaries judged him to be a little aloof and he passed his days with a small group of friends who were of a mildly artistic bent. Apart from lawn tennis, he was not active in the field of sport, but devoted himself seriously to his studies. He chose the unusual school of Oriental Languages and obtained first-class honours in it, becoming, in the process, fluent in Arabic and Persian and an expert in Sanskrit.

In the modern world men find it difficult to lead a genuinely private life. Eden has been notably successful in keeping his private life private. By his first wife he had two sons to whom he has been a devoted father. His eldest son, Simon, was killed on active service in the Royal Air Force during the second world war. The surviving son, Nicholas, has no political aspirations, but is on the closest terms with his father.

For nearly all his adult life Eden has been a full-time politician who has applied himself with assiduity to his chosen profession. Few of his contemporaries have worked as hard as he. The main recreation of his leisure hours has been gardening. He not only knows a great deal about flowers, but works long hours digging in his garden. This he finds takes his mind off politics. Despite his appetite for international conferences he is sometimes bored by the interminable harangues and will close his eyes. When he does so, the odds are that he is re-charging his batteries by thinking about gardening.

Eden is an admirer of Cézanne and while at Oxford wrote a paper on the French impressionist in which he remarked: 'To live entirely for his art, to remove all else: that was the example Cézanne gave to us.' Eden has certainly tried to live up to this maxim in his political life. He is a good judge of Dunoyer de Ségonzac's pictures and though a man of modest means, he has acquired a number of fine pictures including four or five Dunoyer de Ségonzacs which he bought many years ago for five or six pounds apiece and each of which is probably now worth one thousand pounds. He is much better read than the average English politician and is a considerable student of Shakespeare, much of which he knows by heart and which his intimates often encourage him to read aloud.

There are scores of people who have known Eden for thirty years or more who say that they do not know him any better now than they did when they first met him. Is this because he is reserved and somewhat aloof? Or because there isn't really very much more to know? Is he in reality a sphinx without a secret? No epigram or witticism has ever been attributed to him and he has never made a speech which showed any real originality or distinction of thought. Nor has he ever employed any memorable phrase. He has been credited with having coined the phrase 'a property-owning democracy' which has now become the main theme of the philosophy and aspirations of the Tory Party. It was in fact

first used by Mr. Noel Skelton, the Conservative M.P. for
the Scottish Universities.

It has been said of him that he has no enemies and few
friends. There is something in this. He is not at all what
Dr. Johnson called 'a clubbable man'. He is seldom seen
in the smoking room of the House of Commons and, except
for his immediate entourage, much prefers the adulatory
company of young men and women to that of his contemporaries. This, in a busy politician, is perhaps understandable.

In all the spheres of life, and in none perhaps more than
in politics, there is a tremendous gulf between being number
two and being number one. In his long period of tutelage,
Eden has perhaps had to face a more than the average share
of frustration. And this may account for the vanity, pettiness
and occasional tantrums which he has in the past displayed.
His marriage three years ago to Miss Clarissa Churchill
may well have been a turning point in the development of
his character. Someone who knows him better than most
people said recently that instead of being a politician who
was not quite sure of himself, he is now a self-confident
statesman.

Time will tell. Now that he has achieved the peak of his
life-long ambition at an age a good deal earlier than it comes
to most men (Neville Chamberlain became Prime Minister
at sixty-eight; Winston Churchill at sixty-six) he may
mature very rapidly and in the rarefied atmosphere at the
summit may feel himself more at home than he has ever
felt before. It has been cynically observed that there are no
friends at the top. This may make it easier for him to feel at
home.

★

This is what I wrote about Sir Anthony Eden at the time
when he became Prime Minister. It was substantially
published in the *American Weekly* on 15 May 1955, and the
Evening Standard of May 23. It was intended as an objective

appraisal and was based on the observations of a quarter of a century from different angles and different distances. It will be readily apparent that I never supposed that Sir Anthony, despite his lengthy service in a junior station, was likely to be a successful Prime Minister.

In the light of all that has taken place in the last three years it seems of interest to make a new and more searching assessment of his career and to consider to what extent the judgment of four years ago has been confirmed or invalidated.*

* It should be stated at the outset that the author, on the basis of further information, now rejects his earlier view that Lord Cranborne was the prime mover in Mr. Eden's resignation in 1938.

CHAPTER TWO

Youth

Robert Anthony Eden was born at Windlestone, which had for more than three hundred years been the chief seat of the Eden family, on 12 June 1897. The records at Somerset House suggest that it had originally been intended that he should take his first name from his father. His birth was registered in the registration sub-district of Bishop Auckland as William Anthony Eden. However, when two and a half months later he came to be christened at St. James's, Coundon, on September 4 the name Robert, another family name, was substituted for William.

He was the fourth child whom Lady Eden had borne; and the infant Anthony (as he was to be known) found himself in a nursery with a sister, Marjorie, aged ten, and two brothers, John, aged eight, and Timothy, aged four. Three years later a fifth child, Nicholas, was born. Like his eldest brother John he was to die in early manhood in the first world war. John, serving as a lieutenant in the 12th Lancers, was killed in action in France on 17 October 1914. Nicholas, who served as a midshipman in the Royal Navy, was also killed in action almost twenty months later at the Battle of Jutland on 31 May 1916. Thus it came about that on the death of Sir William Eden in 1915 the baronetcy devolved upon Timothy. He had been travelling in Germany when the war came and he was interned in the Ruhleben camp for two years. However, upon his release, he was commissioned as a lieutenant in the late Yorkshire Light Infantry and served from 1917 to 1918.

Anthony, though he had longer war service than any of his brothers and nearly all of it as a regimental officer, was, like Timothy, to survive.

These five children who spent their youth at Windlestone were the product of unusual parents.

Sir William Eden, 7th Baronet of West Auckland and 5th Baronet of Maryland, came of a family which had played a substantial and varied role in the life of the nation. It had been settled in County Durham since the sixteenth century. The five children of Sir William Eden grew up in a prosperous and in some ways an agreeable home.

Some biographers have speculated as to the influence on Anthony of his father, mother and governess. It is not the purpose of this book, which aspires to deal seriously with the political career of its subject, to pry into family matters nor to speculate upon matters which belong more properly to the private than to the public life of a well-known statesman. For the purpose of this biography it is enough to say that the young Anthony grew to manhood in surroundings not markedly different from those of young men of his class in that golden, or at least silver-gilt, Edwardian epoch which preceded the 1914 war. Anthony, like his sister and brothers, went in considerable awe of his father, and though he had a genuine respect and admiration for him there does not seem to have been any of the easy intimacy which characterizes the relationship of so many fathers and sons. His mother, like many other great beauties, was a spoiled woman and she never extended the same love and sympathy towards Anthony as she did towards her first-born John, and Nicholas, the Benjamin of the family. Friends of the family are convinced that Anthony, though he concealed it, felt injured in his self-esteem, and that this injury was the motive force of the quest for self-sufficiency which has dominated his whole life, both private and public; though life at Windlestone was outwardly elegant, gay and varied, there were inward repressions which inevitably affected the character and personality of the growing boy.

Sir William Eden, the heir to long tradition of public service, was in some ways the most extraordinary personality whom this family produced, not excepting any of his children.

Much has been written about Sir William Eden, his talents
and eccentricities, his splendid horsemanship in the hunting-
field, his artistic taste, his unusual ability in water-colour,
his proneness to controversy, especially in minor matters.
His son Sir Timothy Eden, in his penetrating book *The
Tribulations of a Baronet*, gives ample evidence of all these.
Of the last characteristic the following extract, which
concerns a dispute he had at Boodle's Club, seems especially
revealing:

> . . . Sir William Eden, unaware of a new rule that members
> must dine in evening dress, was dining in the club in day
> clothes when he was requested by a waiter, acting apparently
> under the instructions of a member of the committee, to leave
> the room, as he was improperly dressed. Unfortunately we
> have no record of the scene which must thereupon have taken
> place. We can only imagine it. But the ultimate result was that
> Eden resigned from the club.

'*Private, confidential and without prejudice*

'Dear Colonel.—Very many thanks for your letter. As you
say, "the incident was a disagreable one" (disagreeable one,
you should say, Colonel)—to be told by a waiter and, as it
appeared, on the suggestion or instruction of a member of the
committee to leave the dining-room as being improperly
dressed, is an indignity that I do not care to put up with
again. I was not aware of the new rule or should not have
exposed myself to your mercy.

'I have been thirty-five years or so a member of Boodle's,
and had I been in your place, I should have looked the other
way, have sacked the waiter, and held my peace.

'But these things, dear Colonel, are a matter of taste—like
evening clothes. After all, what *are* evening clothes? and who
should wear them? That is a matter of taste and opinion. My
own is certainly against that of Boodle's Club, as now regulated.

'Fortunately, I am still a member of other clubs—the
National Sporting, for instance, where the amiable President
is resplendent, if I mistake not, in a black jumper jacket, a
diamond stud, a black tie and a white waistcoat. Now this
again is evening dress, but not according to my bad taste.

'But Bombardier Billy Wells does, I think, wear faultless evening dress, for I have seen him in my house. But then he too might fail to please at Boodle's for he doesn't wear a yellow waistcoat which I notice is much affected by the committee at Boodle's. Now I haven't got a yellow waistcoat, so what am I to do? I *can* only resign and leave the club—for if I had a yellow waistcoat I really could not wear it, even to please your refined and elegant waiter.

'Fortunately again, I have still other clubs—the Turf and Travellers' to wit, and I cannot find that there are any similar regulations at these pot-houses, or any particular instructions as to how to dress.

"NO, thanks, dear Colonel; the decision is irrevocable, I must meet you with a *coup de chapeau* and wish you good-day, at the same time thanking *you* particularly and most sincerely, and the committee, members and head waiter to boot, for all their past and many kindnesses.'

Mingled in his arrogance and eccentricity and near madness he had an engaging sense of humour, as this further extract from his son's book shows:

. . . The following note was drawn up to greet the butler on his return from a half-holiday:

'LIST OF GRIEVANCES FOR MR. HOUSE'S CONSIDERATION
>   Cold soup.
>   Fish not done.
>   Mutton tough.
>   Cabbage cold.
>   Wild duck tough, cold and high.

———————

>   Floor covered with bread and butter.
>   No toothpicks.
>   Dirty dishes.
>   No ice to the butter.
>   Small soda instead of large.
>   Small spoon instead of large for gravy.
>   *Sic transit gloria mundi.*
>   House to the rescue.
>   Amen.'

But the passages in the book which are pertinent to a study of Sir Anthony Eden's life concern Sir Timothy's relations with his children. Much more is known of the study of psychology today than at the time of which Sir Timothy writes, and the modern reader must form his own view of the likely effect on a sensitive young boy of a father of whom the following is recorded:

> ... He could not endure, for long, even the presence of his own children. He had not the patience to suffer their moods and tears. He was incapable of placing his intellect on a level with theirs. Their casual irresponsibility irritated him. Their language and habit of thought were almost as incomprehensible to him as his to them, and while they got on his nerves, he terrified them. When they were schoolboys, the fear of doing or saying the wrong thing and the public ridicule which would inevitably ensue made association with him, particularly before others, a torment to them.
>
> ... He wishes to make friends of his children, but he does not know how to approach them. He has always fled from them in the holidays. Now, when they are older, he resents their avoidance of him. Now when he wants them, when he is lonely, he cannot get them. They fear him, his rages, his abuse of those nearest to them, the sad silences in his warm room after dinner, when the stir of a log in the grate and the rustling of a newspaper make him jump and exclaim in nervous anger. They are bored with the lack of amusements in his company. They soon weary of the perpetual strain of artificial behaviour which seems necessary in his presence, the constant vigilance they must exert over their lightest words and deeds. They are too young to appreciate him, the harsh savour of his jest, his admiration and love for things which they take for granted or cannot see. And so his letters—'*You*, remember, have *got* to come'—are read with alarm, and every excuse is made to avoid going to him. Sometimes he insists, but rarely. He guesses their feelings. He knows himself to be out of touch with them.

It would probably be a mistake to draw too precise conclusions from the above. Victorian and even Edwardian parents of the upper classes, as they were then called, were by habit and tradition as much as by fashion and inclination far more remote from their children's lives than are their counterparts today. The greater intimacy which has come about in the last forty years between parents and children has not arisen through a radical transmogrification of human nature. Rather has it come from the more restricted accommodation available, the lack of staff, or servants, as the staff used to be called, and the consequent enforced propinquity of the two generations. A father who at the turn of the century thought it natural to send his children out hunting with the groom and had his sons taught to shoot by the keeper today assumes these responsibilities himself with added delight to young and old and increased cohesion to the family. The modern generation of parents, however, should not take undue heart of grace from this family and social transformation or allow itself to be misled into a feeling of smug superiority. It is unlikely that well-to-do parents today are inherently more enlightened and humane than their grandparents, or that they would not if they had the means still leave their children even in their holidays largely in the custody of nannies, governesses and tutors.

In fact many children in the Victorian and Edwardian eras never expected to enjoy much intimacy with their parents, and must have taken their remoteness from them as part of the natural state of society. In these circumstances they often formed strong attachments to their nurses and governesses. Anthony's affection for his governess, Miss Broomhead, was particularly strong. Not only, in common with the rest of the children, did he see so little of his parents; he inwardly felt that even within the narrow bounds of maternal affection he was specially disregarded.

★

In 1907, when he was ten years old, Eden went to the well-known preparatory school Sandroyd, near Cobham in Surrey. This was a fashionable school which in subsequent

years was attended by characters as varied as Sir Gladwyn
Jebb, Mr. Terence Rattigan, King Peter of Yugoslavia and
the author. During the second world war the school moved
to new accommodation near Salisbury in Wiltshire and has
remained there ever since. In his first year Eden won a
prize for French and in 1910 another for history. He does
not seem to have been outstanding in sport and the school
magazine, *The Sandroydian*, records in its issue of August
1907: 'Several new boys have learnt to swim. . . . Four
boys only now are unable to swim two lengths, Eve minor,
St. Clair, Eden, Wilson minor, but judging from their man-
ful efforts . . . it will not be long before they succeed.'
Subsequent issues of *The Sandroydian* do not chronicle if and
when Eden did; but it is known that in manhood he was a
powerful swimmer and derived great pleasure from sun
bathing.

In January 1911 Eden joined Mr. E. L. Churchill's*
house at Eton where he had been preceded by his elder
brother Timothy. Whereas *The Sandroydian* says of Timothy,
who took Upper Fourth at Eton, 'He has always taken more
than his share of prizes and has always been a keen gamester',
it said of his younger brother: 'Anthony Eden has taken the
Middle Fourth at Eton; he has hardly reached the standard
of his brother T.C. but principally owing to interruptions
in his work. Happily the family will still be represented at
Sandroyd after his departure.' The representative was
Nicholas, who on leaving Sandroyd went to the Royal Naval
College at Osborne.

Anthony's four years at Eton did not bring him outstanding distinction in either work or games. Nor do any
of his contemporaries or masters who survive remember
much about him.

Brigadier J. N. Cheney, who was a Lower boy when Eden
was an Upper and who is now Chief Constable of
Buckinghamshire, records that 'he was always very well
dressed and good-looking as a boy at Eton'. Another

* He was widely known as 'Jelly' Churchill.

contemporary, Lieutenant-General Sir Frederick Browning, now Treasurer to the Duke of Edinburgh, writes: 'My memory of him is that though he was not very distinguished at games or particularly at work he always struck all of us as possessing a considerable amount of quality.' Mr. F. W. Dobbs, a master at that time, says that Eden's housemaster told him how highly he thought of him and that Eden was 'liked and highly respected by everybody'. On the other hand Mr. T. F. Cattley, another master, writes: 'Two present masters, who were in the school when he was, make it clear that he was not in any way a conspicuous figure.' This is also confirmed by the Hon. George Lyttelton, also a master at Eton, who comments: 'Like so many Etonians who have distinguished after-careers, he was very inconspicuous at school. . . .'

Another master, Mr. W. Hope-Jones, who instructed him for a period in mathematics, seems to have been disappointed in his work. His remarks are as follows:

> He made no strong impression on me, as the best and the worst do; and for reminiscences of him I have nothing to go by except my mark-book. The last three of the Division (in Lent half, 1913) were:
>
> 16th,   Eden,   199.
> 17th,   Webb,   198.
> 18th,   Bruce,   176.

'Better manners than brains' was probably what I thought of him. . . .

Further rummaging in my mark-books has brought to light the fact, which I had forgotten, that he was up to me again in C4 in the Summer half, 1914. This time the list ended with:

> 14th,   Renton,   211.
> 15th,   Eden,   210.

but because 'equal 14 out of 15' looked more respectable than '15 out of 15', I counted him and Renton as 'equal 14'. In 1949, when the Mathematical Association met at Birmingham University, we were told that the Chancellor of the University would come and welcome us personally: so I took the old mark-book with me to show him how charitable I had been; but an important division in Parliament detained him, and so the poor dog had none.

Mr. Charles de Paravacini, son of the well-known cricketer and another contemporary, writes:

. . . Anthony Eden and I went to Eton the same half, January 1911, and were in the same Division for a couple of years or so. During that time I got to know him pretty well and came to realise, even at that age, that his outstanding characteristic was public spirit and thought for others.

Not being particularly clever, and certainly not very industrious in those days, I was often the object of his kindness in the shape of assistance with my work. His help was always given through sheer good nature and never to show off his own superiority.

At football he did not get his Field* but had his House colours. He was a wet-bob and got his Boats. From some old lists I have here I see he was in the Dreadnought.

Looking back over the years I think that his career has been a logical development of his character in the early days, i.e., sincerity, public spirit, and an immense capacity for taking trouble, added to a good, though not flashy, intellect. . . .

★

Like nearly all his contemporaries at Eton, Eden volunteered for the Army immediately after his eighteenth birthday and in September 1915 he was gazetted a lieutenant in the 21st Battalion the King's Royal Rifle Corps. This Battalion had been newly raised with a particular object which is well described in the *King's Royal Rifle Corps Chronicle* (1916):

. . . In the autumn of 1915, in consequence of the number of men of the farmer and yeomen class who were believed to be holding back from enlisting, it was decided that a Battalion composed of such men should be raised in the hopes that they would welcome service with those of their own ideas and manner of life. This hope was amply justified.

* The school football eleven.

In order to make the Battalion additionally attractive, it formed part of the King's Royal Rifle Corps, but the success of the scheme depended on the choice of the first Commanding Officer, and in the Earl of Feversham an ideal selection was made.

In April 1915, he took to France the Yorkshire Hussars, in which he had long served, but the Regiment being broken up into Divisional Cavalry, its Commanding Officer became surplus to requirements, and when offered the Command of the 'Yeoman Rifles' he gladly accepted. . . .

The men accepted were of a very high standard physically, educationally, and socially, and the Battalion prided itself on having less crime than any other in the service. In B Company there was not a single crime from November 1915, to September 1916. The full establishment was reached in December 1915 and on 24 January 1916 the Battalion moved from Duncombe Park—Lord Feversham's home—to Aldershot, becoming part of the 124th Brigade under Brigadier-General Clemson. Here it made an excellent name for itself both for work and play.

On 4 May 1916, it crossed to France, and after being in billets near Bailleul for about three weeks, went into the line near Ploegsteert, remaining there until the middle of August, at the end of which it moved to the Somme. By then it had attained a high fighting reputation.

On September 15 it took a notable part in an attack on the enemy's position to the East of Flers, carrying three lines of trenches, and establishing itself on, and holding the captured ground until relieved by troops of another division. The Battalion lost heavily, including its most gallant Colonel who fell gloriously at the head of the riflemen he had led further into the enemy's lines than any troops penetrated on that day.

The battalion was then withdrawn, but moving up, took part in the attack of October 7, when, although in support, it suffered greatly from enfilade machine-gun fire. The bravery of the men was beyond all praise, but that day the Yeoman Battalion ceased to exist. Of its original officers and men few were left, and it was completed by drafts composed principally of Londoners.

The remainder of the year was spent in ordinary trench

routine work. In October at Flers until the 16th, when they moved to Meteren and occupied the Bois Carre area and Ridge Wood until the end of December, with occasional periods of 'rest' in reserve at La Clytte.

Ploegsteert was inevitably anglicized to Plug Street. The battalion which K.R.R. relieved was the 6th Royal Scots Fusiliers, commanded at that time by Lieutenant-Colonel Winston Churchill, M.P. Both this and Eden's battalion formed part of the 9th Division, but there is no record that the two men, who were later to work together for so many years in peace and war, ever met at this time.

Eden served for about eighteen months with his battalion, of which he was appointed Adjutant at the exceptionally early age of nineteen. While leading a small trench raid he distinguished himself by rescuing his platoon sergeant, who had been badly wounded in the thigh, and bringing him safely back through the wire. For this act of gallantry he was awarded the Military Cross on 4 June 1917.

Subsequently Eden was promoted to the rank of captain and with the rank of temporary major served for some time at Brigade Headquarters before ending the war on the staff of General Sir Herbert Plumer's First Army.

When Eden was demobilized in 1919 his immediate future was uncertain. One biographer suggests that he considered going into the diplomatic corps. On the advice or insistence of his mother, however, he reluctantly agreed to go up to Christ Church; he felt that after four years of war service, Oxford would be 'going back to school'.

Eden read for the Honours School of Oriental Languages, one of the smallest schools in Oxford; the languages he studied were Persian and Arabic. This was an unorthodox school to choose, and his biographers offer varying explanations for this choice. One is that Eden was advised by Sir George Clark and that the advice fitted in with Eden's interest in the Near East (though we are not told whence this interest was derived). Another biographer states that

Eden already had diplomacy in mind as a career and thought the languages of the Middle East were likely to be diplomatically useful and important. This biographer adds that Eden later regretted not having chosen Russian instead. The third explanation offered is that Eden had become interested in the Near East as a result of his accompanying Sir Mark Sykes on his mission to Mesopotamia during the war.

Eden took his studies seriously and in 1922 he obtained a First Class Honours degree. All his biographers agree that Eden led a rather reclusive existence while at Oxford. He barely participated in college or university life. If he had already decided upon a political career it seems strange that he joined neither the Union nor any of the political societies organized by undergraduates.

One biographer informs us that Eden joined the Oxford University Dramatic Society; this was quite a natural activity, since in his youth there had been much amateur dramatics in the holidays both at Windlestone and at Lord Feversham's house, Norton. But he fails to say what progress if any, Eden made on the stage. It is also recorded that he belonged to the O.U. Asiatic Society, perhaps because he was reading oriental languages.

It seems that Eden moved among a small group of friends. Among these were Lord David Cecil and R. E. Gathorne-Hardy. These three founded in 1920 the Uffizi Society in order to discuss painters and painting. Two biographers quote passages from a paper on Cézanne that Eden read to this society.

One life of Eden says that in order to improve his French, he spent his vacations near La Rochelle with a French Protestant pastor; another that he toured Europe and Asia Minor with Lord David Cecil and others.

Eden's biographers do not agree whether he had decided upon a career by the time he went down from Oxford in the summer of 1922. It would seem that he already had politics in mind, for in November of that year he was engaged in fighting his first election.

CHAPTER THREE

Parliament and Marriage

LLOYD GEORGE's famous Coalition, which had been overwhelmingly endorsed and fortified for the task of peace making by the Coupon Election of December 1918, had been tottering to its ruin for many months. Ireland, Chanak, the scandal about the sales of honours, had produced an uneasiness in the mind of the Tory party both at Westminster and in the country which gave the Government's enemies abundant scope for criticism. The weakness of the Coalition Government was that its most powerful critics were not among the handful of Labour representatives who had been elected in 1918, or among Mr. Asquith's contingent of Liberals, but among its own supporters in the Tory party. Excepting the seventy-three Irish Sinn Feiners who did not take their seats, the Tories had a clear majority of 140 over all other parties. It irked and chafed them to see so many policies pursued which were inimical to all their deepest traditions and prejudices. It irked them too to see that of the triumvirate in whom power really resided in the Government two, Lloyd George and Winston Churchill, were Liberals; and it was small consolation to them that the only Tory in the inner circle was Lord Birkenhead, who, though he enjoyed a wide popularity in the country, had given numerous grounds for offence to many powerful Tory chieftains.

The ground was therefore fertile for the insemination of political dissent; and Tory dissidents such as Lord Salisbury and Lord Beaverbrook, acting from widely different motives, were able to sow and nourish the seeds of discord. There was to be a meeting of the National Union of Conservative and Unionist Associations where it was certain that resolutions hostile to the Government would be moved and probably carried. To forestall this the Conservative ministers who were loyal to the Prime Minister suggested calling a meeting of Conservative Members of Parliament and peers who were ministers at the Carlton Club on October 19. Lloyd George and his Conservative friends believed, and their belief seemed to be based on reasonable calculaation, that the Tory party would not dare to destroy the Government because they had no leader available who could form a government and carry them through a successful election. Bonar Law, the former leader of the Tory party, had quit the Government on the grounds of ill-health a few months before. Of those who were still ministers, Birkenhead, Robert Horne, Worthington-Evans, Curzon and Baldwin, all, save the last, had pledged their word to Lloyd George that they would not join any new government. In these circumstances it was judged unlikely that the Conservative Members of Parliament would wish to destroy the Government and precipitate a general election which, with their leadership divided, they could hardly expect to win.

But from these calculations they omitted a true estimate of the influence which Beaverbrook possessed over Bonar Law. Beaverbrook had decided at the time of Chanak, rightly or wrongly (wrongly as the author believes), that a prolongation of the Coalition Government would be likely to involve Britain in a war in which she would not have the support of the Empire. And after meeting Lloyd George, Birkenhead and Winston Churchill at Lord Wargrave's house on the Thames he had told Bonar Law: 'These men mean war.' As in a number of previous political crises Beaverbrook was able to play a decisive role through his friendship with Bonar Law. And it was he who persuaded Bonar Law to go and speak at the Carlton Club on October 19. No one knew till the last moment that Bonar Law would attend and speak, and thereby throw his hat back in the political ring by making it apparent that he was available to lead the Tory party once more and to form an alternative government.

The meeting at the Carlton Club was not a party meeting in the true sense of the word since it was confined to Members of Parliament and the handful of peers who were ministers. Subsequently, the opponents of the Tory party have sought to make political capital out of the venue and a legend has developed that the Coalition was brought down by a conspiracy of members of the Carlton Club. This, of course, is absurd. Traditionally all Tory Members of Parliament and Tory peers are members of the Carlton Club, but the policy of the party was not decided by the general membership of the Carlton Club which amounted at that time to 2,000 members. The Carlton Club was merely a convenient place for the Tory M.P.s to meet in privacy. The resolution which was proposed and carried and which proved fatal to the Government was that the Tory party would fight the next election on its own. But it would never have been carried and the Coalition could not have been destroyed if Beaverbrook had not been able to adjure or persuade his great friend Bonar Law into a belief that regardless of his ill-health he could once more play a role in the political arena. Despite speeches from Austen Chamberlain, Balfour and Birkenhead the resolution was carried by 187 to 87 votes, in the main because of the reappearance of Bonar Law and a vigorous partisan speech by Stanley Baldwin who said: 'This man [Lloyd George] has already destroyed his own party, let us leave him before he destroys ours.'

Baldwin was the only member of the Cabinet from whom none of Lloyd George's adherents had extracted any pledge of allegiance. Birkenhead used to say in later life: 'We never bothered as he was regarded as the idiot boy of the Cabinet.' This was a strangely injudicious opinion from one whose opinion was so often right.

Lloyd George resigned at once. The King sent for Bonar Law who, after indicating that he would in the existing

confused circumstances try to form a government, said he
would prefer to be installed in the party leadership before he
accepted the King's commission. On Bonar Law's advice
the King immediately proclaimed a dissolution and the
country proceeded to a general election.

It was against this background that Anthony Eden fought
his first election.

The fact that he took no part in the debates at the Oxford
Union and that he did not join either of the leading political
clubs, the Canning or the Chatham, seems to suggest that
in his Oxford days any political ambitions Eden may have
earlier entertained were dormant. However, within a few
months of coming down from Oxford we find him adopted
as the Conservative candidate for the Socialist mining
constituency of Spennymoor near his home in Co. Durham.
As against this the late Mrs. Beatrice Eden told the author
some months before her death that Eden had told her
that he already took a keen interest in politics while he
was still at Eton, even to the extent of keeping a political
map of England with all the safer Conservative seats plainly
marked. Of course it may be that this adolescent political
interest went into cold storage during his years in the Army
and at Oxford and that it needed the excitement of the fall
of the Coalition and the thrill of a general election to thaw the
ice in which his political interest had been frozen. We know
that he had at one time contemplated a career in diplomacy
and the choice of Persian and Arabic as his principal field of
study certainly indicates an interest in the delicate delights of
diplomacy rather than the hurly-burly of the hustings.

Be that as it may, having set his feet on the political ladder
Eden was to climb steadily upward till he reached the top
without ever a glance in another direction. The rung
selected for him at Spennymoor was certainly one of the
lowest on the ladder of politics. This division had indeed
been held in 1918 for the Coalition by a Liberal, Mr. S.
Galbraith, by 9,443 to 8,196 polled by his Labour opponent
M. J. Batey, a majority of 1,247. It is reasonable to suppose

that the Liberal would have had the benefit of virtually the whole Tory vote. In 1922, however, Eden was faced with a three-cornered fight; there was a Liberal candidate to split the anti-Socialist vote. When the poll was declared on November 16, the figures were:

J. Batey, Labour	13,766
Captain R. A. Eden, Unionist	7,567
T. E. Wing, Liberal	6,046

Eden had done well to poll 1,521 votes more than the Liberal; and the combined anti-Socialist vote was only 153 votes fewer than that of Mr. Batey. The fundamentally Socialist character of Spennymoor is shown by the fact that though successive Tory candidates have since had a clear run against the Socialist none of them has ever been able to present a serious challenge, not even in the great 'National' landslide of 1931.

Eden was plainly considered to have proved his electoral merit, and when in the following year the safe Tory seat of Warwick and Leamington became vacant on the appointment of Sir Ernest Pollock, K.C., as Master of the Rolls and his elevation to the peerage as Lord Hanworth, Eden procured this delectable political plum at a time when there were many ambitious Tory stalwarts who had fallen by the wayside in 1922 and who were not only available but anxious to snatch it from him.

Scarcely had Eden opened his campaign than his local fight became merged in a general election. Baldwin had succeeded Bonar Law in May 1923 when the latter resigned on the grounds of ill-health. Baldwin had for a long time been increasingly turning his mind to the idea that some form of tariff was necessary to protect British industry and to cope with unemployment. But the Tory party's hands were tied by numerous pledges which had been given in the past against the introduction of a general tariff. It was thus necessary to secure a mandate at the polls. In normal circumstances a newly chosen Prime Minister, the leadership of whose party was still badly split, would scarcely have entrusted the fortunes of his new government to so precipitate and precarious an election, but Baldwin had heard that Lloyd George, who was in the United States, intended on his return to England to declare his own conversion to a policy of protection. Baldwin concluded that this would perpetuate the split in the Tory party and decided openly to espouse the traditional Tory policy of tariff reform before it could be filched from him by the Liberal leader. In two successive speeches at Plymouth and Manchester Baldwin moved cautiously towards an exposition of the new policy and though he spoke in guarded terms acute political observers could see that he was making an election almost inevitable. However, when on November 16 Baldwin announced the dissolution of Parliament the public generally, and indeed most party politicians, were taken by surprise.

The result of the poll at Warwick and Leamington was declared on December 7. The figures were:

Captain R. A. Eden	16,337
G. Nicholls, Liberal	11,134
Countess of Warwick, Labour	4,015

This was a satisfactory result at an election where the Tories lost ground all over the country. It is difficult to estimate the degree of Eden's success since at the two previous contests in the constituency Sir Ernest Pollock had been returned unopposed. Lady Warwick was the first Socialist to contest this seat and she must in the circumstances be considered to have done well in not losing her deposit.*

This remarkable and beautiful woman had embraced the Socialist cause early in life and threw herself with energy into the campaign. As the chatelaine of Warwick Castle she had considerable local influence. A double piquancy was

---

* To avoid loss of the £150 deposit payable on nomination day a candidate must poll one-eighth of the votes cast. On this occasion the necessary quotient would have been 3,935. Lady Warwick saved her deposit by 80.

added to the contest by the fact that she was closely related both to Eden and to his fiancée, Miss Beatrice Beckett, to whom he had become engaged a short time before the election started. Lady Warwick was the mother-in-law of Eden's sister, Marjorie, who was married to her son, Lord Brooke. She was also step-grandmother to Beatrice since Sir Gervase Beckett's second marriage had been to Lady Marjorie Brooke. Beatrice had a further connection with Eden's opponent. Her late uncle, the 2nd Earl of Feversham, who had been Eden's commanding officer in the war had been the first husband of Lady Marjorie Brooke.

The numerous links between the families were so complex that the reader who wishes to comprehend them had best study the genealogical table shown as endpapers. It shows the wide ramifications and close intermarriages of a number of important families in the north of England whose friendship and support were to prove valuable to Eden in his career.

The election was in a way a family affair and an additional flavour of romance was added when in the middle of the election the engaged couple were married on November 5 at the fashionable church of St. Margaret's, Westminster. Eden's subsequent discreet Parliamentary career belies the idea that there was any significance in the fact that he should have selected the anniversary of the day when Guy Fawkes attempted to blow up the Houses of Parliament as the day of his nuptials.

★

When all the results from the whole kingdom were in it was obvious that the Tory party had suffered a severe defeat. In the previous parliament they had held 344 seats. In the new parliament they held 258, a net loss of 86 seats. The sizeable working majority of 88 votes which Baldwin had inherited from Bonar Law had been thrown away. The Conservatives were still the largest party in the House of Commons—the Socialists numbered 191—but the Lloyd George and Asquith Liberals together amounted to 159 and therefore held the balance of power. For the purpose of the election Lloyd George and Asquith had come together under the nominal leadership of the latter. Since the main issue on which the election had been fought was free trade against protection it was obvious that the Baldwin government would be defeated as soon as it met Parliament. Mr. J. R. Clynes moved an amendment to the Address that 'His Majesty's present advisers had "not the confidence of the House".' This was supported by Mr. Asquith and on a division the Government was defeated by 328 votes to 256.

Baldwin had thus not only set back for many years the Tory party's aspirations towards a tariff policy; he had also created a situation in which a Socialist government could for the first time take office. However, during Christmas and the New Year a chaotic, frenetic situation had developed in which various Tory leaders tried desperately to bring about a Tory-Liberal alliance which would keep the Socialists out of office. In this period three men seem to have kept their heads, the King, Lord Stamfordham, his private secretary, and Mr. Asquith. Once Baldwin had resigned, the King's plain constitutional duty was to send for the leader of the next largest party, Mr. Ramsay MacDonald. Any other solution would have been regarded by the country as a fraud or at the least a trick and would have involved the monarch in party strife. The King was the first to perceive this verity and on January 22 MacDonald was entrusted with forming a government. There had been some fears that he would refuse to do so unless the King gave him the promise of an immediate dissolution. These fears proved illusory. The appetite of the majority of the Socialist leaders for office was sufficient to persuade them to accept their constitutional responsibilities even on a minority basis. MacDonald appeared as Prime Minister before Parliament (which had met earlier, on January 8), the same day. He had already formed his Government and with the support of Mr. Asquith sensibly adjourned Parliament for three weeks until February 12.

CHAPTER FOUR

The House of Commons

A WEEK after the reassembly of Parliament the new member for Warwick and Leamington made his maiden speech. This was an early occasion for someone who had no very novel or urgent opinions to put before his fellow members. Eden spoke on a resolution on Air Defence which had been moved by Sir Samuel Hoare: 'That this House, whilst earnestly desiring the further limitation of armaments so far as is consistent with the safety and integrity of the Empire, affirms the principle laid down by the late Government and accepted by the Imperial Conference that Great Britain must maintain a Home Defence Air Force of sufficient strength to give adequate protection against air attack by the strongest air force within striking distance of her shores.'

In later life Eden's speeches were often to be ghost-written for him, and accordingly his maiden speech, which it is believed that he composed himself, is of exceptional interest and must be quoted textually:

May I, at the outset, ask for the usual courtesy and indulgence which is always extended to a maiden speech. The last speaker (Mr. Wallhead) made great play of a little geographical tour, and he asked us from what quarter we expected an attack from the air. I do not know, but I do not think that is the point we want to discuss. Surely, the point is rather that we should prepare to defend ourselves against an attack from any quarter. There can be little doubt that this question is of exceptional interest in this House, and the reasons are not very far to seek. In the first place, it is not in the nature of things possible to provide hastily and at a moment's notice for air defence; and, in the second place, the very heart of our country, the city of London, is especially vulnerable to attack from the air. For

41

these reasons, I hope that the Government will not be tempted too much by sentiment, and will rather act, as we gather from the speech of the Under-Secretary, not in accordance with his principles, but in accordance with the programme he has inherited from other parties, and that the Government will, as a matter of insurance, protect this country from the danger of attacks from the air.

The Under-Secretary for Air, (Mr. W. Leach) asked what was meant by adequate protection, and he said he believed preparedness was not a good weapon. That may be, but unpreparedness is a very much worse weapon, and it is a double-edged one, likely to hurt us very seriously. The Under-Secretary quoted an old military maxim, and I will quote one, which is: 'Attack is the best possible form of defence.' (*Hon. Members:* 'No, no!') I expected honourable Members opposite would be a little surprised at that doctrine. I was not suggesting that we should drop our bombs on other countries, but simply that we should have the means at our disposal to answer any attack by an attack. It is a natural temptation to honourable Members opposite, some of whose views on defence were fairly well known during the years of the war, to adopt the attitude of that very useful animal the terrier, and roll on their backs and wave their paws in the air with a pathetic expression. But that is not the line on which we can hope to insure this country against an attack from the air. I believe and hope that honourable Members opposite will carry out the programme which they have inherited and will safeguard these shores, so far as they may, from the greatest peril of modern war.

The careful choice of cliché, the avoidance of anything even bordering on the controversial and of any original thought or phrase, seem to have been noted by those who drafted his speeches fifteen and twenty years later. And the ghosts who drafted his speeches and communiqués when he was in a position to procure their services are entitled to commendation on the authentic way in which with his co-operation they conformed to the pattern set in this maiden speech.

New Members are often well advised not to seek too

spectacular a success the first time they address the House of Commons, but to reserve their deepest thoughts and highest oratory for a subsequent occasion. As this biography proceeds the reader may possibly conclude that Eden reserved such expressions of thought and repartee to a period when he was unfortunately inhibited by place and circumstance from putting them before the public which had been so long expectant.

A month later Eden made his second speech. Again he chose to speak about the air. The occasion was the annual Air Estimates. Again he was commendably brief; and on the whole it must be considered a slight improvement on the earlier speech. But from the point of view of any oratorical standard there was still a lot of sad stuff. Instead of seeking for an adjective which would precisely convey to the House the shade of meaning existing in his mind, there was much recourse to the fortification of pedestrian adjectives with the weak word 'very'. This word occurred four times in three successive sentences, being used to animate 'much', 'encouraging', 'disappointing' and 'great'. Then there was the hardy annual which was so often to recur in later speeches: 'I would suggest that nothing should be left undone . . .'

The double negative may have its uses for the purpose of ministerial and legal obfuscation but ought to be eschewed by those whose purpose it is to press their views on the Government of the day. This oratorical and literary device is one of the most irritating tricks into which speakers and writers can fall, and those who allow themselves and their audiences to become its victims almost always find that like most other narcotics its influence is increasingly habit-forming.

This malaise may often be due to intellectual sloppiness; sometimes it may reveal a psychological fear of the positive which, except in the Baldwin-MacDonald era of British politics, might have been thought a handicap in one who aspired to be a man of action. The new Member had no real need of so much recourse to the double negative, since he early showed an ability to obscure or even to contradict his meaning while engaged in positive utterances. He concluded his third speech of 1 April 1924 with this scarcely luminous peroration on the Treaty of Lausanne:

> ... This Treaty, whatever its merits or demerits may be, has brought to an end an era, full, if you will, of doubts and anxieties for the future, but also, I believe, rich in promise of great and increased happiness to come, and more widely, and more usefully developed friendly relations between this country and Turkey.

That the youthful Member who was, as his speech showed, anxious to improve Anglo-Turkish relations should have commended a treaty which was, he believed, to bring to an end 'an era rich in promise of great and increased happiness ... and more widely and more usefully developed friendly relations between this country and Turkey' must surely have baffled the comprehension of his fellow Members. But perhaps they were not giving him their full attention. Nor did he later trouble to revise this meaningless phrase when he published some of his speeches in book form fifteen years later.

★

The first Labour Government was to be short-lived. It lacked Law Officers of the Crown with political experience, and partly through its own fault and partly through the ineptitude of the Attorney-General, Sir Patrick Hastings, it made a grave error of judgment which lost it the support of Mr. Asquith and the Liberal Party and brought about its downfall.

Mr. J. R. Campbell, the acting editor of a Communist paper, the *Workers' Weekly*, had been arrested and charged under the Incitement to Mutiny Act. Under pressure from back-bench Government supporters and advice by the Prime Minister, Mr. Ramsay MacDonald, the Attorney-General withdrew the prosecution. A vote of censure was tabled by the Conservative Opposition to which an amendment was moved by the Liberals calling for a select committee of inquiry. MacDonald chose to treat this no less than the Tory motion as a matter of confidence and the Liberal amendment was carried by 364 to 198. Parliament was dissolved and a general election followed immediately.

Eden once more contested Warwick and Leamington, and though he does not seem to have set the Avon on fire or kindled a flame which had any marked effect on the election, he increased his majority from 5,203 to 6,609. This time his colourful relation Lady Warwick was no longer a candidate and he had a straight fight against the same Liberal opponent. The election was marked by the publication in the *Daily Mail* of a letter by Zinoviev, President of the Praesidium of the Communist International, to the Central Committee of the British Communist Party calling on them to stir up the 'masses of the unemployed proletariat to obtain endorsement of the proposed Anglo-Soviet Treaty which the Socialist Government had been negotiating'. The Red Letter has since been widely denounced as a stunt. What made it effective was that after its publication in the *Daily Mail* it became known that the Foreign Office had already procured a copy of it nine days before; and MacDonald was open to criticism for not having disclosed the matter himself. This was wrong on national grounds and was maladroit even from the point of view of the partisan interests of the Labour Party. Since the document was going to be published anyway, it would have served the interests of the Government better if it had revealed it itself. The attempted suppression aggravated the widespread suspicion in the country that the Government in this matter, as in the Campbell case, was too much under the influence of the crypto-Communists in the Socialist Party.

In the circumstances Mr. Baldwin and the Conservative Party, now reunited under his leadership, secured a majority of more than 220. MacDonald resigned and Baldwin and his new Government met the new Parliament for the first time on December 9. In the new Parliament Eden

widened the scope of the topics on which he spoke, and
in the course of the year 1925 we find him speaking on
the Geneva protocol, unemployment relief and the situation
in Iraq. Early in the year he became Parliamentary Private
Secretary to Mr. Godfrey Locker-Lampson, who was at that
time Under-Secretary of State at the Home Office. The
office of P.P.S. is a first shallow rung on the political ladder to
which many Members aspire; though it is unpaid and
requires considerable additional attendance in the House.
The P.P.S. sits on the bench behind his Minister and runs
and fetches for him. It is a serviceable though scarcely heroic
way in which to climb the greasy pole of higher politics, and
one which precludes the Member from many controversial
aspects of House of Commons life. At the same time it
affords him access to a Government department where he
may observe at first hand how the country is governed.
Such minor political activity was lampooned long ago in the
Gilbert and Sullivan opera *The Gondoliers*:

> But the privilege and pleasure
> That we treasure beyond measure
> Is to run on little errands for the Ministers of State.

Eden, like many other ambitious young men of the party,
early observed that under the leadership of Baldwin advancement would come by discreet and unquestioning services to
the party and the Government rather than by trying to
impose his own personality or will-power upon the House of
Commons. Baldwin was perhaps the most successful party
manager seen in British politics since Sir Robert Walpole.
He did not, like Asquith, search around among his adherents
for those with the most outstanding political and intellectual
attainments. In order to reunite the party it was true he
had taken back into his Cabinet Lord Birkenhead, Mr.
Austen Chamberlain and Sir Laming Worthington-Evans,
who had split with him and Bonar Law at the Carlton Club
meeting when Mr. Lloyd George's Coalition was brought
down, and though he put up with this political necessity he

saw no need to encourage the advancement of other such adventurous spirits (even if they could have been observed on the political horizon). His only striking and surprising appointment was that of Mr. Winston Churchill to the Treasury. Baldwin made this appointment for two reasons. He was alarmed at the damage that might be done to his Government by the combination in opposition of Mr. Churchill and Mr. Lloyd George. Moreover Mr. Churchill's appointment to the Treasury was a guarantee to the country that there would be no more experiments with tariffs. Promotion in the main went not by merit or outstanding abilities, but by solid devoted services to the party and the Government. Eden not only perceived correctly what was the right ladder to climb and the method of climbing it; he was also the recipient of a small, but perhaps in retrospect decisive, piece of good fortune. A few months after he had allied himself to Locker-Lampson the latter was transferred to the Foreign Office as Under-Secretary to Mr. Austen Chamberlain.

Seven months afterwards Chamberlain's Parliamentary Private Secretary, the Hon. Roger Lumley, resigned and Locker-Lampson recommended Eden to his chief as a suitable successor. Henceforward the pattern of his career was largely fixed. Eden's interests and talents already lay in the field of foreign affairs. Early in 1925 he had visited the Persian oilfields as a member of a parliamentary delegation. During his early years in Parliament Eden contributed regularly to the *Yorkshire Post*, which was partly owned by his father-in-law, Sir Gervase Beckett, under the pseudonym 'Backbencher', and also wrote from time to time on artistic and literary subjects.

In the summer of 1925 he went as the representative of the *Yorkshire Post* to Australia for the third meeting of the Imperial Press Conference. Among others on the British delegation were the proprietor of *The Times*, Colonel John Astor (now Lord Astor of Hever) and Mr. A. P. Herbert (now Sir Alan Herbert). The delegation went to Australia across Canada and returned the other way, visiting New Zealand and Ceylon, thus circumnavigating the globe. This trip gave Eden an invaluable insight into many aspects of the British Empire and confirmed his faith in the Empire as a beneficent instrument of human progress. His dispatches to the *Yorkshire Post* were subsequently published in book form under the title *Places in the Sun*. Most of the writing was of an undistinguished character and though it included a preface by the Prime Minister, Mr. Baldwin, made no great literary stir. Eden took his mission seriously and did all he could to profit by its opportunities. Sir Alan Herbert writes: 'I didn't, as a matter of fact, see an awful lot of the great man, but I remember him as looking very young and Etonian and making a good impression with two or three speeches—even on the tough Canadians and Australians. . . .'

On the voyage out the party stopped at Honolulu. In his book *Independent Member* Sir Alan has preserved an agreeable memory of the visit, from which it appears that he contrived to have more fun than did the other members of the delegation:

. . . In 1925 I represented *Punch* at the Third Imperial Press Conference in Australia. One evening we landed at the famed Honolulu. The ship was to leave after lunch the next day. The official programme for the morning was: '(1) Inspect Naval Base, (2) Visit Pineapple Cannery and (3) Visit Industrial District of Pali.' In all the six months of that expedition I was, I think, a pretty good boy. I went where I was told and made speeches when required. But now I said, 'This will probably be the only morning of my life that I shall spend in storied Honolulu. Am I going to spend it looking at a pineapple cannery, an industrial district, or even a naval base?' 'No,' I answered quickly. 'I am not Lord Burnham, our great leader; I am not John Astor, proprietor of *The Times;* I am not Anthony Eden or Sir Francis Newnes. They, of course, must follow the plan and see the pineapple cannery. But I am only a humble young contributor to *Punch*, who matters little. And, if they execute me afterwards, I am going to spend this one unrepeatable morning trying to surf-ride on Waikiki Beach.' So, in the morning, after

breakfast, I hid in the lavatory. I heard them calling for me
as the fleet of cars assembled and departed. And, when all was
silent, I crept quietly down to the beach. A Hawaiian 'boy'
said, 'Yes, I teach you surf-ride,' and away to the sea (300 yards
or so) we went. There are no motor-boats, no ropes or harness
here. All you have is a heavy board, about eight feet long, and
the ocean. But with the gorgeous luck of the beginner, I stood—
stood—on my first wave—at about the speed of a Derby winner
—all the way to the shore. I never did it so well again. But all
the morning I tried; and it was one of the luminous, unforget-
table mornings of my life. I behaved like a toad, no doubt. But
was I wrong?

Austen Chamberlain's tenure of the Foreign Office has
been inadequately appraised by most writers of the period.
In the Treaty of Locarno he achieved a measure of European
pacification which seemed remarkable at the time. The fact
that Locarno, which obliged Britain to go to the aid of either
France or Germany in the event of aggression by the other,
proved as inadequate as did the League of Nations to
prevent the second world war was certainly not Chamberlain's fault. And if successive governments had pursued a
comparable policy of European unity instead of fretting
and fidgeting about chimerical hopes of disarmament that
ghastly catastrophe might have been avoided.

Eden now had the opportunity of studying the foreign
scene at first hand. He had access to the Foreign Office
telegrams and was able to accompany the Foreign Secretary
to some of the international conferences of the period. This
was invaluable training and provided the background and
experience which were to enable him in later years to display
such remarkable gifts for diplomacy and negotiation.

An integral feature of Locarno had been Germany's
admission to the League of Nations. It seemed at the time an
immense achievement for the combined statesmanship of
Stresemann, Briand and Austen Chamberlain. Until then
France had chiefly looked upon the League as an instrument
for maintaining the Treaty of Versailles, which was indeed

incorporated in the Covenant of the League of Nations, and of resisting any possible German aggression in the future. Now it seemed there was a hope that the League might become the means by which the safety and peaceful advancement of the whole European family might be procured. The system could, of course, only work so long as France and her allies of the Little Entente felt secure. And it was the incessant agitation for disarmament and for an approximation in French and German military power (which was inaugurated by Ramsay MacDonald when the Labour Party took office in 1929) that destroyed these hopeful possibilities.

Winston Churchill was soon to be proclaiming that the 'redress of the grievances of the vanquished should precede the disarmament of the victors'. This, however, all lay in the future. At the time when Eden first began to be intimately associated with British foreign policy all men of good will had the right to feel that an era of reconciliation in Europe was about to dawn.

It was not until the thirties that Eden was to become identified in the public mind not only in England, but in many other countries, as the young Sir Galahad who was capable of producing a new brand of international idealism and good faith to supplant the discredited power politics of an earlier generation. His rise to fame and power was to be associated with the League of Nations and the whole international conception implied by the word 'Geneva'.

No more ideal setting could have been found for the League of Nations than this placid lakeside in a small civilized country which had managed to maintain its neutrality, guarded by its Alps and the good sense and discretion of its politicians, since it was invaded by Napoleon in 1797. The cynics mocked at the international conceptions which the League embodied; realists doubted if the concept would succeed without the United States, the Soviet Union* and Germany.

But there were others, some visionaries, some pacifists,

* The Soviet Union was not admitted until 18 September 1934.

some simpletons, who believed that the forming of the
League of Nations, coupled with disarmament, could without much further thought or sacrifice achieve an automatic
rule of law and peace. Eden was never among those; yet he
became fixed in the public mind as a symbol of many of the
facile hopes to which large sections of the public pinned their
unthinking and uncritical faith.

The first step on the ladder for Eden had been his entry
into Parliament; the second had been his association with
the Foreign Office; the third was his introduction to the
earnest, optimistic and pious rigmaroles of Geneva.

★

While the face of Europe had begun to wear a more genial
glow, recovery at home was to receive a severe setback from
the General Strike and Coal Strike of 1926. The General
Strike was beaten by the collective will of the nation in a
few days and Britain's trade unions have never since
attempted to use this dire and certainly illegal weapon. The
effects passed away without leaving any permanent injury.
It was otherwise with the Coal Strike, which dragged on for
seven months. This left a bitterness in the coalfields some of
which prevails to this day, and lost us many markets which
have never been recovered. It also affected for several years
the whole economy of the nation.

Eden does not seem to be on record for any pronounce-
ment during the General Strike, but in December he made
a speech in the House about coal:

> . . . Now that we are at the end of a very prolonged dispute,
> we have got the same situation as we have had at the end of
> each one of these industrial disputes, with suffering on all sides,
> devastation, and impoverishment of industry. Regardless of
> who is to blame, has this sort of thing got to go on? Is there no
> way out? We all admit how barbarous is the weapon, call it
> lock-out, as the right hon. gentleman the Member for Platting
> (Mr. Clynes) did, or strike; the name does not matter—but
> have we to go on paying this price every few months or years?

We cannot afford it. No country in the world, no industry in the world, can possibly afford it.

The strike or lock-out, whichever you call it, is the scalping knife of the twentieth century, abhorrent alike to reason and truth, and yet it is still new. We all know what its eventual effect will be. It has no place in the armoury of a sane man. Can we not devise some means by which it shall not be used? The right hon. gentleman the Member for Carmarthen (Sir A. Mond) made an appeal for some form of arbitration or outside court of appeal by some body similar to the League of Nations. I care not what form it takes, but it should surely be possible for all parties in this House, by their united efforts, to find some formula which will assist us to meet this difficulty. It cannot be beyond the wit of man to devise some method by which we can meet this evil. Unless we do, there is certainly no future for British industry. Unless we do, we shall certainly never recover our national prosperity, and I would suggest to the right hon. gentleman who is going to speak for the Opposition and to the representative of this Government that they cannot do better than unite in such endeavours. We know perfectly well that if anything is to come of it, we shall all have to make sacrifices for the common pool. . . .

In response to ironic cries of 'Hear, hear' from the Labour benches Eden went on:

Oh yes, we shall. Hon. Members opposite, by their sus-picion, show how much harm the present spirit can do. They may not believe me, but I was thinking of our party and not of theirs at that moment. I was thinking that we would have to put some sacrifice into that pool. . . .

This speech of Eden's revealed greater debating force than he had exhibited up to this time, and the last three sentences quoted above are good examples of his skill in disarming his critics, a technique which he was progressively to develop over the years.

Earlier in the year, in March, Eden had intervened with an effective speech on the League of Nations. Since Locarno a year before, it had been the agreed policy of France and Britain to grant Germany a permanent seat on the Council.

However, when the Council met at the beginning of March great difficulties emerged consequent upon a welter of secret intrigue. Poland also aspired to a permanent seat, while Spain and Brazil threatened to leave the League unless their Council seats were made permanent. As a result of this squabble the matter had to be deferred. Eden concluded his speech:

> The League has suffered in some senses a rebuff, but the work of Locarno is there. It is safe; it is secure; it is strengthened by the ordeal through which it has passed, and the work of Locarno was to secure that those countries which previously had been enemies should arbitrate by conference instead of arbitrating by the sword. That was the value of Locarno. It was that that made the Treaties possible. It was that we called the 'spirit of Locarno'. That work is not destroyed. That spirit is not dead, and that wine is not corked. That wine has only been delayed in delivery, and has not suffered in quality through the delay. On the contrary, it is maturing, I can assure the right hon. gentleman, and it will still prove to be a source of strength and a stimulant, not only to the brain, but to the heart of man.

Eden's qualified optimism was soon to be vindicated. Later in the year the Council was reorganized and Germany duly received what she had been promised at Locarno.

In June 1926 Eden spoke on the committee stage of the Finance Bill. He concentrated principally on the question of Imperial Preference. Like his leader Baldwin, under whose influence he was more and more to come, he had learnt the lesson of the 1923 election and in common with the vast majority of his party was opposed to any form of food taxes. In the course of his speech he said:

> . . . Certainly the Dominions are building up industries in their own orbit; equally certainly they realize that we in our country cannot put duties on foodstuffs. Within these two limits, then, we have to circumscribe our efforts and work out a policy of preference which will help us both as far as possible. These are the limitations within which we have to realize our aims. I do not think that tariffs are by any means the be-all

and end-all, and we do get, I believe, far more value from
preferences of a sentimental character. What we have to do is
to persuade our people in this country that a sentimental
preference can be made of greater value to the Dominions than
a tariff preference. We have to realize the ambitions of our
Dominions, and equally the sentiments of this country. If we
can combine these as we should combine them, if we can
evolve a scheme of collective Imperial preference, then this
Committee will have done valuable work. . . .

Eden did not expatiate upon what he meant by 'a scheme
of collective Imperial preference' nor did he define what he
meant by 'preference of a sentimental character'. Presumably by the latter he was expressing the hope that people
here and in the Dominions would buy each other's goods in
defiance of practical business considerations and without any
governmental organization, purely because they liked each
other better than they did those outside the Empire.
Subsequent events have afforded little validity to such
aspirations.

The debate on the funding of the French debt, which had
been negotiated by the Chancellor, Mr. Winston Churchill,
and the French Finance Minister, M. Caillaux, led to
another short speech by Eden in July of the same year.

. . . It is very natural that there should have been irritation. It
is not pleasant to owe money to, or to be owed money by, one's
friends, and it is not pleasant for one nation to owe money to
another friendly nation. Financial arrangements of any kind
between friends are more likely to irritate friendship than to
cement it. It is a good maxim never to borrow money from
your friends. It is far better to be in debt to your tailor or your
dentist! The same argument applies equally among nations.
It is a good maxim never if you can help it to borrow money
from your allies. You had better borrow it from neutrals, or
even from those who are or were your enemies. . . .

On 23 March 1927 Eden was successful in the ballot
for Private Members, and introduced a resolution on
Empire topics. The motion was:

That this House observes that over a period of widespread depression in trade the proportion of our trade with the Empire has increased and continues to increase; and is of the opinion that, in order to benefit the people of this country by developing our best and most productive markets, and in order to assist those Dominions which so desire it further to increase the British population within these territories, no effort should be spared, in co-operation with the Governments of the Dominions, to initiate new proposals and to increase the existing facilities for settlement in the Empire overseas.

Competition to speak in the debate was keen, perhaps as a result of Eden's appeal for suggestions which might make migration 'smoother, and even a little more rapid, than it is today', and Eden made a successful speech. He diagnosed two causes of a low rate of emigration: poor trade and a high proportion of failures. Ignorance of the conditions of life and work in the Dominions, which he thought was one of the principal causes of failure, could best be rectified by teachers in school. 'I think, for instance, that it would be a great advantage to the education of this country if more time could be devoted to a study of the rapid progress of New Zealand and the development of Australia, and rather less time, say, to the hunting habits of William Rufus, or the passion for shellfish of our Norman kings.' He also referred to the work of the Australian Migration and Development Commission, and suggested that a similar body be set up in England to deal with the inquiries of prospective emigrants, and to 'co-ordinate their knowledge with the knowledge which the Dominions would be able to give them'. He also suggested that a commission be sent round the various training establishments to decide which form of training was best. He was seconded by his friend Mr. Lumley, and the motion was carried without a division.

Earl Winterton in his *Orders of the Day* has preserved his impressions of some of the young men in this Parliament:

. . . Three young men, all with a fine record in the 1914 war—Captain Crookshank, Captain Macmillan and Captain

Anthony Eden—were among those whose names began to be familiar to the public in the 1927 session, from parliamentary press reports. Even in those days I had been long enough in the House of Common to be, or to flatter myself that I was, a fairly good judge of those among the young and new members who were likely eventually to attain high office; I was confident that such a position in the future would be reached by the three captains in question. . . .

Of the three captains, Eden and Macmillan were to become Prime Minister, while Crookshank rose to be Leader of the House of Commons, an exacting task which he discharged from 1951 to 1955.

Baldwin and his colleagues fought the 1929 election under the slogan of 'Safety First'. The country was covered with huge posters with a reassuring photograph of Baldwin and his pipe with the caption 'You Know You Can Trust Me'. The election proved generally disastrous to the Tories, who lost 152 seats; though few people foretold its outcome correctly and on the whole it was a quiet campaign. In Warwick and Leamington the figures were:

Captain R. A. Eden, Conservative	23,045
Captain W. Dingley, Liberal	17,585
G. C. Garton, Labour	7,741

Eden's majority of 5,460 was more than a thousand less than it had been in 1924, despite the fact that the electorate had risen from 44,191 to 62,406. Indeed for the first and only time he was elected on a minority vote, since his Liberal and Labour opponents polled 52 per cent of the votes cast. Had it been a straight fight against a Liberal as it was in 1924 it would probably have been a very close-run affair and Eden could possibly have lost the seat. However, thenceforward the Liberal dropped out and at subsequent elections the Tories at Warwick and Leamington always had a straight fight with Labour.

In the new Parliament, which met on June 8, the parties were represented as follows:

Labour	287
Conservative	261
Liberal	59

Of the twenty-five Communist candidates none was returned and twenty-one of them forfeited their deposits. Baldwin did not wait to receive his dismissal from Parliament. He resigned on June 4. The King sent for Mr. Ramsay MacDonald, who completed the formation of his second minority Labour Government on June 8 and met the new Parliament the same day. He did not, as in 1924, arrogate to himself the Foreign Office. Instead this key position was allotted to Mr. Arthur Henderson. Mr. Philip Snowden took the Treasury. Mr. J. H. Thomas, the former railway trade union leader, was appointed Lord Privy Seal, Mr. George Lansbury First Commissioner of Works and Sir Oswald Mosley Chancellor of the Duchy of Lancaster. This last whimsically assorted trio was entrusted by MacDonald with the task of grappling with the problem of unemployment. When he fell from office two years later, unemployment had nearly trebled. This unhappy outcome of Socialist aspirations—for which they were partly to blame—has never deterred Socialist spokesmen from the double-barrelled and hollow allegation that their opponents deliberately seek mass unemployment and that the Socialists alone have a sovereign cure for this social and economic malady.

★

In opposition Eden began to speak much more frequently than he had when his own party had been in power. In November he addressed the House on no fewer than four occasions, on Anglo-Russian relations, on widows' pensions, and twice on the Singapore base. At the end of December he spoke twice, on Anglo-Russian relations and on the Anglo-Egyptian Treaty. He also, at the end of November, made a speech to the Unionists' Canvassing Corps at the Caxton Hall. This speech is worthy of recall as showing the lines along which his thought was moving:

The fundamental divergence between Conservatism and Socialism was that Conservatism believed in the private ownership of property and Socialism did not. Their objective therefore must be to spread the private ownership of property as widely as possible to enable every worker to become a capitalist and not the State to be the sole capitalist. The status of the worker in industry must be raised. This Socialism could never do. In order to achieve this, the first task was to assist productive industry to a greater prosperity than ruled today. . . .

How could the State help industry? First by the maintenance of stability, which did not mean doing nothing, but the pursuit of an active policy for the stabilization of peace at home and abroad. Secondly, stability once assured, it must be the task of the Government to ease existing burdens on industries so that industry might prosper effectively and the share of wealth of all concerned in it, including of course the wage-earner, might grow in volume and in value. The rating relief scheme of the late Government was most useful to this end. . . . Thirdly, by assisting industry to the use of new markets for the greater development of old. For the attainment of this objective the British Empire afforded the greatest scope. There lay the most generous opportunities for a growing mutual trade. There are certain difficulties admittedly, and these were to be found not only at home, but in the Dominions also. The Conservative Party should, during its enforced period in the wilderness, devote a full measure of its energies to the study of the problem and strive to evolve ways and means to secure an increasing growth in the volume of inter-imperial trade. Some mutual adjustments, even some sacrifice, might be called for, but the result and benefits to every part of the Empire would assuredly be well worth while.

There was a fourth line of advance along which progress must be recorded if their ideal was to be attained. There must be steady and ever-growing development in schemes of co-partnership in industry. If the Conservative ideal was to be attained, the workers in industry must have an increasing personal share of its progress with which would then march a greater personal concern for its well-being. There were many schemes of co-partnership of one kind and another in industry today. A careful re-examination of their mechanism and their results should be undertaken and the Conservative Party should, in his judgment, concern itself actively with the extension of the best among them.

In July 1931 the country became involved in the worst financial crisis which has ever struck it before or since. The report of the May Committee, which called for economies of £96,000,000 and increased taxation of £24,000,000, shocked public opinion both at home and abroad. Foreign investors began to dispose of their sterling assets and a strong run on the pound began. The foreign withdrawals of gold became very heavy. The £50,000,000 credit which the Bank of England arranged failed to stop the rot. MacDonald recalled the two Opposition leaders Baldwin and Samuel from their holidays and asked them for their support in the harsh measures which would be necessary to restore the situation, and during the last ten days of August MacDonald and Snowden had repeated conversations with them in order to discover the severity of the measures required to obtain their parliamentary support. The £50,000,000 loan which the Bank of England had secured from the Federal Reserve Bank in New York and the Central Bank in Paris had already been spent and an attempt to secure another £80,000,000, which Paris and Washington were quite prepared to lend, became contingent upon satisfying the banks concerned that Britain was determined to establish a viable economy. It was this fact which led to that part of the modern Socialist mythology known as 'the Bankers' Ramp'. In fact, as Mr. Snowden later Viscount Snowden, pointed out in his autobiography:

. . . Contrary to reports which were circulated that the present crisis was due to a conspiracy on the part of the bankers, the fact was that throughout the banks had shown great willingness to render financial assistance to the Government. All that the foreign banks had insisted upon was that they should be reasonably sure of the security for the advances they were ready to make. The representatives of the Bank of England made it quite clear that if the economies of £56,000,000 represented the Government's final word, the scheme would be of no value in restoring foreign confidence. They pointed out quite truly that an analysis of that figure showed that the real savings in the expenditure amounted only to about £42,000,000, the remainder being further taxation upon the employers and workpeople. . . .

Since the matter of how far the Labour Cabinet was prepared to go in the matter of economies is still disputed by interested partisans, it may be a good thing to put on record the exact nature of the economies which were backed by the unanimous agreement of the Labour Cabinet:

	£
Unemployment Insurance (limitation of insurance benefit to twenty-six weeks, means test after that for transitional benefit, removal of 'anomalies', and increased contributions)	22,000,000
Education (including 15 per cent reduction in teachers' salaries)	10,700,000
Defence (including present reductions in pay of the Forces)	9,000,000
Roads	7,800,000
Police Pay—First year..	500,000
(Second year, £1,000,000)	
Unemployment Grants	500,000
Afforestation	500,000
Agriculture	700,000
Health—Doctors	700,000
Other Economies	1,000,000
Empire Marketing Board	250,000
Colonial Development Fund	250,000
Miscellaneous (including reductions for Cabinet Ministers and others)	2,500,000
	£56,400,000

The only economy which the dissident Socialists would not swallow, and it was on this that they broke up the Government, was a 10 per cent cut in unemployment benefits. This was a harsh measure, and even the handful of Socialist Ministers who were prepared to support it did so with the greatest reluctance. However, they drew some comfort from the fact that there had in recent years been a fall of 30 per cent in the cost of living.

Meanwhile MacDonald had been having increasingly intimate contacts with the Opposition leaders. The minds of both MacDonald and Baldwin, even before Parliament got up in July, had been working along the lines of a Council of State. When the majority of the Labour Cabinet showed themselves unwilling to adopt the full measures that were thought to be essential to the solution of the crisis Mac-Donald called for their resignations and immediately urged the King to send for Baldwin and Samuel with a view to forming a National Government. The continued drain on the pound compelled urgency and in a few days the new Government was installed. It was intended to be a purely stop-gap Administration. Indeed, an official statement issued from Downing Street on the day the National Government was formed stated:

The specific job for which the new Government is being formed is to deal with the national emergency which now exists. It will not be a Coalition Government in the usual sense of the term, but a Government of co-operation for this one purpose. When that purpose is achieved the political parties will resume their respective positions.

Snowden, J. H. Thomas, Lord Sankey and William Graham who alone among the Cabinet clave to MacDonald did so with hearts heavy at the prospect of quarrelling with the friends and associates of a lifetime. MacDonald, however, was delighted at the event and was in a state of euphoria. Some years later Snowden, who by then had quarrelled with MacDonald, revealed how he said to him the day after the National Government was formed that he would now find himself very popular in strange quarters. 'He replied,' wrote Snowden, 'gleefully rubbing his hands: "Yes, tomorrow every Duchess in London will be wanting to kiss me!" '

CHAPTER FIVE

Office

THE new Coalition or 'National' Government, as its supporters preferred to call it, was formed under the leadership of Mr. Ramsay MacDonald as Prime Minister. Its membership was announced on August 29. The Cabinet was limited to ten members instead of the usual sixteen or seventeen. Despite the fact that only a score of Labour M.P.s followed Mr. MacDonald, four of the ten were members of the Labour Party. In addition to Mr. MacDonald, Mr. Snowden was confirmed as Chancellor of the Exchequer; Mr. J. H. Thomas as Secretary of State for the Dominions and Colonies; and Lord Sankey as Lord Chancellor. The Conservatives, despite their overwhelming numerical superiority to the National Labour Party, had only an equal representation. Mr. Baldwin, who had once declared that he would never again serve in a Coalition, became Lord President of the Council; Mr. Neville Chamberlain Minister of Health; Sir Samuel Hoare Secretary of State for India, and Sir Philip Cunliffe-Lister President of the Board of Trade. Two Liberals completed the Cabinet. Lord Reading went to the Foreign Office, and Sir Herbert Samuel became Home Secretary.

It was in these circumstances that Eden first obtained ministerial office. He was appointed Under-Secretary of State for Foreign Affairs. Save for the Financial Secretaryship to the Treasury, this is the juiciest plum among the junior offices. And the plum was sugared by the fact that as his chief, Lord Reading, was in the Lords, Eden would have the responsibility and opportunity of answering for the Government's foreign policy in the House of Commons. No one can deny that he was well suited to the post. The interest he had long taken in foreign affairs, coupled with his apprenticeship as Parliamentary Private Secretary to Sir Austen Chamberlain, gave him credentials possessed by no other back-bencher. He also knew his way about the Foreign Office and, to a large extent, about Europe and the Near and Middle East.

Six years previously this important office had fallen vacant, when the late Mr. Ronald McNeill, later Lord Cushendun, had been promoted to the Financial Secretaryship to the Treasury; and Alfred Duff Cooper, who had only recently been elected to Parliament, was seriously considered for the job. It would have been remarkably swift promotion from the back benches, but he had exceptional qualifications. He had served for many years in the Foreign Office and was a brilliant speaker with an original and cultivated mind. He was recommended for the appointment by his former Foreign Office chief, Sir William Tyrrell, Permanent Under-Secretary, and the *Manchester Guardian*, a detached observer, said that he was 'obviously the man for the job'. In the event, the post fell to Mr. Godfrey Locker-Lampson, who was soon to start Eden on the political ladder by appointing him his Parliamentary Private Secretary. It is interesting to speculate what might have happened if Duff Cooper had been appointed. He might well have done what Godfrey Locker-Lampson did, and appointed Eden his Parliamentary Private Secretary. But Duff Cooper would have been a decisive lap ahead of Eden, and all the opportunities that fell to the latter would have been open to the former. If in fact Duff Cooper had been Foreign Secretary in the thirties instead of Simon, Hoare, Eden and Halifax, the history of the world might have been very different. His sharp insight into the German danger, his love of France, his instinctive knowledge of the articulation of Europe, his robust and dauntless nature, his intimate friendship with Mr. Winston Churchill—with all this, is it fanciful to speculate on the possibility that Nazism might have been throttled in its cradle? This, however, was not to be. In the event, Duff Cooper rose in the political hierarchy by more laborious means. He too, like Eden, was to resign from the Government on a matter of principle. It may usefully be noted that he resigned at the time of Munich on the real issue of the threat of Hitler, and not on the relatively trumpery one of the threat of Mussolini.

The new Government introduced an emergency budget to balance the nation's internal finances. But though some measure of international confidence was restored, the run on sterling continued; within three weeks the Government was compelled to suspend the gold standard and devalue the pound—the very things that it had come into office to avoid. Having balanced the budget, the Government, according to the pledges given by MacDonald, should have wound itself up, but the widespread alarm caused by the devaluation of the pound decided the Government to widen its task, and for this purpose to dissolve Parliament and seek a fresh mandate from the electorate. Parliament was dissolved on October 7 and polling took place on October 27.

The public showed how alarmed it was by the way it voted, which was more like a stampede than an election— 558 Government candidates were returned, while the Opposition amounted to fifty-six. The majority of 502 was the largest ever secured in a British election. Fourteen and a half million voters supported the Government; only six and a half million the Labour Party.

Eden himself had a straight fight at Warwick and Leamington against a Socialist, and had one of the largest majorities in the country—29,323, polling 38,584 against 9,261. Henceforward this constituency was to prove a secure base for the rest of his political life.

Prior to the election there had been a lot of bargaining between the leaders of the three parties as to their tariff policy. The time certainly required some import duties to correct the balance of trade and to secure protection for home industries; and such a policy was, of course, historically greatly to the liking of the Tory Party. But the suggestion of a general tariff naturally excited all the Liberal susceptibilities over Free Trade. The Chancellor, Mr. Snowden, was also an ardent Free Trader. A compromise was achieved for a 'doctor's mandate' under which it was stated that the Government would not exclude tariffs from its future policy. Under this decision it would be possible to deal with each case on its merits. Such a solution was most acceptable to Eden, who had never held doctrinaire views on the controversy between Free Trade and Protection. A speech he made attacking Snowden's Budget in 1929 makes this clear:

> Perhaps it is true of the younger members, certainly the younger members of our party, that we are merely opportunists in these fiscal matters. I, personally, am prepared to plead guilty to the charge. It seems to me that the only useful test which can be applied in these fiscal controversies, which have no academic interest whatever, is the result which is actually achieved.

Immediately after the election the Government was reconstituted, the notable changes being that Mr. Neville Chamberlain went to the Treasury in the place of Mr. Philip Snowden, who accepted the sinecure of Lord Privy Seal, and that Sir John Simon replaced Lord Reading at the Foreign Office. Eden thus had a new chief. Though he no longer had the advantage of being alone answerable to the Commons the complexities of foreign policy soon gave him scope for his talents. This situation was assisted by his own attractive personality and growing popularity and the increasing distrust with which Sir John Simon was soon to be regarded. Simon's advent to the Foreign Office was to commence a disastrous era in which under successive Foreign Secretaries, himself, Hoare, Eden and Halifax, British power and influence steadily declined, and Britain was fatuously conducted towards the second world war. Eden, as we shall see, was to resign on a matter of principle;

but he must share with Simon, Hoare and Halifax, all of whom were removed from their offices, responsibility for this disastrous period. In 1931, as Under-Secretary, later as Minister for League of Nations Affairs, and ultimately as Foreign Secretary until his resignation in 1938, he participated with growing authority in the work of the Foreign Office and indeed provides among the political leaders the one continuing link of this period of seven years.

Whatever may have been his private views in this period, his public declarations are on record. He cannot therefore be absolved from complicity in a general decline of British power and a progressive diminution of British authority and safety which are scarcely paralleled in any other period in British history, save perhaps in those of Charles II and of Ethelred the Unready. Eden must share the culpability of Simon, Hoare and Halifax; this despite his ultimate resignation (on what was in any case a minor point), which was made at a time when the policy of the previous seven years, which he had helped to form or in which he had acquiesced, had borne bitter fruit which would anyway have then to be eaten. Succeeding chapters will show the measure of Eden's responsibility and the reader will have to judge for himself whether the foregoing judgment be unduly severe.

★

Eden's first political visit to Geneva, in which city he was destined to spend so much time, had been in August 1928. Among Eden's contemporaries one who was also paying his first visit to Geneva (though it proved his last) was Mr. Alfred Duff Cooper, Financial Secretary to the War Office. The atmosphere in Geneva at this time was admirably set out in his book *Old Men Forget*:

> ... the numbers of committees which talked interminably and accomplished nothing, which indeed never hoped to accomplish anything, the gossip of the cosmopolitan politicians, the huge dreary dinner-parties and receptions, created an impression of confusion and gloom. The contrast with the

Congress of Vienna struck me. That Congress was accused of dancing, and dance it did, but behind that genuinely gay façade it also worked, and to the sound of music made a Europe that lasted for a hundred years.

Duff Cooper was already a Minister and was assigned to serve on the committee dealing on an international basis with the evils of alcoholism. His account of this committee provides an illuminating vignette of the League's activities:

Our first meeting was in the evening, and before proceedings started we were served with port and other aperitifs. After the danger of alcohol had been roundly denounced by all, our chairman, a Frenchman, explained that wine of course was not alcohol nor, for that matter, were the products of the Cognac district, which were all derived from the grape. His views were warmly supported by the representatives of Italy, Portugal and Spain. I then felt bound to remind the meeting that, while I entirely shared the views of the previous speakers, my country did not enjoy the same quantity of sunshine as blessed their happier lands, and that its inhabitants had even greater need than had their fellow creatures of that internal warmth and stimulus which the fermented juice of the grape bestows. Unfortunately the vine did not flourish in Great Britain, but we had made an effort, especially in the northern and coldest part of the kingdom, to produce a substitute, which had been found so satisfactory that we were now able to export it in considerable quantities to foreign countries, and I felt confident that this agreeable and beneficent beverage, which many doctors recommended in preference to wine, would not come within the purview of our inquiries.

I think that this committee met two or three times. I cannot remember reading its report, if it presented one, but it accomplished as much as many of the other League committees, which was precisely nothing, and it must have left in the minds of most of its members, as it left in mine, an impression of futility and farce.

Early in 1932 Eden was dispatched to Geneva as substitute Head of the British Delegation to the Disarmament Conference. For the next four or five years it fell to him to be increasingly involved in vexatious, illusory and abortive discussions on this increasingly dismal theme. All the leading delegates paid lip-service to the cause of disarmament, and while the democracies generally believed that their interests were involved in a far-reaching effort for disarmament, the dictators were busily rearming. The statesmen of the West encouraged the supine pacifism and complacency of the democracies and behind the façade of all the smooth words that were spoken and all the laborious discussions that took place the democracies were day by day losing ground and war was coming remorselessly nearer. The inherent folly of the leaders of the democracies was in failing to detect that Hitler from the outset meant war. A minor folly was in supposing that disarmament, even if it could have been achieved, could have prevented war. Successive British Prime Ministers and Foreign Secretaries, all of them upright, honourable patriotic men, with Mr. Geoffrey Dawson of *The Times* newspaper as their bellwether, succeeded in closing their eyes to the facts of life which were there for all to see. A few voices, notably that of Mr. Churchill, were raised in agonized warning; but he was easily written off as a warmonger. The fantastic postulate was allowed to be accepted that to warn of the possibility or likelihood of war was to bring war nearer. A cant phrase of those times was that 'war was unthinkable'. The people who dread to think of the dangers ahead of them only bring those dangers upon themselves more rapidly.

For several years before the war Mr. Churchill was made privy to all the knowledge of the British Secret Service on German industrial rearmament. This was done with the full knowledge and authority of Mr. Baldwin. It seems incredible that Mr. Churchill should have drawn the true conclusion while Mr. Baldwin and his colleagues misled themselves.

In all this process of unwittingly hoodwinking the British public, Eden played a leading part. The frivolity of the popular Press concentrated on the good looks, the personal charm and the exquisite raiment of England's new Sir

Galahad. The generality of the public was gratified that Britain should be represented abroad by so debonair a young man. It suited its mood. Peace-loving idealists were reassured that though he invariably spoke in clichés, they were clichés that were acceptable to them.

It would be unkind to Eden to revive lengthy extracts from the speeches he made at this time. They are shot through with pious hopes and aspirations, all of which were doomed to disappointment. No one should underrate the toil he put into his negotiations, no less than into his clichés, which were not the result of casual inattention but of strong midnight oil. He worked long hours and days in a cause doomed to frustration and one which, if it had succeeded, might have brought ruin to civilization. Arms are the defence of the peace-loving. If there were no arms the barbarians would triumph by sheer weight of numbers.

Apart from the fundamental fallacies underlying the whole conception of disarmament, a menagerie of other chimeras could soon be discerned by those who had the eye for detecting such beasts. An issue much disputed was whether a disarmament agreement should be reached on a quantitative or a qualitative basis. There was the proposal of President Hoover for a straight cut of one-third in the armaments of all the nations; but then there were those who said this was too crude; it should be on a qualitative basis; weapons should be classified as offensive or defensive. Offensive ones should be banned and defensive ones should be permitted; but then no one could agree as to what was offensive and what was defensive. Those nations with large battle fleets like Britain and the United States naturally thought that submarines were excessively offensive. Small countries with long coastlines whose seaboard cities might be bombarded by the battle fleets of powerful nations naturally thought the submarine an admirable weapon of self-defence. A heavy gun in a fortress was presumably defensive, but if it was taken out and put on a gun-carriage it became potentially offensive. The same argument could be used in regard to fighter and bomber aircraft. And so on, and so on; so forth and so forth. The topics for discussion seemed limitless, and so indeed they proved. This aspect of the disarmament controversy had been satirized some years before in a little-known speech made by Mr. Churchill in October 1928 while he was still Chancellor of the Exchequer. Mr. Baldwin thought it was one of the happiest that Mr. Churchill had ever made. Mr. Churchill called it a 'disarmament fable':

Once upon a time all the animals in the Zoo decided that they would disarm, and they arranged to have a conference to arrange the matter. So the Rhinoceros said when he opened the proceedings that the use of teeth was barbarous and horrible and ought to be strictly prohibited by general consent. Horns, which were mainly defensive weapons, would, of course, have to be allowed. The Buffalo, the Stag, the Porcupine, and even the little Hedgehog all said they would vote with the Rhino, but the Lion and the Tiger took a different view. They defended teeth and even claws, which they described as honourable weapons of immemorial antiquity. The Panther, the Leopard, the Puma, and the whole tribe of small cats all supported the Lion and the Tiger. Then the Bear spoke. He proposed that both teeth and horns should be banned and never used again for fighting by any animal. It would be quite enough if animals were allowed to give each other a good hug when they quarrelled. No one could object to that. It was so fraternal, and that would be a great step towards peace. However, all the other animals were very offended with the Bear, and the Turkey fell into a perfect panic.

The discussion got so hot and angry, and all these animals began thinking so much about horns and teeth and hugging when they argued about the peaceful intentions that had brought them together that they began to look at one another in a very nasty way. Luckily the keepers were able to calm them down and persuade them to go back quietly to their cages, and they began to feel quite friendly with one another again.*

* Unhappily, the Keepers turn out to be no good.

It is time to reassure the reader that we have no intention of conducting him through the labyrinthine corridors of the League of Nations at Geneva. The student can find the voluminous records of these farcical, abortive transactions in the records of that defunct organization. Suffice it to say that nothing contributed so much to the death of the League as its concentration on disarmament. If it had devoted a tithe of the thought which it gave to that sterile topic to considering ways and means by which the League could effectively deter or punish an aggressor, the world might have been spared the second world war. The trouble was that nearly all those who believed most in the League were terrified of the use of force or the threat of force. Few people saw the truth at the time. It is to be hoped that everyone sees it now.

As the international situation deteriorated so Eden's fortunes rose. The growing unpopularity of the Foreign Secretary, Sir John Simon, led the Prime Minister, Mr. Ramsay MacDonald, with the approval and perhaps at the suggestion of Mr. Baldwin, to promote Eden to the office of Lord Privy Seal, on 1 January 1934. This, in the hierarchy of Government, is one of the highest offices there is, and normally carries with it a seat in the Cabinet. For the moment, however, Eden was to exercise the sinecure functions of this office outside the Cabinet; but this promotion was meant to increase his status and, of course, he frequently had to report direct to the Cabinet. He was seconded to the Foreign Office and came nominally under the jurisdiction of Simon. This unusual arrangement can hardly have given pleasure to Simon, and it certainly was a blow at his prestige.

The general condition of world affairs meanwhile had continued to deteriorate. The League had been ineffectively trying to cope with the Japanese invasion of China; the disarmament conference was meandering drearily on; Hitler had come to power and had walked out of the League of Nations. In these circumstances it was decided that Eden should proceed on a grand tour of Europe,

visiting Paris, Berlin and Rome. The object of his mission
was to revive the disarmament conference by hawking round
the MacDonald Plan. There was no precise plan or agenda
for the talks that were to ensue. It is not surprising in the
circumstances that nothing was achieved save an exchange of
divergent opinions. The Paris visit was ill-timed. The Lord
Privy Seal arrived at a moment when there had been
considerable disorders in the streets of Paris following upon
the Stavisky scandals. In the riot in the Place de la Concorde
fifteen people had been killed and above two hundred
wounded. M. Daladier's Government fell and a new
Government was formed under the aged M. Gaston
Doumergue, former President of the Republic. The Lord
Privy Seal moved on to Berlin, where he had some conversation with Herr Hitler.

The Times reported that '. . . Mr. Eden and Herr Hitler
appeared to have got on very well together. They found
common ground in their service in the trenches, which
appealed particularly to the German Chancellor. . . .' The
next stop was Rome. Here Eden had his first encounter
with Signor Mussolini. There were agreeable social and
diplomatic functions. Many newspapers have suggested
that it was on this early occasion that Eden and Mussolini
first formed an aversion to each other, though a close
scrutiny has failed to reveal on what authority this assertion
rests. From Rome, Eden returned to London via Paris.

It may be of interest in view of its authorship to rescue
from oblivion a somewhat unorthodox view which was
entertained of Eden at this time:

The latest political fad is the cult of Mr. Anthony Eden. He
first leapt into international fame last summer when a French
newspaper decided he was the best-dressed Englishman. Since
then the political prophets and wiseacres have been tipping
him as the next leader of the Conservative Party.
Mr. Anthony Eden is what the Americans call a 'stuffed-
shirt politician'. He has a fine presence, a deferential manner,
a courteous word for everybody, and unlimited patience and

docility towards his elders. In addition, through his wife, he is connected with the powerful Beckett family, pundits not only of the Westminster Bank but also of the *Yorkshire Post*, that pillar of orthodox Conservatism. Many powerful individuals and groups are uniting at the moment in an effort to puff him. We are told how remarkable it is that such a young man should have attained such high office. Considering his limited abilities, it is remarkable. But he is not really so young. He is thirty-six.

How odd it is that it should be considered remarkable for a man of thirty-six to hold such a minor office as Lord Privy Seal. He has not even attained to Cabinet rank. In the past most politicians of real merit have got further at that age. The late Lord Salisbury was in the Cabinet at thirty-three, the late Lord Balfour at thirty-seven, Lord John Russell at thirty-eight, Lord Randolph Churchill at thirty-five, and Mr. Winston Churchill at thirty-three.

I have never been one of those who have subscribed to the foolish campaign which has sought to boost youth at the expense of the old men. The plain fact today is that most of the old men are much better than the young men.

Instead of clamouring to get rid of the old men, political controversialists would do much better to agitate against the old women of politics. These are to be found of every age. Starting with Mr. Ramsay MacDonald at the top, right down to the minor mugwumps at the bottom among the younger members.

I would be the last person to wish to see a man so astute, resolute, tough and formidable as Mr. Baldwin replaced by any one of the hundred or more mediocre young men who are in the House of Commons today.

It is always the mediocre young men who are crying that youth should be given a chance. How foolish and how vain to utter this cry! If youth is any good at all it will make its own chances. Many of the old men are far more virile than the milk-and-water young men who today permeate the Tory Party. The young men who do get advancement only do so by a sedulous aping of the older men. Mr. Anthony Eden has none of the qualities of youth. He is sedate, not fiery; respectable, not dashing. That is why he has been successful—but only by kind permission of the older men. His success will continue only so long as he continues to serve them.

The old men are able to fob off young men of promise by saying: 'Look at the splendid promotion we have given that young man, Mr. Anthony Eden,' knowing all the while that he is no menace to them.

No one can blame the old men for this action. It is merely the instinct of self-preservation. The sad truth is that 90 per cent of young men who go into politics are not really ambitious. They are avid of office, not of power. I have never seen the attraction of politics apart from the desire for power. Men like Mr. Lloyd George never sought office for its own sake.

Someone wrote of William the Silent, 'While he lived he was the guiding star of a whole great nation, and when he died little children cried in the streets'. Perhaps it is asking too much to expect our modern politicians to desire to be worthy of such an epitaph. But they might at least be ambitious to *do something*. Unfortunately, they merely wish to *be Something*. Thus glamour, romance, and independence are almost totally absent from our political life. Instead the most obvious feature is squalid intrigue for office and position.

Captain Eden certainly does not possess half the abilities and talents of Mr. Duff Cooper. Mr. Duff Cooper is older than Captain Eden, but he still languishes as Financial Secretary to the War Office. His utility to Mr. Baldwin has long ago passed. At the time of the St. George's election it was Mr. Duff Cooper who rescued Mr. Baldwin from political annihilation. He has never been rewarded for this action, though he not only showed great political flair, but fine courage. The moral is obvious. A really able young man will find it hard to rise in politics by climbing the conventional ladder.

The Anthony Edens will win every time, as the old gang will always encourage mediocrity rather than brilliance. Real ability will always be suppressed. Hence the only chance is to be a rebel and to seek to master the old men, not to serve them.

The history of Lord Randolph Churchill furnishes a good example of how power may be exercised without office. When Lord Salisbury was forming his Government in 1885 Lord Randolph was only thirty-six. He had only been actively engaged in politics for about five years; yet so great was the position he had established for himself in the country by his attack upon the old gang that he was virtually able to dictate the line upon which the Administration should be formed. An interesting letter of Queen Victoria's is still preserved in which she writes to Lord Salisbury, who had informed her about the claims which Lord Randolph was making: 'With due consideration to Lord Randolph Churchill, I do not think he should be allowed to dictate entirely his own terms, especially as he has never held office before.'

The political commentator quoted above was twenty-two years old at the time. Now that he is writing this book a quarter of a century later, he finds little need to alter the judgment he formed in his youth.

CHAPTER SIX

Talks with Dictators

D
URING 1934 the menace of the German and Italian
dictators was to become increasingly manifest in
Europe. Assassination as a prelude to aggression
became the order of the day. Hitler was active both at home
and abroad. On June 30 took place the notorious night of
the long knife, when Hitler used the Army, the State Police
and the S.S. to seize the headquarters of the storm-troopers
who represented the cream of his proletarian backing and to
execute their leader Roehm and more than a hundred other
leaders. Advantage was taken of the emergency to pay off
many private scores. Among others, General Schleicher was
murdered.

Three weeks later the Austrian Nazis sought to seize power
in Vienna, and murdered the Chancellor, Dr. Dollfuss.
Mussolini reacted sharply to this event and placed three
army corps on the Brenner. This for the moment caused
Hitler to pause. On August 2 President von Hindenburg
died at the age of eighty-six in his bed, of old age. Henceforward in Hitler's Reich, though the death rate rose, an
increasingly small number of people were to die from old age
or in their beds.

On October 9 King Alexander of Yugoslavia, who was
paying a State visit to France, was assassinated together with
the French Foreign Minister, M. Louis Barthou, at Marseilles. The assassin was a Croat terrorist who had been
trained in Italy and had been furnished by Italy's Hungarian
ally with an Hungarian passport.

★

Eden had been on a goodwill tour of Scandinavia at the
time of the international outrage in Marseilles, but he was

soon back at Geneva for a meeting of the League's Council
in October as the British representative, when the Council
had to consider an appeal alleging Hungarian complicity in
the assassination of King Alexander. By general consent
Eden was appointed as *rapporteur*. His appointment was
largely due to the prestige he had gained in the world of
international affairs and to the goodwill he was continuing
to develop among nearly all foreign statesmen with whom
he was increasingly being brought into contact. The Council
was in a grave mood and wished to face its responsibilities.
At the outset Dr. Benes, who was at that time Foreign
Minister of Czechoslovakia, said: 'if the case which was
before the Council had happened before the war or before
the League existed, war between the two states concerned
would have been a sad reality today.' The fact that power
politics even if they had been assuaged had not been eliminated by the new spirit of the League was early emphasized
when the French Foreign Minister openly supported the
Yugoslav Government and Italy showed that she favoured
the case of Hungary. This for no better reason than that
France was the ally of Yugoslavia and Italy of Hungary.

It looked as if the merits and demerits of the case would
be entirely subordinated to a decision in the Lobby depend-
ing on how many of their clientele among the smaller Powers
the great Powers could muster on their side. It was Eden's
leadership which avoided this clash of naked partisanship.
Behind the scenes he persuaded France and Italy of the
paramount importance of securing a peaceful settlement of
the dispute. He succeeded in drafting a resolution which
while condemning the Marseilles murders in strong terms
also expressed sympathy for Yugoslavia and France. It
pointed out that international terrorism was contrary to
Article 10 of the League Covenant, since it constituted the
violation of the political independence of nations. Eden's
skilful diplomatic negotiations were widely hailed at the
time. In addition, the decision was arrived at to set up a
committee to consider the preparation of a draft convention

to suppress terrorist activities. Eden had scored a notable diplomatic success and his prestige was further enhanced. The resolution which he had drafted was carried unanimously, partly since it did not call for any action by anybody.

During the course of this year Eden was also much concerned at Geneva in seeking an accommodation between France and Germany in the matter of the Saar dispute. Here again he helped to 'reduce tension' and added to his growing reputation. By the end of the year Eden had made a name for himself both at home and abroad, but his career was about to be caught up in three great crises, Abyssinia, the Rhineland Occupation and the Spanish Civil War. Graver still, German rearmament was to continue all the time.

★

During the latter part of 1934 Italy began to agitate her long-standing grievance against Abyssinia. As was so often to be the case in this period, an act of aggression was preceded by high protestations of friendship and non-aggression. Early in October, the Governments of Italy and Abyssinia exchanged notes of friendship. But throughout November and December these protestations of friendship were followed by accusations on either side of frontier attacks. On December 26 Abyssinia protested that Italian forces were attacking her at Walwal; and on New Year's Day 1935 Abyssinia appealed to the League, accusing Italy of aggression under Article XI of the Covenant.

At the end of January 1935 the French Prime Minister and Foreign Secretary, MM. Flandin and Laval, came on a visit to London. Just before the end of the year M. Laval had been to Rome, where he had entered into an agreement with Signor Mussolini. The pact between Italy and France had been signed on January 7. Italy was to receive 43,000 square miles of French territory by a revision of the frontier between Italian Libya, French West Africa and French Equatorial Africa. Italy's possession of Eritrea was also to be enlarged by a small tract of land, formerly part of French

Somaliland. France further recognized Italy's sovereignty over the island of Doumeirah.

For some time Britain had been pressing France to abate her disputes with Italy so that a joint Anglo-French-Italian front could be formed against the menace of Hitler. Flandin and Laval had evidently become convinced that this was in France's interest. If a genuine agreement could be made with Italy, France would no longer have the same demands on her Alpine frontier, and could redeploy the numerous divisions stationed there against the more massive threats arising against her on her frontiers with Germany.

Flandin and Laval were able to report to the British Ministers, with whom they conferred for forty-eight hours, that some progress had been achieved in the Rome talks; that Mussolini was himself apprehensive of the German menace; and was ready to have discussions with France and Britain somewhere in Italy with a view to making a common front against German aggression.

Immediately after these talks in London it was decided that Sir John Simon should accept an invitation to visit Hitler in Berlin early in March.

Meanwhile on March 4 the British Government published a White Paper on defence. It protested in strong terms against German rearmament:

> Rearmament, if continued at the present rate, unabated and uncontrolled, will aggravate the existing anxieties of the neighbours of Germany, and may consequently produce a situation where peace is in peril.
>
> His Majesty's Government have noted and welcomed the declarations of the leaders of Germany that they desire peace. They cannot, however, fail to recognize that not only the forces but the spirit in which the population, and especially the youth of the country, are being organized, lend colour to, and substantiate, the general feeling of insecurity which has already been incontestably generated.

Two days later the German Government notified the

British Government that Hitler was suffering from a severe cold. Sir John Simon's visit was therefore postponed.

★

The late Lord Simon, in his book *Retrospect*, describes Hitler's reaction:

> Hitler took great umbrage at this plain speaking and postponed the date of our visit to Berlin on the ground that he had caught cold when speaking in the open air at the Saar celebrations and was thus too hoarse to talk with us. The cold was genuine, but so was the indignation; though the facts stated [in the White Paper] were indisputable.
>
> Following the Commons' debate there came news that Hitler's cold was better and his fever over the White Paper appeared to have abated. It was arranged that Eden and I should go to Berlin.

On March 11 Government Defence Policy was debated in the House of Commons. In the course of it, Mr. Baldwin somewhat retracted the force of the arguments predicated in the White Paper. He explained that the references to Germany were meant in no invidious sense and were not intended to throw on Germany the sole blame for all the competition in armaments. Hitler took note of this obeisance and immediately signified that he would be graciously pleased to receive Sir John Simon in Berlin on March 24.

Almost immediately it was further announced from Berlin that at a special meeting of the German Cabinet, held on March 16, it had been decided to pass immediately a law introducing compulsory military service, and that the strength of the German forces would be set at thirty-six divisions—totalling about 500,000 men. This was in flat contradiction of the Treaty of Versailles, which was an integral part of the Covenant of the League.

Sir John Simon, who had been in South Wales, returned to London. The Prime Minister came up from Chequers the next morning. A Cabinet Meeting was held the following day, March 18, and a Note was dispatched to Germany which denounced any step taken by the German Government as a further example of unilateral action which was seriously to increase uneasiness in Europe. The Note went on to indicate the basis on which the British Ministers had been prepared to accept the German invitation to Berlin and that what had been in their mind was 'a general settlement freely negotiated between Germany and the other Powers', and 'agreements regarding armaments which in the case of Germany would replace the provisions of Part V of the Treaty of Versailles'. The Note suggested that Germany's decision to raise her military strength so unexpectedly was bound to make agreement more difficult if not impossible; and added that the British Government were most unwilling to abandon the visit but desired before undertaking it to be sure that the German Government still wished the visit to take place with the object previously agreed, namely 'to carry consultation a stage further on all the matters referred to in the Anglo-French communiqué'.

The British Government, for once, were not abasing themselves before a dictator. And the dictator immediately, for a brief period, appeared to be a trifle civil. The invitation to Berlin was renewed, and Sir John Simon and Mr. Eden proceeded to Berlin, where they arrived on March 24.

Hitler was not going to let the British boobies escape from the trap which he had contrived for them as easily as all that. When Simon was admitted into the presence of the no longer infectious Führer, he was to receive startling news. Later Simon was to explain that his conversations had revealed considerable 'divergence of view between the two Governments'. Indeed they did. Hitler was not interested in the proposed Eastern Pact of mutual guarantee. He did not care for a collective system of peace and security. Though he might return to the League of Nations on terms he was not prepared to give any guarantees with regard to Austria nor was he prepared to withdraw the recently announced law for German conscription. And as a *bonne-bouche* he told Sir John Simon that Germany had now achieved parity with Great Britain in the air.

Such were the bitter fruits of the visit for whose sake a mighty nation had been prepared to abase herself, which visit it had then been indicated the host no longer desired, but in which he was speedily led to acquiesce once more as soon as he felt in the mood to spring his surprise.

This is a particularly unhappy example of what happens when statesmen, to gratify a feckless democracy, insist on 'exploring every avenue to peace' and spread abroad the idea that no sacrifices will be necessary and no action need be taken so long as everyone goes on talking.

Conferences held on this basis inevitably end in affronts and humiliations for those who desire peace on any terms, and in advantages for those who desire war. The period we are examining is, alas, rich in examples of this diplomatic ineptitude. Those who, as Clarendon said of Falkland, 'With a shrill cry ingeminate ... Peace, Peace', nearly always bring war upon themselves. British statesmen of this period as well as the helpless British public were soon to learn this lesson the hard way. (They could have learned it by reading history.)

Unfortunately, most of the lucky survivors of the catastrophe have already forgotten it. Doubtless further generations will have to be immolated before the lesson becomes ingrained and instinctive in the bone. However, it seems that after the next lesson there will be few pupils left.

★

From Berlin Simon returned to London: Eden, on another of his grand tours of Europe, went on to Moscow and visited Warsaw and Prague on his way home. The Foreign Minister, Litvinov, gave an official reception for him and the next day he had talks with Stalin, Litvinov, Molotov and Krestinsky. At the end of his two-day visit a joint communiqué was issued.

Since it was meatier than most such documents it deserves quotation in full:

Conversations have taken place in Moscow in the last few days between Mr. Eden, Lord Privy Seal, and M. Litvinov, People's Commissar for Foreign Affairs, upon the principal elements of the present international situation, including the proposed Eastern Pact and the other questions set forth in the Anglo-French communiqué of February 3, as well as regards further developments and improvement of Anglo-Soviet relations. In the course of the conversations, Mr. Eden informed M. Litvinov of the recent talks between the British Ministers and the head of the German Government.

It was agreed that these talks had helped to clarify the European situation. Mr. Eden, M. Stalin, M. Molotov and M. Litvinov were of the opinion that in the present international situation it was more than ever necessary to pursue the endeavour to promote the building up of a system of collective security in Europe as contemplated in the Anglo-French communiqué, and in conformity with the principles of the League of Nations.

It was emphasized in the conversations by MM. Stalin, Molotov and Litvinov that the organization of security in Eastern Europe and the proposed pact of mutual assistance had not aimed at the isolation or the encirclement of any State, but at the creation of equal security for all participants, and that the participation in the pact of Germany and Poland would therefore be welcome as affording the best solution of the problem. The representatives of the two Governments were confirmed in the opinion that the friendly co-operation of the two countries in the general work for the collective organization of peace and security is of primary importance for the furtherance of international efforts to this end.

In Warsaw Eden had talks with Marshal Pilsudski and Colonel Beck. The talks in Warsaw were cordial but Poland would have none of the proposed Eastern Pact. In Prague Eden was received by President Masaryk and had talks with him and with the Foreign Minister, Dr. Benes. On his way back to London Eden had a very rough air trip between Prague and Cologne. A journalist, Mr. Douglas Reed, who was on board, gave the following account of what must have been a most unpleasant experience:

> . . . a foul trip, the worst I ever made. . . . We flew into thick cloud and then suddenly snow was beating about us, and the machine was thrown here and there and let down with a bump into a deep void and then again rocketed upwards and given a smack on one wing and a smack on the other, and a bang on the solar plexus and a kidney punch that sent the tail spinning round. I knew that we were flying over wooded and mountainous country with no hope of a forced landing.

On his arrival in London Eden was so exhausted that he had to take a complete rest for six weeks. Meanwhile during his absence plans had been concerted for the Anglo-French-Italian conference. It had been arranged that the meeting should be held at Stresa; and it had been intended that Eden should accompany the Foreign Secretary, Simon. As it was, he could not do so and the Prime Minister, Mr. Ramsay MacDonald, decided to go himself.

★

The three Powers met at Stresa on April 11. The meetings were held in the Palazzo Borromeo on the Isola Bella on Lake Maggiore. The British and French delegations were accommodated on the shores of the lake and were ferried back and forth to the conference each day in motor launches. Springtime on Lake Maggiore must have provided an idyllic setting for the labours of the assembled statesmen and diplomats. The objectives of the British and French delegations were, in the light of German rearmament and of Germany's growing threat to her neighbours, to build a solid front and thereafter from a position of strength to negotiate with Germany about the scale of her rearmament. It was with the intention of keeping Mussolini sweet and bringing him along that France had made minor territorial concessions to Italy at the end of the previous year. Mussolini at that time not only feared the expansion of Germany but entertained a very lively contempt for Hitler. Their meeting in Venice in June of the previous year had not been a success. Mussolini was proud of how Hitler had paused when the three Italian army corps were put on the Brenner following the assassination of Dollfuss, and it was plainly in his interest to make a collective stand. In these circumstances it was quite easy to get agreement since the interest of all three Powers was in harmony. Moreover, it is almost certain that as well as the minor territorial concessions which France had made to Italy in December 1934 Laval had already let Mussolini know that France would not resist the invasion of Abyssinia which he had long been contemplating and preparing.

Outwardly it seemed that the Stresa agreement was the high-water mark of European statesmanship since Hitler had come into power. But there was a snag which was not apparent to those who merely read the communiqué, but which could not have failed to be patent to all who attended the concluding session where Mussolini read out the terms of the agreement. When he reached the final clause which pledged the three Powers to oppose 'with all suitable means the unilateral repudiation of treaties calculated to endanger the peace of Europe . . .', he paused and looked for a challenging moment around the table, and then read on. Of course he meant that this guarantee of the *status quo* only applied to Europe and had no bearing on Africa. The late Lord Vansittart, then Sir Robert Vansittart, accompanied MacDonald and Simon to Stresa in his capacity as Permanent Under-Secretary at the Foreign Office. In later years he told the author how a few moments later he pointed this out to MacDonald, who replied rather tetchily in that irritating Scottish burr: 'Don't be tiresome, Van, we don't want any trouble. What we want is an agreement that we can put before the House of Commons.'

Of course the British should have had it out with Mussolini, and on a lower level this was done. Vansittart explained to his opposite number in the Italian Foreign Office that if Italy invaded Abyssinia it would wreck the Stresa agreement since British public opinion would not tolerate it. In his book, *Lessons of my Life*, Vansittart says:

> It has often been asked why Mussolini was not warned at Stresa against the consequences of invading Abyssinia. . . . I did, of course, warn the Italians in personal talks; but it seemed better tactics, with an eye on Laval, first to secure agreement on Austria, that is, to provide a bait before administering a monition. The bait, however, was not enough. It was notorious that Britain had still a horror of 'commitments', while Mussolini, besotted with dreams 'of Africa and golden joys', was speculatively bent on making the best of both continents by acquiring Abyssinia and preserving Austria—an impossible combination.

So MacDonald had his little hour of Parliamentary triumph, Mussolini had his war and conquered Abyssinia, Hitler remilitarized the Rhineland and got Austria; Britain and France merely had to pay the bill. It is true that it was all put right in the end after a major world war, but some may think that rather a heavy price for the luxury of a Parliamentary triumph. Hitler showed what he thought of the determination of the three great Powers that concerted against him at Stresa by almost immediately announcing a further breach of the Treaty of Versailles. He intended to start construction of U-boats.

★

While the Stresa talks had been going on the British Government had been exploring with the German Government how advantage might be taken (if advantage be the right word in the circumstances) of suggestions which Hitler had made to Simon and Eden when they were in Berlin. Perhaps to soften the blow of his intransigence over German conscription, his lack of interest in the proposed Eastern Locarno, and his alarming claim that Germany had achieved parity in the air with Britain, he had dangled before his British guests the possibility of an Anglo-German Naval Agreement. This idea seems to have commended itself to the selfishly unrealistic mind of the British Government. And the Germans were encouraged to make proposals; on June 3 Herr Ribbentrop came to London with some German naval experts with precise proposals, namely that Germany should limit her Navy to 35 per cent of that of the British Empire, and that Germany should have the right to possess a submarine tonnage the equal of that of the British Empire.

The British Government appear to have accepted these proposals with the minimum of negotiation or argument and sought to commend the agreement, which was signed on June 18, as a step which would make it easier to bring about a new treaty of general naval limitation among all the naval Powers of the world. This extraordinary act of appeasement, indeed of abasement, and so soon after Stresa, passes human comprehension. That admirable and indispensable reference work, the *Annual Register* for 1935, commented at the time, in words which cannot be bettered:

> What, however, most struck observers in France and Italy, and many critics in England, was the fact that after having a few weeks before severely criticized Germany for a unilateral repudiation of the Versailles Treaty, England now openly abetted her in doing the very same thing once more. While the content of the Anglo-German Agreement was regarded as on the whole not unsatisfactory, the manner in which it had been brought about was deeply resented both in France and in Italy, and was declared in both countries to be an evil precedent and a breach of the 'united front' formed at Stresa. The British Government showed itself very sensitive to these criticisms, and sent Mr. Eden on a tour to Paris and Rome to soothe the ruffled tempers and explain that no harm had been done. Mr. Eden was unable to convince M. Laval and Signor Mussolini that England's action had been correct, but he succeeded in reassuring them as to British intentions, and restored the friendly feeling which had been disturbed for a time.

Who has the right to say that appeasement and abasement started with Neville Chamberlain?

★

The negotiation and signing of the Anglo-German Naval Treaty was the first and very typical action for which Sir Samuel Hoare, who had moved from the India Office to the Foreign Office on June 6 when Mr. Baldwin became Prime Minister, was responsible. The account he gives of this period in his own book *Nine Troubled Years* is lamentably self-revealing.

Hoare was a little worried as to whether his relationship with Eden would not result in dyarchy at the Foreign Office, and expected Baldwin to define a *modus operandi*. Baldwin, however, 'would not involve himself in the details' and merely passed a pencil note at the Cabinet Meeting 'asking me to settle direct with the young man'.

This condescending attitude towards a Minister whose widespread popularity he was exploiting tells us a lot about Mr. Baldwin. It also adds to our understanding of Eden's true stature in the political hierarchy. Eden had been promoted to the Cabinet and made Minister without Portfolio for League of Nations Affairs when Baldwin became Prime Minister and sent Hoare to the Foreign Office in place of Simon. It is clear that Eden was still to be kept in tutelage and was to have little power in the shaping of policy.

Hoare was not the only one who had doubts as to the wisdom of this double-headed arrangement. Speaking in the House of Commons on July 11 Mr. Winston Churchill said:

> That brings me to the new plan of having two equal Foreign Secretaries. I was very glad indeed that the Prime Minister [Mr. Baldwin] said yesterday that this was only a temporary experiment. I cannot feel that it will last long or ever be renewed. At any rate, it is in the nature of poetic justice that the Foreign Secretary [Sir Samuel Hoare] should, on leaving the India Office, have a personal experience of dyarchy in its most direct and homely aspect. What we want in foreign affairs is not, as the Prime Minister suggested, a team, however loyal— and it certainly will be loyal—and however well disciplined it

may be. What we need is a plain, simple policy which can be declared in Parliament and to the nation and can be generally approved by both.

★

Mussolini had for some time been trying to fasten a quarrel on Abyssinia and to agitate claims for large parts of that country to be ceded to Italy.

Abyssinia is a part of a wide tract of land known in ancient times as Ethiopia. It first received Christian missionaries in A.D. 330. There was a Portuguese mission in the sixteenth century and rival British and French missions in the first half of the nineteenth century. Italy first took an interest in Abyssinia in 1870 when an Italian company bought the port of Assab at the southern end of the Red Sea. The Italians gradually penetrated inland; fighting occurred intermittently from 1887 onwards and culminated in the Battle of Adowa in 1896. The Italians suffered a disastrous defeat at the hands of a large barbarian army. Several thousand Italian prisoners were castrated in accordance with the immemorial martial tradition of that part of the world. Italy had long brooded on this savage and humiliating reverse. Revenge was a national aspiration and one which it naturally suited Mussolini to gratify as a means of rallying round himself a far from united nation.

Abyssinia had already complained to the League under Article XI of the Covenant at the end of 1935. The Walwal frontier clash which was the cause of the complaint was for some months before a Conciliation Committee which by the end of May issued a report of a hopeful nature. It seemed that Italy and Abyssinia, which were both represented on the Committee of Five, were prepared to accept arbitration not only in the Walwal dispute but on some other frontier incidents which had arisen while the conciliators had been at work.

The League Committee concluded its report of September 18 with a paragraph stressing the role that France and

Britain were expected by the League to play in any agreement:

> The representatives of France and the United Kingdom have informed the Committee of Five that, with a view to contributing to the peaceful settlement of the Italo-Ethiopian dispute, their respective Governments are ready to facilitate territorial adjustments between Italy and Ethiopia by offering Ethiopia, if necessary, certain sacrifices in the region of the Somaliland coast.

> In negotiating on this subject, the Governments of the French Republic and of the United Kingdom will take care to obtain from the Ethiopian Government guarantees regarding the execution, in the territories to be acquired by it, of the obligations by which Ethiopia is bound in regard to slavery and to traffic in arms.

> The representatives of France and of the United Kingdom have further informed the Committee of Five that their respective Governments, without wishing to impair the existing régime in regard to the treatment of foreigners and in regard to external trade, are prepared to recognize a special Italian interest in the economic development of Ethiopia. Consequently, these governments will look with favour on the conclusion of economic agreements between Italy and Ethiopia, on condition that the existing rights of French and British nationals and protected persons are respected by the two parties, and that the recognized interests of France and the United Kingdom under all agreements already in force are safeguarded.

A series of bombastic utterances by the Duce, in the course of the summer, soon made it clear that Mussolini did not mean to be cheated out of his war. Eden at his meeting with Mussolini in Rome was authorized to offer some parts of British Somaliland to Italy in return for a general agreement. But this had only further provoked Mussolini. In the course of the summer, Britain proposed another formal Conference of the Three Powers, France, Britain and Italy under the 1906 Treaty. But Mussolini would not agree to a formal conference. In consequence Eden and Vansittart went to Paris for informal talks at the Italian Embassy with

Signor Cerutti and Laval. No progress was made towards conciliation; Mussolini merely increased his demands.

It was ironical that Italy should have attacked Abyssinia and thereby have fallen into the toils, however ineffective, of the League of Nations. For it was Italy which had procured Abyssinia's entry into the League in 1923. It was also ironical that Britain should have taken the lead, however ineffectively, in denouncing Italy and supporting Abyssinia. For Britain had opposed Abyssinia's entry into the League on the grounds that that country had not yet reached the stage of civilization which entitled her to admission to the comity of nations.

Parliament adjourned at the end of July and most of the British Ministers went on holiday. Hoare has described in his memoirs how he, Eden and Vansittart had managed to catch the Prime Minister, Mr. Baldwin, before his departure and to obtain his general approval of what he was trying to do. A letter which Hoare wrote to Neville Chamberlain, who was having a holiday in Switzerland, puts very clearly the difficulties of the situation and the methods by which Hoare was planning to cope with it:

> I believe that we have done everything possible to keep in step with the French and to do nothing to provoke the Italians. None the less, at the time of writing it looks to me as if the Italians will be entirely unreasonable, and as a result there will be a first-class crisis in the League at the beginning of September. It is urgently necessary for the Cabinet to consider what in these circumstances our attitude should be on two assumptions: (1) that the French are completely with us; (2) that the French have backed out. It is equally urgent for the Cabinet to consider what preparations should be made to meet a possible mad dog act by the Italians. As to the latter question, I have been in great difficulties. On the one hand, I was anxious to suggest no action which would even give the impression of provocation to the Italians or of war to the British public. On the other hand I have been very nervous of leaving undone anything that might make a mad dog act more dangerous.
>
> In the circumstances it seemed to me that I could do no

more than get the Chiefs of Staff and the Planning Committee to investigate the position, and to leave it to the Cabinet to decide upon what action should be taken. I am having the reports circulated to the Cabinet and you will be receiving them in this bag. It seemed to me even at the risk of a dangerous period of delay best to defer any action until the Cabinet.

As you may imagine I have received little or no help from other quarters. Stanley [Baldwin] would think about nothing but his holiday and the necessity of keeping out of the whole business almost at any cost. Ramsay [MacDonald] has written me a curious and almost unintelligible letter warning me of all the dangers that surround us, generally taking the side of the Italians and making the amazing suggestion that the Italians are likely to be our Great Empire rivals in the future and will almost certainly be stronger than ourselves.

Outside the Cabinet public opinion has been greatly hardening against Italy. Papers like the *Birmingham Post* are getting very restive over the arms embargo and over the ineffectiveness of the League. I see myself the making of a first-class crisis in which the Government will lose heavily if we appear to be repudiating the Covenant.

When I say this I do not mean that I have changed my views since we both discussed the question in London. What, however, I do mean is that if we adopt Stanley's attitude of indifference or Ramsay's alarmist and pusillanimous surrender to the Italians, we shall get the worst of every conceivable world. Our line, I am sure, is to keep in step with the French, and, whether now or at Geneva, to act with them.

The Council of the League had to meet on September 4 to consider the whole question of Italo-Ethiopian relations. It had long been apparent that the efforts of the Conciliation Committee had totally broken down and that war was inevitable. On July 7 Signor Mussolini had declared: 'Our decision is irrevocable. There can be no turning back. Government and nation are now engaged in a conflict which we have decided to carry on to the bitter end.'

The Annual Meeting of the Assembly of the League was due to meet on September 11, and the imminence of this

Assembly meeting considerably overshadowed the deliberations of the Council. Sir Samuel Hoare, despite a painful arthritic attack of the leg, had come to Geneva himself two days before to participate in what was perhaps the most historic of the sixteen Annual Meetings so far held by the Assembly. The menace of war had aroused unusual interest in the Assembly's proceedings and when Hoare rose to open the discussion the great Conference Hall which overlooks the Lake of Geneva was packed as it had never been before with an excited and expectant throng. One passage in Hoare's speech thrilled the Assembly and electrified the world:

> In conformity with its precise and explicit obligations, the League stands, and my country stands with it, for the collective maintenance of the Covenant in its entirety, and particularly for steady and collective resistance to all acts of unprovoked aggression.

M. Laval of France, though less precise, did not demur; the world believed that Britain and France meant business and sat back to see whether the will of the League could be made effective against a self-proclaimed aggressor and whether the assertion of a rule of law would prove a sure guarantee of peace.

As early as January 1935 Eden had made a statement of remarkable prescience: '1935 will be the most challenging year in postwar history. It will show whether we can make the League—the collective system—effective, or whether nations are determined to pursue a selfish course.' At this time, the prospects that the League might provide an adequate system of collective security seemed fair. The Saar controversy had been settled by the plebiscite which passed off peacefully without disorder on January 13. The inhabitants voted with an overwhelming majority in favour of joining Germany; and unanimous agreement was reached at Geneva transferring the territory to the Reich. In the spring of 1935 it really seemed as if the League might establish itself as a body effective for the maintenance of peace.

CHAPTER SEVEN

Hoare–Laval

DESPITE Hoare's heroic words at Geneva on September 11, Italy attacked Abyssinia on October 3. Mr. Baldwin's colleagues had found it difficult to interest him in foreign affairs, but even he could observe that this international episode might be turned to favourable account on the home front. Accordingly, on October 23, he announced that Parliament would be dissolved two days later and that a general election would be held on November 14.

The Government's election programme was issued on October 27. It stressed that the League of Nations would remain the keystone of British foreign policy. The manifesto contained a significant passage: 'We shall continue to do all in our power to uphold the Covenant and to maintain and increase the efficiency of the League. In the present unhappy dispute between Italy and Abyssinia there will be no wavering in the policy we have hitherto pursued. We shall take no action in isolation, but we shall be prepared faithfully to take our part in collective action decided upon by the League and shared in by its members. We shall endeavour to further any discussions which may offer the hope of a just and fair settlement, provided that it be within the framework of the League and acceptable to the three parties to the dispute—Italy, Abyssinia, and the League itself.' Further promises were that gaps in national defence would be filled in the next few years, but at the same time there would be further efforts to bring about a general limitation of arms.

The National Government went to the country in 1935 with the huge majority it had obtained in 1931 almost intact.

It was obvious that it would lose many seats; but the Government's losses were much smaller than most observers and party managers had anticipated. Of the 450 seats held by the Conservatives, 385 were retained, and the Conservatives still had a clear majority over all other parties combined. With the 32 National Liberals and 8 National Labourites, the Government held 428 seats compared with 513 in the previous Parliament. The Labour Party only managed to increase its representation of 95 seats to a total of 154.

While Mr. Baldwin was cashing in at the election on Sir Samuel Hoare's great ovation at Geneva, Mussolini was prosecuting his war with vigour and poison gas. Within four days of Mussolini's attack the Council of the League unanimously branded Italy as an aggressor. This was quick work by League standards. Three days later a committee was set up to impose a series of sanctions against the aggressor. An arms embargo and various economic and financial sanctions were speedily agreed upon. Eden went to Geneva and himself introduced a resolution calling for an embargo by all League members on the purchase of Italian goods. This was carried unanimously by the committee of eighteen. On the same day the co-ordinating committee of fifty-two nations carried a resolution detailing an impressive-looking list of warlike metals and materials which were to be denied to Italy.

On the third day of the debate on the Address in the House of Commons Sir Samuel Hoare, speaking as Foreign Secretary, told the House that the League machinery was working well with the imposition of sanctions. This was scarcely surprising since the committee of eighteen charged with the application of sanctions was taking especial pains not to impose any which might interfere with Italy's prosecution of her war against Abyssinia, but was confining itself to sanctions which merely imposed privations on the civilian population of Italy. For instance, in the course of the campaign of sanctions, the export of aluminium into Italy was banned. However, aluminium was almost the only warlike metal of which Italy had a surplus. Scrap iron and iron ore were similarly black-listed. This impressed unthinking people, as it was known that Italy was short of scrap and ore. But as steel billets and pig-iron were not included in the list of banned supplies, the Italian dictator suffered no inconvenience to his war plans. Such economic sanctions as were imposed merely struck at the civilian population of Italy. Instead of making the war unpopular they merely served to stimulate a patriotic spirit.

Already by the time that Parliament met it was clear that an oil sanction was the crux of the business. On this Hoare replied that though Britain was prepared to play her part it could only be in company with the rest of the eighteen, and Britain did not seem anxious to take the lead even in proposing what would have been an effective sanction. The position was soon reached that no sanctions would be imposed to which Mussolini might object: that might mean war. Laval was playing Mussolini's hand for him at Geneva and French representatives in Rome were carefully instructed to find out from the Duce each morning which sanctions would be inconvenient to him. Mussolini in a statesmanlike and sensible way entered into this merry conspiracy, which suited him admirably. The League of Nations hoped they were bravely doing their duty, the Italian people rallied behind their Government, and the Italian Army got on with winning the war. The Geneva policy of 'sanctions with no teeth in them' was to continue throughout the spring and early summer of the following year.

★

In the same speech Hoare explained to the House of Commons 'our double policy of negotiation with Italy and loyalty to the League'. Laval had suggested coming to London to discuss the situation with Hoare. The latter was in ill health and was planning to go for two or three weeks to Switzerland. He therefore explained to Laval that it was inconvenient for him to come to London. Laval suggested that Hoare should break his journey to Switzerland in Paris. This seemed an oddly accidental way of conducting great affairs. Indeed Hoare himself in his memoirs writes:

It may be that I was so pulled down by overwork that my judgment was out of gear. In any case, I weakly agreed to the invitation, not realizing that it would in every way have been better if I had either let Laval come to London, where I should have had my colleagues around me, or dropped altogether out of the negotiation during the short period of my leave. Baldwin, who was fully occupied with the many details connected with the new Government, had little time for discussing with me the implications of my Paris visit. His advice was very simple: 'Have a good leave, and get your health back. That is the most important thing. By all means stop in Paris, and push Laval as far as you can, but on no account get this country into war.' Looking back, I am certain that I should have insisted upon the summoning of a special Cabinet, and a clear agreement as to how far I could go with Laval. This precaution, that has since seemed so elementary, I failed to take.

In Paris Hoare and Laval met for talks at the Quai d'Orsay. 'More than once', Hoare writes in his book, Laval 'rang up Mussolini, with whom he seemed to have a direct and secret line'. The talks lasted for two days, ending on the evening of December 8.

Hoare ultimately agreed to the plan proposed by Laval. Then, having collected 'Lady Maud and the luggage', as he quaintly put it, he took the night train to Switzerland.

Sir Samuel describes his holiday in Switzerland with feeling:

For months past I had been looking forward to my skating holiday in Switzerland. The sport that I loved above all others was to set me up after a long period of overwork. I had arranged for one of the best rinks in the Engadine to be ready for me before the usual time of opening, and everything was prepared for a few weeks of Swiss paradise. The day after my arrival at Zuoz was one of those perfect days of blue sky, white snow and black ice. I hurried on to the rink, feeling that there was no turn or step that I could not accomplish. There followed a complete black-out, even blacker than those I had had several times in the previous months, and when I came to myself, it was clear something serious was wrong with my face. Having tottered back to the hotel and summoned a doctor, I learnt that my nose was badly broken in two places. . . . I had . . . to quiet my mental and physical pains as best I could and count the hours until I could leave for London.

While Sir Samuel was on his way to Switzerland, the text of what had been agreed with Laval was telegraphed to London. The Cabinet met next day and approved it after a long discussion.

On the same morning various newspapers in Paris carried reports of the plan. Pertinax, who wrote for the *Echo de Paris*, was one of the earliest with the news. The versions differed considerably, but all alleged that the plan offered far greater concessions to Italy than the proposals of the Committee of Five.

It is not certain whether Laval himself was responsible for the leak at the Quai d'Orsay. Vansittart in *The Mist Procession* writes:

> While all was yet in confidence the usual indiscretion occurred at the Quai d'Orsay. At first I thought that Laval had inspired it in a clumsy attempt to force our hand. Such was, and remained, the general view, but I soon discarded it. Though one need not be tender to Laval, one must be fair. His Foreign Office disliked him and was probably trying to bring him down before either the French or British could reflect.

On December 10 in Hoare's absence it fell to Eden to defend the Hoare-Laval plan in the House of Commons. He laid stress on the fact that the efforts of the two Foreign Secretaries to find a basis for peace had been carried on at the request of the co-ordinating committee of the League, and that therefore they had merely been trying to interpret the League's wish. Eden asserted that the reports that had appeared in the Press contained many inaccuracies, though he refused to specify what these were, since it would not be right to divulge the plan before it had been submitted to the

League. He admitted, however, that the plan went somewhat beyond the earlier proposals of the Committee of Five
in that they contained plans for an exchange of territory in
detail. He said that they were based on three main principles:
an exchange of territory conveying definite advantages to
both sides; economic help organized by the League for
Ethiopia; and special facilities for Italian settlers and Italian
companies in the economic development of the country. If
the plan was unacceptable to the League and objectionable
to the Covenant it was for the League to say so, and if the
League objected, the Government would make no complaint;
it would accept its judgment.

Though the Cabinet had approved the Hoare-Laval
plan it is obvious that it had misgivings. Eden was dispatched to Geneva to tell the committee of eighteen on the
12th that the plan was not sacrosanct and that it could be
amended. Indeed this had always been Hoare's understanding. The following day the official text was published,
and the popular outcry in the Press and Parliament in
Britain redoubled in intensity. It was seen that the plan in
some respects made even greater concessions than the leaked
versions had suggested. On the 16th *The Times*, in a
murderous leader entitled 'Corridor for Camels', dealt the
plan and Hoare a deadly blow. The Cabinet unanimously
decided to abandon the plan *in toto*, and to persevere,
however half-heartedly, with its policy of sanctions. Hoare
had returned from Switzerland and was ill in bed. He refused
to repudiate the plan for which he was responsible and in
consequence was forced to resign. When Parliament met on
the 19th Hoare explained in a manly and dignified fashion
the steps which had led him into his entanglement with Laval.
He still had plaster on his nose but his general bearing won
him the sympathy, though not the approval, of the House.

Too many tears need not be wasted on Hoare's broken
career. He was soon to be resuscitated and to rejoin the
Government as First Lord of the Admiralty. Hoare cannot be
exculpated of either deceiving the nation or of deceiving

himself. There can be no doubt that he did not believe in the efficacy of collective security or sanctions. Yet he recommended both to the League and to the electorate only to betray them as soon as the election was over. That Hoare did not believe that collective security could be made a reality can be shown by what he wrote nearly twenty years later in his *Nine Troubled Years* on the situation as it was when he went to the Foreign Office in June. He writes: 'collective security, the panacea of the Labour Party, had ceased to be either collective or secure'. Writing in retirement, he provides the most damning evidence of his political fecklessness and of his utter unsuitability ever to have had charge of the nation's responsibilities. For in a brief three months what had only been the 'panacea' of the Labour Party had become the policy of the British Government.

Not since Saul was converted on the road to Damascus had there been so extraordinary a transmogrification in deep-set convictions. What was the explanation? Perhaps the clue can be found in the second clause quoted above about the attitude of the Labour Party. By this date Baldwin had certainly resolved upon a general election. And 'panaceas', whatever their origins, were doubtless much in demand.

It would be wrong to allow Sir Samuel Hoare to pass even temporarily from the scene without a brief scrutiny of his attitude on national defence. In his book he represents himself as one of those who was eager to put Britain's defences in order. He more than once alleges that the Government could not rearm because they had no mandate prior to the 1935 election. In particular he says:

> Should the National Government in these circumstances have taken up the challenge and with or without a mandate embarked in 1933 or 1934 upon a full-scale programme of rearmament? Churchill in 1936 attacked Baldwin for failing to act in these years even though he had no mandate.

But does a Government, especially a 'National' Government, need a special mandate to provide adequate defence?

The defence of the country is implicit and inherent in the function of Government.

On December 19 Mr. Attlee on behalf of the Opposition moved a resolution criticizing the foreign policy of the Government. He moved:

> That the terms put forward by His Majesty's Government as a basis for an Italo-Abyssinian settlement reward the declared aggressor at the expense of the victim, destroy collective security, and conflict with the express will of the country and with the Covenant of the League of Nations, to the support of which the honour of Great Britain is pledged; this House therefore demands that these terms be immediately repudiated.

Attlee summed up the Hoare-Laval plan as involving the surrender to the aggressor of half an empire in exchange for a corridor of camels. (Under the Hoare-Laval plan the Abyssinians were to be denied the right of building a railway to the coast.) Attlee went on to say that the responsibility belonged to the Government as a whole, and since Sir Samuel Hoare had resigned the whole Government should follow his example. Attlee made the tactical mistake of impugning the honour of the Prime Minister, who, he said, had won the election on one policy and immediately afterwards had been ready to carry out another. The other issue, according to Attlee, was the question of the honour of the country. He accused the Government of destroying all faith in the word of honour of Great Britain. To some extent, Baldwin now proceeded to unseal his lips.

Mr. Baldwin said that as Prime Minister he was fully responsible for the plan. Out of loyalty he had decided to support a colleague who had not been present. But he did not attempt to defend the proposals themselves:

> I was not expecting that deeper feeling which was manifested ...in many parts of the country on what I may call the ground of conscience and of honour. The moment I am confronted with that, I know that something has happened that has appealed to the deepest feelings of our countrymen.... It is perfectly obvious now that these proposals are absolutely and completely

dead, and this Government is certainly not going to make any attempt to resurrect them.

He declared that the League of Nations would remain the keystone of British foreign policy. He added a warning:

> If by adherence to the League of Nations we find ourselves standing alone to do what ought to be done by everybody, the country will say: this is the last time we will allow a Government to commit itself with regard to collective security, because, for all we know, the next time the field may be nearer home than the Mediterranean.

He finished by asking for the confidence of the House.

Mr. Churchill at this time was away on holiday in Spain. In his absence the leading Conservative critic of the Government was Sir Austen Chamberlain. It was his opposition which was largely responsible for compelling Baldwin to abandon Hoare and his proposals. Chamberlain when he spoke in the debate said that he would vote in favour of the Government, not because of the argument which Baldwin had advanced, but because the Prime Minister's honour had been impugned. This gave an easy way out to many Government supporters who might otherwise have abstained or even have voted in the Opposition Lobby. Accordingly the Government accepted an amendment which was moved by Earl Winterton:

> That this House, holding that any terms for settling the Italo-Abyssinian dispute should be such as the League can accept, assures His Majesty's Government of its full support in pursuing the foreign policy outlined in the Government manifesto and endorsed by the country at the recent General Election.

At the close of the debate the Labour motion was rejected by 397 votes against 165. Earl Winterton's artful amendment was carried by 390 votes to 165. In a crowded House there were thirty-one Government absentees or abstainers. It would seem that there were at least twenty Government supporters who deliberately withheld their votes.

And what are we to say about Mr. Baldwin? He was grievously stricken in the esteem of the public and in his own, as his speech implied. He never knew about foreign politics, which bored him profoundly, but he thought he understood the innate instincts of the British people. He found that he had altogether underestimated the conviction with which the large majority of his fellow countrymen had accepted the good faith of the repeated pronouncements of his colleagues. In retrospect it seems incredible that a man of his sagacity could have made such an extraordinary error of judgment. Seen in his own lights he was an honest man, and by any lights not wilfully dishonest. It must be to mental sloth and general distaste of all public affairs save those of party management and the winning of elections that we must attribute his dubious role in these transactions.

'You know you can trust me' said the posters when Mr. Baldwin had gone to the country in 1929. Evidently they didn't, for in that year Mr. Baldwin and the Tories suffered a major electoral defeat. For some obscure reason, however, by 1935, they trusted him whatever he did and he took the fullest advantage of this new situation. So the country did not seem to mind when, after the ghastly fiasco of Hoare-Laval, Baldwin told them in almost successive sentences that the proposals which he had endorsed were 'absolutely and completely dead'; that 'the League of Nations would remain the keystone of foreign policy'; and added: 'this is the last time we will allow the Government to commit itself with regard to collective security, because, for all we know, the next time the field may be nearer home than the Mediterranean'. Mr. Baldwin, as was his wont, spoke as if he were an elector rather than a governor, and was naturally more concerned if anything should happen at home than abroad. He was at one with the most stupid and cowardly of his fellow-countrymen, at least in this.

The sort of ignorant rot which was the common parlance at this time of people like Baldwin, MacDonald, Chamberlain, Hoare, Simon, Halifax and Eden, and *The Times* newspaper, was to the effect that any firm stand anywhere would automatically produce a war for which we were by supine inattention unprepared. This sort of talk, much ventilated at All Souls, Cliveden and Printing House Square, was inevitably reported to the dictators, and naturally encouraged them in their forward marches.

Baldwin's unthinking hack phrase that 'sanctions that would be effective inevitably spelled war' was much circulated in every defeatist corridor, *salon* and saloon. This sort of stuff was day by day elegantly dished up in the columns of *The Times*, to the edification of all those who were looking for some respectable excuse for running away, in company with the Archbishop of Canterbury, Mr. Geoffrey Dawson and other Top People. In these defeatist circles to which the mandates of despair had already percolated and been accepted, it was natural to assume that the defence of the country had been so much neglected that we could not even take on a parcel of Italians. Generals, admirals, air marshals (with few air fleets to marshal) rapidly became infected with this defeatism. Cowardice, like courage, is infectious, and in the thirties we lived in a cowardly age in which money was more effective in promoting the virus of cowardice than that of stout-hearted courage.

It was put around by the Cliveden set that we could not stand up to Mussolini because of our patent lack of defence. We had no anti-aircraft defence at Malta; so the fleet was withdrawn to Alexandria. But a squadron was moved from home waters to Gibraltar. Alexandria and Gibraltar were beyond Italian bombing range. But was it true that, single-handed, Britain could not have stopped Mussolini's attack upon Abyssinia? The Suez Canal is by international treaty open to the warships and mercantile marine of all nations both in peace and war. But there was nothing to prevent a British squadron based on Aden scooping up all Italian transport ships bound for the Abyssinian war and escorting them into the wide anchorage at Aden. What would have happened then? Where could Mussolini have struck—

even though Baldwin, MacDonald, Chamberlain, Hoare, Simon, Halifax and Eden had so grievously neglected our defences? Of course Mussolini could have been licked. But Baldwin in his artless fashion proclaimed to the world that Britain was scared of a war, even with Italians. Hitler comprehended, chuckled and soon struck.

★

Mr. Baldwin's reiterated aversion to war and love of peace was a green light to Hitler, who was a somewhat abler man than many people at this time supposed. Hitler must have noted that Baldwin had predicated that in no circumstances would he fight against Mussolini, and have drawn some conclusions (particularly after the phrase 'the last time'). He took note and was to act in a short while. He had a certain flair for action, unlike Baldwin, who quickly relapsed after this disagreeable interlude into his normally comatose condition.

It was always a great argument of Stanley Baldwin's in the hours when he was alert that sanctions meant war. Hitler took note of this also; and so Britain was conducted ineluctably, step by step, by Baldwin, MacDonald, Chamberlain, Hoare, Simon, Halifax and Eden (loudly proclaim the names of the boobies!) to a position where we had to fight almost alone at a time not of our own choosing.

CHAPTER EIGHT

Foreign Secretary

HOARE fallen, Baldwin stricken, the Government abashed, Laval tarnished, Abyssinia betrayed, the League crippled, Mussolini encouraged, Hitler immensely strengthened. That was the bill which the world had to pay for Baldwin's electoral victory. Alone—on our side—Eden benefited by what had happened. After a brief delay during which the names of Halifax and Austen Chamberlain were canvassed, he stepped into Hoare's shoes, and on 22 December 1935 received the seals of the Foreign Office at the age of thirty-eight. As a member of the Cabinet he had been as responsible as anyone else for what had been done and what had not been done; in two senses more responsible. He had made the running at Geneva and had encouraged all the false expectations of what the League could do. When Hoare and Laval betrayed everything for which he stood, Eden was, in Hoare's absence, in charge of the Foreign Office, and while discharging this function was responsible for the telegram that was sent to the British Minister in Addis Ababa, urging the Emperor Haile Selassie to accept the evil work to which Hoare and Laval had set their hands in Paris.

However, no one seemed to think that Eden was in any way to blame. The public thought a lot of his glamorous appearances at Geneva; and in a sense he embodied all the hopes which the silliest people in the country—and they were particularly numerous during this period of British affairs—entertained about how Geneva and not their own strength could bring them peace. Young people growing up today will scarcely give credence to the folly and cowardice which their elders were showing at this time.

Nearly everyone seems to have supposed that the appointment of Mr. Eden as Foreign Secretary in place of Sir Samuel Hoare would usher in a prolonged period of peace. For instance:

His promotion answers accurately to the requirements both of public opinion and of last Thursday's debates in both Houses. In another respect the clearly expressed wishes of the House of Commons are being carried into execution.

With Mr. Eden's appointment the Government go forward again, newly and firmly authorized by public opinion to support the twofold policy of resolutely maintaining the common front against aggression and of finding the means compatible with common obligations of ending an unwarranted and disastrous war by a peaceful settlement.

The Times, 23 December 1935.

The very circumstances out of which the vacancy unhappily arose marked Mr. Eden out as the most appropriate and reassuring choice. He is a strong League of Nations man. Not long after his appointment last June as Minister for League Affairs he said, 'We believe in the League; we hold by the League; we will in no circumstances abandon our conviction of its indispensability'. He has never modified that strong emphasis. With him it has been the League first and last and all the time. Hence his appointment, quite apart from his personal qualifications and past record, should reassure all those whose confidence was shaken by the Paris Agreement, which seemed to them to mark a change in the British Government's attitude towards the League.

Daily Telegraph, 23 December 1935.

Any other choice than that of Mr. Eden as Foreign Secretary would have been a blunder of the first magnitude, and this not merely because he has patently the best qualifications of all the available candidates. It would have been taken as a proof that the Prime Minister was till intending to ride two horses, that he still regarded Mr. Eden as so much a 'League man' that he must be checked and controlled by a Secretary of State holding other, or less definite, views. It would have excited new and dangerous hopes in Italy: it would have aroused new fears and suspicions among the most loyal members of the League.

Daily Herald, 23 December 1935.

Just as the appointment will no doubt be commended by a section of public opinion at home, so it will bring relief in certain countries abroad. The arrival of Mr. Eden (whose attachment to the League of Nations and to the phrase 'collective security' is unwavering) may be understood abroad as a sign that Great Britain has gained second wind for Continental exploits. In Rome there is likely to be a gap in the acclamations, but from the small nations clustered under Geneva's wing there will come a grateful chirping.

Morning Post, 23 December 1935.

Mr. Eden, by his training and experience and marked ability, appears to be precisely the man needed for the present British emergency.

New York Times, 23 December 1935.

It is certain Mr. Eden considers that British policy should be based on the League. . . . It is to be hoped, however, that he will become conscious of the dangers of this policy if pushed to extremes and that he will agree with M. Laval that no opportunity should be allowed to go by for a peaceful settlement.

Journal des Débats, 23 December 1935.

The new Foreign Secretary, who faces a difficult task, will accentuate his efforts in the direction of sanctions as regards the Italo-Ethiopian conflict.

Le Matin, 23 December 1935.

This nomination will be welcomed abroad in all countries whose policy consists in making the League a real force in the service of peace.

Le Petit Parisien, 23 December 1935.

This choice shows a new orientation of British policy concerning collective security in general and the Ethiopian crisis in particular. England having decided to uphold the League and the cause of collective security, there can be no illusions on the

Italian side as to the developments in the diplomatic situation in the coming weeks.

Le Temps, 23 December 1935.

The situation is serious. A retreat from Italian violence would sharpen the land hunger of other dissatisfied Powers. With Mr. Eden's appointment England apparently desires to take the lead again.

Algemeen Handelsblad, 23 December 1935.

Through the appointment of Eden clarity is restored, the vacillation ended. Sureness of purpose is always a gain, for it enables others to make their dispositions.

Neue Freie Presse, 23 December 1935.

Italy must now see the 'point' directed towards her. The League need no longer doubt Britain's fidelity.

Deutsche Allgemeine Zeitung, 23 December 1935.

It is under the protection of Mr. Baldwin that Anthony Eden has grown up so young to such high honours. Mr. Baldwin took him to his heart, and it is this friendship across the gulf of generations that gives Mr. Eden a chance to prove his worth.

Berliner Tageblatt, 23 December 1935.

Mr. Eden is no stranger to Germany. It can only be a good thing that a man with expert knowledge of the German standpoint in all European questions has been placed at the head of the British Foreign Office. How far he sympathizes with Germany it is hard to say. He shows, however, that he is a realist and not merely a League of Nations idealist.

Frankfurter Zeitung, 23 December 1935.

It is Eden who caused the failure of the Laval-Hoare peace plans by first giving out to two French newspaper men, then in London, the text of the agreement and secondly by disavowing his Government's proposal at Geneva. What exactly Eden will do in his new position is not quite clear, but probably he will utilize the month remaining before the meeting of the League Council to line up once more the defaulting League front.

Giornale d'Italia, 23 December 1935.

The *New Statesman* in one of its silliest moods described Eden's appointment as Foreign Secretary as 'Mr. Baldwin's Christmas present to the nation'.

Eden was as compromised as Hoare and all his other colleagues in the Hoare-Laval transaction. But for some strange reason, perhaps of national sanctity, it suited everyone to pretend that he had no responsibility in the matter and that he was still the Sir Galahad of Geneva. The nation *wanted* a Christmas present. So, in a sense, he got off to a very good start. But it was essentially a bogus and broken-backed policy which he was now compelled to take over. All discerning observers could see that we had not the moral fibre to win, that Mussolini could do as he chose and that Hitler would swiftly profit from British folly and cowardice. This was the melancholy heritage that Eden accepted from Hoare.

Now the plush, plump, unthinking, pleasure-loving West was to be sharply confronted with the facts of life. On March 7 Hitler reoccupied the Rhineland. MacDonald, Hoare and Eden had destroyed the Stresa front, and Hitler was free to act. He acted. There has been much speculation since the event as to what would have happened if England and France had reacted violently against this gross breach of the Treaty of Versailles, but such speculation is idle. With Baldwin as Prime Minister, Eden as Foreign Secretary, anyone, even an ignorant, jumped-up Austrian house-painter like Hitler, could have guessed the result. The West gave in. Why not? Had not Baldwin already proclaimed that Britain would never fight? If Hitler had been confronted by men of courage and renown and, in spite of these obstacles, had achieved what he did achieve—and it was quite a lot—that might have ranked him as a genius. But as all he had against him was Baldwin and Eden, and since the Labour Party was unwittingly on his side, it was not difficult for him to prevail.

★

When the first unpleasantness ended in 1918 Clemenceau and Foch wished to annex the left bank of the Rhine in order to insure France against further acts of German aggression. This idea was distasteful to President Wilson, who arrived in Paris with all sorts of ideas about self-determination. He, perhaps rightly, thought it very shocking that several million Germans should be incorporated into the French Republic. Accordingly he produced the idea that the United States and Britain would guarantee the existing frontiers of France, plus Alsace and Lorraine, and would be ready jointly to fight on behalf of France if Germany were ever to attack again.

This was a tremendous offer. Clemenceau accepted it. Foch still preferred the left bank of the Rhine to the Anglo-American guarantee. In the end, of course, France got neither. The American Senate repudiated the signature of President Wilson and refused to ratify the Treaty of Versailles. The British guarantee was contingent upon the American guarantee, and thus France was left with no secure frontier and no guarantee of either British or American aid should her frontiers once more be violated.

No appraisal of France's conduct between the two wars and during the second war is realistic except against this sombre and tragic background. Frenchmen had poured out their blood as never before and thought at the end of it they had achieved security. Instead, they found they had been robbed of the legitimate fruits of the Allied victory and were again at the mercy of the German aggressor. Small wonder that there was bitterness. Small wonder that many of the finest and most patriotic men of France began to think in terms of coming to an accommodation with Germany. There were 40 million Frenchmen; there were 70 million Germans. Each year nearly twice as many Germans came of military age and were called to the colours as in France. The French are a logical people. They surveyed the scene. They did not like the look of it. They had no right or reason to suppose that Britain and America would rescue them again. They felt that they had better settle with their enemy while he was still at the gate.

The only tiny sop that was flung to the French was that the right bank of the Rhine should be demilitarized. On paper, and politicians are very fond of paper—it can always be thrown in the fire—it looked very good and peaceful and sensible. Until, on 7 March 1936, Hitler sent his army into these demilitarized zones, 'reoccupied' them, and quite soon proclaimed the building of the Siegfried Line on which some premature English songster, to the embarrassment of all thoughtful people, was, in 1939, to proclaim that 'we would hang out the washing'.

One man knew his own mind—the French Prime Minister, M. Pierre-Etienne Flandin. He was for fighting, and came to London to try to persuade Mr. Baldwin and his colleagues that France and Britain, in accordance with their obligations under the Treaties of Versailles and Locarno, should turn the Germans out of the Rhineland. Mr. Baldwin was eloquent about the misfortunes which seemed to plague him at this time of year, so that instead of seeing the plum and apple blossoms in the Vale of Evesham some tiresome international episode almost invariably detained him in the metropolis. Flandin was in a weak position since his soldiers, airmen and sailors were not at all keen to fight. Still, he might have talked them into it, if he had received some encouragement from the English. Alas, the English were presided over at that time by Baldwin and the new Foreign Secretary, Eden; and resolute though Eden may have felt himself, he did not carry sufficient political guns in the Cabinet for him to be a determining factor in British policy.

It was unlucky for Eden that he should have been confronted by a crisis of this magnitude so early in his tenure of the Foreign Office. Hitler, of course, as was to be his wont, coupled his illegal aggression with reassuring noises: 'we have no territorial demands to make in Europe', he told the Reichstag. This was highly gratifying to those in the West who wanted to give in—and they were numerous. Eden, after seeing the German Ambassador, Herr von Hoesch, in London and indicating his concern at what had been done, bustled off to Paris with Halifax to comfort the French. Baldwin had considered Halifax for the Foreign Office. The fact that he was detailed to accompany the Foreign Secretary showed that Baldwin still felt that the 'young man' should not be allowed abroad on really important occasions involving peace and war without the *chaperonage* of a member of the inner Cabinet. Eden, though his office should have made him among the two or three most powerful members of the Cabinet, had not yet, despite his popularity at home and abroad, achieved a comparable political stature in the Cabinet to that enjoyed by Lord Halifax, who only occupied the sinecure office of Lord Privy Seal.

In Paris, Eden and Halifax proposed that the Rhineland question should be referred to the Council of the League, which should meet in London. The four Locarno Powers, Britain, France, Belgium and Italy, met in London on March 12; it was unanimously recognized that Germany had violated Articles 42 and 43 of the Treaty of Versailles. Two days later the League Council met; at the end of the discussions the Council invited Germany to attend its next meeting. The Council met again on March 17, 18 and 19; Ribbentrop delivered a long speech on the third of these dates. When he addressed the House of Commons on the following day, Eden said that the discussion between the Locarno Powers had been both long and complicated:

It was clear from the outset that the occupation of the demilitarized zone by German troops presented a *fait accompli* which made the opening of negotiations with Germany very difficult. It was strongly held that negotiations could not begin until this breach of international law had been in some measure restored. Immediately on my return from Paris, therefore, I suggested to the German Government that they should make a contribution to ease the situation created by their action. The suggestion was, briefly, that pending negotiations they should withdraw troops in sufficient number to warrant the description of the reoccupation as symbolic, and that, similarly, they should abstain from the construction of fortifications. Though the German Chancellor publicly expressed his willingness not further to increase the number of troops sent in, this was not sufficient to enable much progress to be made.

Eden told the House that it was now proposed to submit to the League Council certain resolutions enjoining 'scrupulous respect for treaty obligations, proposing the reference to the Permanent Court of International Justice . . . and taking note of the reaffirmation which Belgium, France, Italy and ourselves propose to make of their rights and obligations under the Treaty of Locarno'.

It was by now perfectly plain that neither Britain nor France intended to turn Hitler out of the Rhineland, though the task would have been quite easy, even with the limited resources available. Instead France was fobbed off with a promise of immediate Anglo-French staff talks in London. And that was that. We had passed another milestone on the road to war, down which we were all unknowingly being shepherded by Baldwin, MacDonald, Chamberlain, Hoare, Simon, Halifax and Eden.

Mussolini was meanwhile getting on in a businesslike fashion with the conquest of Abyssinia. During the dispute which had preceded the outbreak of hostilities in Abyssinia, the League had placed an embargo on the export of arms. This was thought a particularly wise act of statesmanship, since it ensured that the country which the League was so anxious to defend against threatened aggression should be quite incapable of defending itself.

However, despite this restraint, the Italians were soon complaining that the Abyssinians were shooting at their troops with dumdum bullets of British manufacture, a weapon which is obviously far more deadly at close range than poison gas, and which, like poison gas, was a breach of the rules of war and a further example of the barbarous character of the Abyssinians. Fortunately, the Foreign Secretary, 'in the interests of British industry and of the good name of the country', was in a position to announce that the licence for the export of this ammunition had been issued before the embargo and that, in any case, the ammunition had been intended 'for sporting purposes'. Everyone sighed with relief at this plausible explanation, which did not, however, receive an encomium from the Royal Society for the Prevention of Cruelty to Animals.

By the early summer it was clear to everyone that sanctions had failed and that Mussolini had conquered virtually the whole of Abyssinia. His troops had entered the capital, Addis Ababa, on May 5. The Emperor fled and arrived in England on June 3. There he was to live in exile until British arms restored him to his throne in 1941.

There did not seem much point in going on with sanctions. They had, not surprisingly, failed to save Abyssinia; it seemed irrelevant to persevere with them merely to punish Mussolini, particularly as there were not lacking people who hoped that all might be forgiven and that Mussolini might be detached from Hitler and the Stresa front rebuilt.

The first speech which openly advocated the dropping of sanctions was made by Sir Austen Chamberlain in the House of Commons on May 6. This was followed on June 10 by Neville Chamberlain's famous 'midsummer madness' speech given to the 1900 Club:

I see . . . the other day that the President of the League of Nations Union issued a circular to its members in which . . . he urged them to commence a campaign of pressure . . . with the idea that, if we were to pursue the policy of sanctions, and even to intensify it, it is still possible to preserve the independence of Abyssinia. That seems to me the very midsummer of madness. . . . Is it not apparent that the policy of sanctions involves, I do not say war, but a risk of war? . . . is it not also apparent from what has happened that, in the presence of such a risk, nations cannot be relied upon to proceed to the last extremity unless their vital interests are threatened?

On June 18, Eden announced the decision of the Government to abandon sanctions against Italy:

It might be argued that collective action should have been more thorough or more complete, but nobody can argue that in the action that has been taken the British Government have not played their full part.

We have no intention of departing from that principle now. On the contrary, we shall continue to take our full share in any decision which the League of Nations in its Assembly at the end of this month may decide to take. The Government is responsible to the League—responsible not only for compliance, but also for guidance.

When it came in October to the actual organization and application of the collective action which fifty nations of the League had decided, for the first time in history, that they would take, again it was this Government which took the lead both in proposing and in organizing the work of these committees. Now that the League is perplexed, it is the view of the Government that it is their duty to take the lead again.

Whatever view we take of the course of action which the League should follow, here is one fact upon which we must all be agreed. We have to admit that the purpose for which sanctions were imposed has not been realized. The Italian military campaign succeeded. That is a situation which has got to be faced. It is a situation which nothing but military action from outside the country can reverse.

Taking all these facts into consideration, His Majesty's Government have come to the conclusion that there is no longer any utility in continuing sanctions as a means of pressure upon Italy. We have got to comprise within one organization the willing collaboration of Governments of totally divergent character. I say this to give some indication of the nature of the problem, and unless we do face it, we cannot expect the League in the future effectively to meet these problems. There is one aim upon which we are all united—that peace, not chaos and catastrophe, should rule.

Peace is the one essential need of the world. It is because I believe profoundly that the policy I have outlined is that which in the present anxious, difficult, critical situation is most likely to preserve peace, that I submit it with deep conviction and with a full sense of responsibility.

While the melancholy masquerade of sanctions was grinding to its pathetic conclusion, a new problem arose to occupy the attention of the statesmen of Europe—the Spanish Civil War. This episode was to have wide and persistent repercussions in several European countries. It was to become a touchstone of high political significance. In many people's eyes it made Communism more respectable and encouraged ideas of a popular front. It was 'liberal' and 'progressive' to support the 'loyalists'. It was reactionary to support General Franco. Eden and the British Cabinet decided to accept the French proposal for a policy of 'non-intervention'. This was mainly devised to spare the embarrassment of the French Prime Minister, M. Léon Blum, whose left-wing coalition Government was based on the Popular Front and was, to some extent, dependent on Communist support for its survival. But as the official Government of Spain increasingly fell into the hands of Anarchists and Communists, the French increasingly began to wonder how they would be advantaged by a Communist Spain. Non-intervention, though unheroic, was probably the best method of preventing a civil war in France and the likely possibility that all Europe might become involved.

In March 1936 there had been elections in Spain in which a left-wing coalition had united in a Popular Front and scored a victory. A Government was formed by Señor Cesares Quiroga, friend and associate of Señor Caballero, the Marxist leader. The early months of this Government were disfigured by much disorder, most of it due to provocation by organizations of the extreme Right and of a Fascist complexion. The period was marked by many strikes. Despite a large number of incidents and outrages, which raised doubts as to the capacity of the Government to maintain law and order, the situation did not get wholly out of hand. Indeed, the Government seemed to be getting some grip upon the administration of the country, when, in July, Lieutenant Castillo of the shock police, who was known to have Socialist sympathies, was shot dead by right-wing terrorists. The next day in retaliation a group of shock police tried to arrest Señor Calvo Sotelo, the leader of the right-wing opposition. A scuffle ensued and Sotelo was shot dead. This was the event which decided the Army that it was time to take over. Risings took place in a number of cities simultaneously; a careful plan had obviously been concerted well in advance. The rebels immediately gained control of Seville, Cadiz and Saragossa. In Madrid and Barcelona, after considerable bloodshed, the revolt was put down. Many of the leading military figures had been posted abroad by the Government as a precaution. They immediately returned to Spain to take command of the military rebellion. The natural leader, General Sanjurjo, was, however, killed in an aeroplane smash taking off from Lisbon. General Mola rallied the Army in Morocco, while General Franco, who had been serving in the Canaries, flew to Tetuan to place himself at the head of the movement following the death of Sanjurjo.

To begin with, the insurgents made rapid progress. They captured Badajoz in the middle of August and advanced rapidly up the Tagus valley via Talavera and Toledo, and by the middle of November had arrived in front of Madrid. Franco had from the outset benefited from weapons supplied by Germany and Italy and the Government was much less well equipped. However, as the year wore on the Government forces began to receive the weapons which were being feverishly manufactured in industrial centres such as Barcelona and Bilbao, and with the advent of the International Brigade the defence of Madrid seemed assured for many months ahead.

France and Britain pressed ahead with their plans for non-intervention. They sought to set up an international committee which would include Germany, Italy, Portugal and

Russia. This committee met in London at the beginning of September. Portugal did not adhere till a little later.

*

While this was going on, Eden signed at the end of August an Anglo-Egyptian treaty of alliance. In view of the importance which Egyptian affairs assume later in this biography, it may be for the convenience of the reader if a detailed summary of what was signed in 1936 is set down here.

The following were the main heads of agreement:

Military Clauses:

1. The transfer of British troops from Cairo to the Canal zone (the occupation to be limited to twenty years), with a gradual reduction of the British Army in Egypt, though not until the Egyptian forces are strengthened.
2. The creation of a British naval base at Alexandria, for which rent will be paid by the British Government to Egypt.
3. A considerable increase in the strength of the Royal Air Force.
4. The construction by the Egyptian Government of suitable strategic roads to allow British forces to be moved rapidly across Egypt if necessary.

Sudan Clauses:

1. Measures to be taken to facilitate Egyptian immigration to the Sudan.
2. Egyptians to be permitted to own property in the Sudan.
3. Units of the Egyptian Army to return to the Sudan.
4. Certain Egyptian officials to be appointed to the Sudan Government Service, including a senior official of the Governor's Council and two officials for finance and justice.

Capitulations Clauses:

1. The abolition in principle of the Capitulatory régime.
2. The transfer of the jurisdiction of the Consular courts (which deal with criminal cases) to the mixed courts (which deal with civil cases only).
3. Collection of taxes from foreigners the same as from Egyptians.
4. Convocation of an international conference at Cairo to discuss proposals to abolish the mixed courts.

At the ceremony which marked the signing of the treaty, Eden said:

I have seen it said that the treaty marks the end of an epoch in Anglo-Egyptian relations; I would prefer to regard it as the beginning of a new stage. . . .

The treaty which we are about to sign is the pledge and instrument of our future collaboration. We earnestly hope that the alliance which we thereby inaugurate today may be at once the means of enabling the Governments of our two countries to work together in close amity for the furtherance of their common interests, and the symbol of a freely agreed and enduring partnership between the British and Egyptian peoples.

The Egyptian Prime Minister, who signed the treaty, was Nahas Pasha, of whom we shall hear more as the story of Anglo-Egyptian relations becomes increasingly dominant in these pages.

★

On 1 November 1936, the Rome-Berlin Axis was proclaimed by Mussolini in Rome. This was the outcome of talks held first at Berlin and then at Berchtesgaden between Ciano and Hitler in the middle of October. The Reich gave formal recognition to the Empire of Ethiopia.

By a maladroit policy Britain had failed either to make a friend of Mussolini or to destroy him. We had merely driven him into Hitler's artful arms. Henceforward Britain was to seek persistently but unavailingly to detach Mussolini from the Axis. An Anglo-Italian Mediterranean Agreement was signed in Rome early in the New Year by Count Ciano and Sir Eric Drummond, the British Ambassador. This was a 'gentleman's agreement', 'concerning assurances with regard to the Mediterranean'.

In the House of Commons Eden declared that we were prepared to co-operate in the common work of political appeasement and economic collaboration.

Economic collaboration and political appeasement must go hand in hand. If economical and financial accommodation merely result in more armaments and more political disturbance the cause of peace will be hindered rather than helped. On the other hand a new and freer economic and financial collaboration, based upon solid and well-conceived political undertakings, will be a powerful aid towards the establishment of a unity of purpose in Europe. . . . We do not accept that the alternative for Europe lies between dictatorships of the Right and the Left.

★

1937 was to be a relatively quiet year. The scene at home in the early summer was largely dominated by the Coronation of King George VI; abroad by the execution of Marshal Tukhachevsky together with several hundred other senior officers of the Red Army. Hitler was digesting and fortifying the Rhineland and his armament factories were now getting into their stride and were pouring forth the copious supply of weapons which was so soon to make him the master of Europe. Mussolini was digesting Abyssinia and consolidating his position on the home front. He had involved himself in a scrape in Spain, but this was all to turn out quite satisfactorily for him.

Shortly after the Coronation Baldwin's long-heralded resignation took place. He was succeeded, as had been expected, by Neville Chamberlain. The new Prime Minister only made consequential changes in the Administration. Simon was brought from the Home Office to replace Chamberlain at the Treasury; Hoare came from the Admiralty to replace Simon; Duff Cooper came from the War Office to the Admiralty; Hore-Belisha came from Transport to the War Office. Chamberlain made no attempt to make a new Government of his own or introduce any new blood save that of Dr. Leslie Burgin. It was merely a game of musical chairs. Chamberlain inherited Eden as Foreign Secretary with, as the auctioneers say, 'the livestock on the premises'. Though the two men were temperamentally unsuited and their views on foreign policy remarkably divergent, it does not seem to have occurred to Chamberlain to make any change in this crucial office.

A comical episode which lent light relief to the darkening scene was a visit by Halifax in his capacity as Master of the Middleton Foxhounds to Berlin as the guest of Goering, Chief Huntsman of the Reich, who was presiding over a hunting exhibition in Berlin. Though Halifax devoted the time that had been allotted to a *battue* of foxes to talking to Goering and Hitler, the diplomatic results of his visit were scarcely more impressive than was the proffered sport in the eyes of an English master of hounds. Hitler was shortly to lay violent hands upon Vienna. Naturally Halifax did not suspect this; naturally Hitler was not deterred from a new outrage by anything he heard from Halifax.

Though for the most part British merchant ships complied with the Government request not to trade with either side in Spain, there were some hardy spirits who disregarded diplomatic niceties and continued to carry goods indifferently to either side. One who caught the popular fancy was 'Potato' Jones. Since he was a Welshman he also gained the enthusiastic plaudits of Mr. Lloyd George. Italian submarines were very active in the Mediterranean and frequently molested and sank British shipping. Eden was most energetic in this matter and took the leading part in the conference of the principal Mediterranean Powers which met at Nyon on the Lake of Geneva in September.

In a broadcast from Geneva at the conclusion of the Nyon Conference on September 14, Mr. Eden said:

> Recent submarine sinkings have constituted a kind of gangster terrorism of the seas. They took no account of the sufferings and loss of life of the crews attacked. By setting up a police force in the Mediterranean, we believe that we have put a stop to submarine piracy in that sea. If any submarine attempts again to embark on evil courses it will, I hope and believe, receive the punishment it deserves.
>
> The problem that confronted the Powers at the Nyon Conference was that of the masked highwayman who does not

stop short of manslaughter or even murder. What we have done is to authorize the patrolling vessels to counter-attack, and, if possible, destroy any submarine actually engaged in piracy.

The success of this conference evoked a tribute from Mr. Churchill in the House of Commons. It was one of the few he was able to pay to His Majesty's Ministers during this period:

Let me recall the ugly situation which existed before the Nyon Conference. Eight or nine pirate submarines were loose in the Mediterranean, sinking ships from one end of it to the other, and leaving crews to drown with the most atrocious inhumanity. All of a sudden Great Britain and France decided that these outrages must be stopped, and stopped if necessary by armed force. Anyone could feel, although it was not expressed in words, the stiffening and surge of resolution which accompanied the summoning of that conference. That was a great responsibility for our Foreign Secretary to take, but he was able to take it, and the results were most satisfactory. From that moment not a single torpedo has been fired by any submarine in the Mediterranean at any ship carrying any cargo under any flag. The success of these measures should be recognized even by those who criticize the course which the Government have pursued, but I must pay my tribute to Signor Mussolini, who joined in the common exertions of the Mediterranean Powers, and whose prestige and authority—by the mere terror of his name—quelled the wicked depradations of these marauders. Since the days of Caesar himself there has been no more salutary clearance of pirates from the Mediterranean.

CHAPTER NINE

Resignation

SHORTLY before the close of 1937, Sir Robert Vansittart, Permanent Under-Secretary of State at the Foreign Office, was 'kicked upstairs'. He was given the honorific position of Chief Diplomatic Adviser to the Secretary of State and was replaced in his key post by his deputy, Sir Alexander Cadogan. Vansittart's new functions were stated to be 'analogous to those fulfilled by the occupants of similar posts attached to other Departments (the Chief Industrial and the Chief Economic Advisers to the Government)'. His functions were to include 'advising the Secretary of State upon all major questions of policy concerning foreign affairs *remitted to him for that purpose*, and representing the Foreign Office on any occasions, whether at home or abroad, on which the Secretary of State might wish to avail himself of his services'. The *Annual Register* of 1938 commented:

> The reasons given for the new departure seemed at the time genuine enough; but in the light of subsequent developments it came to be regarded as a subtle device for removing from close contact with foreign affairs a man who was in general sympathy with Mr. Eden and replacing him with one who could be relied upon to give unquestioning support to Mr. Chamberlain.

The *Annual Register* for once failed in its insight to the truth. Eden was every bit as eager to dispense with Vansittart as was Chamberlain. The last words which Vansittart wrote in his memoirs *The Mist Procession* are decisive on this point. After describing how he had consulted Sir Austen Chamberlain about his difficulties, he tells how he received a devastating reply. ' "You had better go," Austen

said, "you are getting rattled." Each word was a blow.
"We've lost," I said to my wife. "Even Austen doesn't see."
I decided to stick it out in spite of him', but 'Vansittart was
considered to have compromised himself over the Hoare-
Laval Pact'. So spake Eden by his biographer Broad.

Vansittart was no more compromised save in the undis-
criminating eye of the public over Hoare-Laval than had
been Eden, and it is doubtful if Mr. Broad (so long after the
event) had diagnosed Eden's true attitude much more accurately than it was diagnosed at the time in the *Annual Register*.
It is one of the many merits of Vansittart's book that, while
illuminating in a thousand ways the perplexities of these
times, he never writes a disloyal word about any of the varied
chiefs—Baldwin, Simon, Hoare, Eden—under whom he
served. But there is one phrase in *The Mist Procession* which
gives the reader exceptional pause for thought. Whether it
was artless or artful the reader must judge for himself.
Writing of the Cliveden set, who were intriguing at this
time to get rid of Vansittart from the Foreign Office, he
records:

> I told Eden, who was welcome there, that his visits were
> unfair to me while animosity ran so high; but I knew that I
> was unreasonable and did not expect him to discontinue them.

★

It is impossible to form a just view of Eden's resignation
in February 1938 unless one bears in mind the time-table of
European events which advertised and delivered ill tidings
with the punctilio of a Prussian mathematician. Hitler had
completed his digestive process in 1937. '*L'appétit*,' say the
French, '*arrive en mangeant*.' Hitler's gastric juices were now
flowing once more. He needed a new victim. Another
meal, this time Austria, was on the bill of fare, though this
naturally was not apparent to Chamberlain or Simon or
Hoare or Halifax or Eden. They still accepted Hitler's
reiterated and thrice-perjured assurances. On February 12,
Dr. Schuschnigg, who had succeeded the murdered Dollfuss

as Chancellor of Austria, was summoned to Berchtesgaden by Hitler. Schuschnigg found himself confronted by Hitler and his generals, whose hands were bristling with maps and blueprints for the invasion of Austria. Schuschnigg was told at the top of Hitler's voice that he must release all the Nazis that he had imprisoned, give full liberty of action to the Nazi Party and hand over the Ministry of the Interior to Herr Seyss-Inquart, Hitler's personal representative in Austria. Schuschnigg felt himself compelled to accept these humiliating terms. The support which Austria had obtained from Italy nearly four years before, after the assassination of Dollfuss, could no longer be counted on. The Stresa front was a dead duck. Mussolini, having quarrelled with France and England, was not in the mood to quarrel with Hitler, and could not have afforded to even if he had wanted to. On February 20 Hitler graciously informed the Reichstag of what he had done and declared it to be imperative that the 10 million Germans in Austria and Czechoslovakia should achieve 'the right of self-determination'.

★

Eden's enemies, both at the time and later, have sought to establish that he resigned out of petulance on a trumpery issue. There were certainly more important issues on which Eden might, with advantage to the nation and himself, have chosen to separate himself from his colleagues—the failure to cope with the German menace or national defence. But though the ostensible grounds of Eden's resignation can be made to seem, if not trumpery, at least trivial, he had solid reasons for his action.

Many accounts have been given of the just and heavy grievance which Eden had against the Prime Minister as to the way an important telegram from President Roosevelt was mishandled in his absence on holiday in the South of France. Those who have read all these accounts and compared them carefully may perhaps conclude that the most complete and authoritative to be published so far is that of

Sir Winston Churchill in *The Gathering Storm*, the first volume
of his war memoirs:

On the evening of 11 January 1938, Mr. Sumner Welles,
the American Under-Secretary of State, called upon the British
Ambassador in Washington. He was the bearer of a secret and
confidential message from President Roosevelt to Mr. Chamberlain. The President was deeply anxious at the deterioration of
the international situation, and proposed to take the initiative
by inviting the representatives of certain Governments to
Washington to discuss the underlying causes of present difficulties. Before taking this step, however, he wished to consult
the British Government on their view of such a plan, and
stipulated that no other Government should be informed either
of the nature or the existence of such a proposal. He asked that
not later than January 17 he should be given a reply to his
message, and intimated that only if his suggestion met with
'the cordial approval and whole-hearted support of His
Majesty's Government' would he then approach the Governments of France, Germany, and Italy. Here was a formidable
and measureless step.

In forwarding this most secret message to London the British
Ambassador, Sir Ronald Lindsay, commented that in his view
the President's plan was a genuine effort to relax international
tension, and that if His Majesty's Government withheld their
support the progress which had been made in Anglo-American
co-operation during the previous two years would be destroyed.
He urged in the most earnest manner acceptance of the proposal by the British Government. The Foreign Office received the
Washington telegram on January 12, and copies were sent
to the Prime Minister in the country that evening. On the
following morning he came to London, and on his instructions
a reply was sent to the President's message. Mr. Eden was at
this time on a brief holiday in the South of France. Mr.
Chamberlain's reply was to the effect that he appreciated the
confidence of President Roosevelt in consulting him in this
fashion upon his proposed plan to alleviate the existing tension
in Europe, but he wished to explain the position of his own
efforts to reach agreement with Germany and Italy, particularly
in the case of the latter.

'His Majesty's Government would be prepared, for their part, if possible with the authority of the League of Nations, to recognize *de jure* the Italian occupation of Abyssinia, if they found that the Italian Government on their side were ready to give evidence of their desire to contribute to the restoration of confidence and friendly relations.' The Prime Minister mentioned these facts, the message continued, so that the President might consider whether his present proposal might not cut across the British efforts. Would it not therefore be wiser to postpone the launching of the American plan?

This reply was received by the President with some disappointment. He intimated that he would reply by letter to Mr. Chamberlain on January 17. On the evening of January 15 the Foreign Secretary returned to England. He had been urged to come back, not by his chief, who was content to act without him, but by his devoted officials at the Foreign Office. The vigilant Alexander Cadogan awaited him upon the pier at Dover. Mr. Eden, who had worked long and hard to improve Anglo-American relations, was deeply perturbed. He immediately sent a telegram to Sir Ronald Lindsay attempting to minimize the effects of Mr. Chamberlain's chilling answer. The President's letter reached London on the morning of January 18. In it he agreed to postpone making his proposal in view of the fact that the British Government were contemplating direct negotiations, but he added that he was gravely concerned at the suggestion that His Majesty's Government might accord recognition to the Italian position in Abyssinia. He thought that this would have a most harmful effect upon Japanese policy in the Far East and upon American public opinion. Mr. Cordell Hull, in delivering this letter to the British Ambassador in Washington, expressed himself even more emphatically. He said that such a recognition would 'rouse a feeling of disgust, would revive and multiply all fears of pulling the chestnuts out of the fire; it would be represented as a corrupt bargain completed in Europe at the expense of interests in the Far East in which America was intimately concerned'.

The President's letter was considered at a series of meetings of the Foreign Affairs Committee of the Cabinet. Mr. Eden succeeded in procuring a considerable modification of the

previous attitude. Most of the Ministers thought he was satisfied. He did not make it clear to them that he was not. Following these discussions two messages were sent to Washington on
the evening of January 21. The substance of these replies was
that the Prime Minister warmly welcomed the President's
initiative, but was not anxious to bear any responsibility for its
failure if American overtures were badly received. Mr.
Chamberlain wished to point out that we did not accept in an
unqualified manner the President's suggested procedure, which
would clearly irritate both the Dictators and Japan. Nor did
His Majesty's Government feel that the President had fully
understood our position in regard to *de jure* recognition. The
second message was in fact an explanation of our attitude in this
matter. We intended to accord such recognition only as part of
a general settlement with Italy.

The British Ambassador reported his conversation with Mr.
Sumner Welles when he handed these messages to the President
on January 22. He stated that Mr. Welles told him that 'the
President regarded recognition as an unpleasant pill which we
should both swallow together'.

Thus it was that President Roosevelt's proposal to use American influence for the purpose of bringing together the leading
European Powers to discuss the chances of a general settlement,
this of course involving however tentatively the mighty power
of the United States, was rebuffed by Mr. Chamberlain. This
attitude defined in a decisive manner the difference of view
between the British Prime Minister and his Foreign Secretary.
Their disagreements were still confined to the circle of the
Cabinet for a little time longer; but the split was fundamental.
The comments of Mr. Chamberlain's biographer, Professor
Feiling, upon this episode, are not without interest. 'While
Chamberlain feared the Dictators would pay no heed or else
would use this line-up of the Democracies as pretext for a break, it was
found on Eden's return that he would rather risk that calamity
than the loss of American goodwill. There was the first breath
of resignation.'

If the reader feels that a corrective is needed to the above
account, he should have recourse to Lord Templewood's
Nine Troubled Years, which was published six years after Sir

Winston's *The Gathering Storm*. Templewood, though he puts a very different gloss upon the story, does not at any point invalidate Churchill's account, to which, indeed, he does not allude. One quotation from Templewood's story is essential:

> Accordingly there followed a series of telegrams with the object of clarifying any differences between Washington and London, and ending with what practically amounted to a reversal of our respective positions. It was, in fact, we who finally agreed to support the proposal, and Roosevelt who decided that the moment was no longer suitable for pressing it.

Who would suspect from Templewood's story that it was Eden, who, on his speedy return from the South of France, insisted that these more conciliatory telegrams should be sent? This was one of Eden's finest hours. It is inevitably obfuscated in *Nine Troubled Years*.

Before this story ends it will be necessary to draw the reader's attention to some other occasions on which Templewood in his studiously *rusé* memoirs has done something less than justice to former colleagues of his, in one case where the colleague was dead and could not answer.

Eden, when he came to the first great crisis of his political life, was suffering from a number of disadvantages, some of which he probably did not detect. Though he was still on good social terms with many members of the Cliveden set,* few of them agreed with him on foreign policy. And though they had encouraged and approved of his acquiescence in kicking Vansittart upstairs and regarded this as a great triumph

---

* For a worm's-eye view of the Cliveden set, see Tom Jones's *Diary with Letters*, particularly the following passage—of 24 October 1937:

'Here the house is pretty full. Thirty to lunch today but this included three boys from Eton. The Edens are the highest lights and Nevile Henderson the newest. Sir Alex Cadogan and his brother, the Speaker and his Lady, Curzon's two daughters, Lady Alex Metcalfe and Lady Ravensdale, Geoffrey Dawson, Lothian, Brand and Curtis, Nicholls [sic] of the F.O., married to Spender-Clay's daughter, Bernays M.P. and so forth. Politics all day and all night. Eden has aged since I saw him six months ago and is dog-tired at the start of the Session. I sat between him and Henderson after the ladies left last night and found they

for their little fidgety, busybody faction, they were far
from believing that Eden would prove more malleable
than Vansittart in their plans for coming to terms with the
dictators at the expense of the smaller nations.

The author does not wish to obtrude his own opinions
unduly upon this grisly scene. Far be it from him to lay down
the law in these intricate matters. Let us, therefore, once
more summon into court three credible and contemporary
witnesses, so that the reader may pronounce for himself.
Templewood, in his *Nine Troubled Years*, writes:

> Eden wished to discover Mussolini's reactions to Hitler's
> Austrian *coup*, and to postpone the start of the negotiations
> until the position was clarified. Chamberlain, on the other
> hand, felt that any delay would destroy the goodwill between
> the two countries that he had created since he became Prime
> Minister, and that, once lost, might be very difficult to recover.
> Grandi was even more anxious than Chamberlain to avoid the
> Austrian issue and restrict any discussion to the question of
> Anglo-Italian relations. When, therefore, Eden asked him to
> come to the Foreign Office, the Ambassador made the excuse
> of a golf engagement for not accepting the invitation. Chamber-
> lain, at the same time, urgently wished to see Grandi about the
> Italian negotiations, and Grandi, guessing what was in
> Chamberlain's mind, was ready to go to Downing Street, as
> he rightly assumed that the talk would not be about Mussolini's
> reactions to Hitler's *coup*, but about Mussolini's relations with
> Great Britain. Whilst this was the position in London, Ciano
> in Rome was pressing Perth for direct talks between the Prime
> Minister and Grandi. It was to break the deadlock between the

differed widely in policy. Henderson struck me as sensible and informed without
distinction. He has lived in the countries we talked about and Eden has not and
this was apparent. . . . Eden himself thinks the Cabinet very weak and the
armament programme far in arrears. On the other hand, he seems to argue that
we can't do business with Germany until we are armed—say in 1940. This assumes that we can catch up with Germany—which we cannot, and that Hitler
takes no dramatic step in the meantime, which is unlike Hitler. We have
spurned his repeated offers. They will not be kept open indefinitely. His price
will mount and he will want the naval agreement revised in his favour. It is
believed that Mussolini has sold Austria to him at the recent meeting, in return
for what, I don't know.'

Foreign Office and the Italian Embassy that Chamberlain stepped outside the channel of regular communication, and used as a go-between an official* in the Conservative Party office, who had worked for him for many years, to propose to Grandi a meeting in Downing Street. The background of this unconventional approach was found in a long-standing contact between Chamberlain's messenger and a subordinate member of the Italian Embassy.

Whilst the Foreign Office knew of the association and attached little importance to it, it had occasionally provided Chamberlain with scraps of information that had helped him to assess Mussolini's attitude towards the negotiations, and in particular, towards the question of the withdrawal of Italian troops from Spain. When, therefore, an *impasse* had been reached between the Foreign Office and the Italian Embassy he turned to his old confidant, and authorized him to make it known to the Ambassador, through the intermediary at the Embassy, that he would welcome a visit to Downing Street.

Churchill, in *The Gathering Storm*, writes:

It must have been with declining confidence in the future that Mr. Eden went to Paris on January 25 to consult with the French. Everything now turned upon the success of the approach to Italy, of which we had made such a point in our replies to the President. The French Ministers impressed upon Mr. Eden the necessity of the inclusion of Spain in any general settlement with the Italians; on this he needed little convincing. On February 10 the Prime Minister and the Foreign Secretary met Count Grandi, who declared that the Italians were ready in principle to open the conversations.

On February 15 the news came of the submission of the Austrian Chancellor, Schuschnigg, to the German demand for the introduction into the Austrian Cabinet of the Chief Nazi agent, Seyss-Inquart, as Minister of the Interior and Head of the Austrian Police. This grave event did not avert the personal crisis between Mr. Chamberlain and Mr. Eden. On February 18 they saw Count Grandi again. This was the last business they conducted together. The Ambassador refused either to discuss the Italian position towards Austria, or to consider the

* Mr. Joseph Ball, later knighted for his services to the nation.

British plan for the withdrawal of volunteers, or so-called volunteers—in this case five divisions of the regular Italian Army—from Spain. Grandi asked, however, for general conversations to be opened in Rome. The Prime Minister wished for these, and the Foreign Secretary was strongly opposed to such a step.

Our third witness must be called into court, though he comes from the grave. Mr. Duff Cooper writes in his *Old Men Forget*:

> I was unhappy about Anthony Eden's departure. I wrote to tell him so and to say that I had always found myself in agreement with him, except on this one question of Italy. He knew more than I did, but neither he nor I knew that behind his back our own Prime Minister was in secret communication with the Italian Ambassador. The three of them (Chamberlain, Eden and Grandi) had met together on February 18, and on the very day we were discussing whether Eden should remain in the Cabinet, Grandi was reporting to his Foreign Minister, Count Ciano:

>> 'Chamberlain, in fact, in addressing his questions directly to me, expected from me—this was obvious—nothing more nor less than those details and definite answers which were useful to him as ammunition against Eden. This I at once realized and naturally tried to supply Chamberlain with all the ammunition which I considered might be useful to him to this end. There is no doubt that in this connection the contacts previously established between myself and Chamberlain through his confidential agent proved to be very valuable. Purely as a matter of historical interest, I inform Your Excellency that yesterday evening, after the Downing Street meeting, Chamberlain secretly sent his agent to me (we made an appointment in an ordinary public taxi*) to say

* But see Lord Templewood's *Nine Troubled Years*, where he denies the story of the meeting in the taxi-cab:
'Grandi's claim that he had "almost daily contacts" with Chamberlain's messenger greatly exaggerated what had actually happened. In point of fact, he himself seldom saw the messenger, and the later story that had been circulated, that they met in a taxi, is entirely untrue.'
Those who, like the author, know Count Grandi, judge him to be an able

[*continued overleaf*]

that "he sent me cordial greetings, that he had appreciated my statements, which had been very useful to him, and that he was confident that everything would go very well next day".'

The Prime Minister was, in fact, deliberately playing a part throughout the Cabinet discussions. While allowing his colleagues to suppose that he was as anxious as any of them to dissuade the Foreign Secretary from resigning, he had, in reality, determined to get rid of him, and had secretly informed the Italian Ambassador that he hoped to succeed in doing so. Had I known this at the time, not only would I have resigned with Eden, but I should have found it difficult to sit in Cabinet with Neville Chamberlain again.

★

According to his official biographer, Keith Feiling, Neville Chamberlain wrote in his diary on February 17, three days before Eden's resignation:

To intimate now that this was not the moment for conversations would be to convince Mussolini that he must consider talks with us off, and act accordingly.... Italian public opinion would be raised to a white heat against us. There might indeed be some overt act of hostility, and in any case the dictatorships would be driven closer together, the last shred of Austrian independence would be lost, the Balkan countries would feel compelled to turn towards their powerful neighbours, Czechoslovakia would be swallowed, France would either have to submit to German domination or fight, in which case we should almost certainly be drawn in. I could not face the responsibility for allowing such a series of catastrophes.

There seem to be no fewer than six false assumptions contained in this short diary entry. He assumes that six

---

and honourable man. It seems inconceivable that he would have fabricated the story of the meeting in the taxi-cab in order to gain a fugitive prestige for omniscience with his own Government, with whom he was not in sympathy. It is astonishing that Templewood, writing many years later, should flatly deny this story without producing any evidence or argument, in default of which historians will inevitably accept Grandi's current report rather than Hoare's laggardly and lame-dog apologia.

misfortunes would come upon our country if Eden had been
able to frustrate him from his urgent desire for a chat with
Mussolini: (1) '. . . the dictatorships would be driven closer
together.' Although Chamberlain had his way and had his
chat, they were. (2) '. . . the last shred of Austrian independence would be lost.' This event occurred twenty-two
days later. (3) '. . . the Balkan countries would feel compelled
to turn to their powerful neighbours.' They did. (4)
'. . . Czechoslovakia would be swallowed.' With Chamberlain's help it was. (5) '. . . France would either have to
submit to German domination or fight.' France did both,
but in a different order. (6) '. . . in which case we should
almost certainly be drawn in.' We were.

As to Chamberlain's apprehension that the Italian people
might be 'raised to a white heat against us', what could they
have done against us, even if that improbable conjuncture
had arisen? Mr. Feiling does not record that Chamberlain
had, up to this point, met any Italians save Count Grandi,
nor does he recount any travels which Chamberlain under-
took in the Italian peninsula. Those who have had the
pleasure of visiting Italy on frequent occasions and have had
the opportunity of seeing Italians of all classes, Popes, Duces,
business men, peasants, Count Grandi himself, will find
it particularly difficult to swallow Chamberlain's imaginative
exercise of seeing the Italians 'raised to a white heat against
us'—that was certainly not the experience of the Eighth
Army who had the fun of encountering them in the Libyan
desert. But Chamberlain, like Gallio, 'cared for none of these
things'.

Chamberlain added in his diary: 'I could not face the
responsibility for allowing such a series of catastrophes.'
Chamberlain, on this occasion, underrated his own courage.
He took the responsibility and all the catastrophes which he
sought to avert descended upon the free world, and notably
upon the French and British peoples. But Chamberlain
never thought that he had made a mistake. He was conscious
of his rectitude and realism to the very end. It is not for

nothing that Lord Birkenhead, when Bonar Law destroyed the Coalition Government in 1922 and appointed Chamberlain as Minister of Health, remarked of him: 'He was, I believe, considered an adequate Lord Mayor of Birmingham in a rather lean year.'

On February 21 Eden explained his reason for resignation to the House of Commons:

I rise to ask the leave of the House to make a personal explanation. This is for me, both on personal and political grounds, a most painful occasion. No man would willingly sever the links which bind him with colleagues and friends, still less when, as in my case, I am only too conscious to how great an extent those colleagues have encouraged and sustained me during the two years that I have held the responsible office from which I have just resigned. But, Sir, there are occasions when strong political convictions must override all other considerations. Of such occasions only the individual himself can be the judge; no man can be the keeper of another man's conscience. Therefore, I stand before the House today to give the House in a few brief sentences an account of my reasons for having resigned the office of Foreign Secretary.

First let me make it plain that the ultimate aim of us all, the objective of the foreign policy of this country, is, and, must always be, the maintenance of peace. If, however, peace is to be enduring it must rest on foundations of frank reciprocity and mutual respect. If we accept this basis for our foreign policy it follows that we must be ready to negotiate with all countries, whatever their form of government, in order to promote international understanding, but we must also be watchful that in our conception of such negotiations, and in the method by which we seek to further them, we are in fact strengthening, not undermining, the foundations upon which international confidence rests. With that introduction I come to the immediate issue which unhappily divides me from my colleagues. It will be known to the House that certain exchanges of views have been taking place between the Italian Government and His Majesty's Government in respect to the opening of conversations between the two Governments.

Indeed, His Majesty's Government have been committed to

the principle of such conversations ever since my Right
Honourable Friend the Prime Minister himself exchanged
letters with Signor Mussolini last summer. There is no dispute
anywhere about that. The immediate issue is as to whether
such official conversations should be opened in Rome now. It
is my conviction that the attitude of the Italian Government to
international problems in general, and to this country in particular, is not yet such as to justify this course. The ground has
been in no respect prepared. Propaganda against this country
by the Italian Government is rife throughout the world. I am
myself pledged to this House not to open conversations with
Italy until this hostile propaganda ceases. I do not want to
stress the personal position, which is relatively unimportant,
but I must mention, in passing, the difficult position in which I
must have been placed had I had to announce to the House in
existing conditions the opening of such conversations. Moreover,
little progress, in fact, though much in promise, has yet been
made with the solution of the Spanish problem. Let me make
it plain. I do not suggest and I would not advocate that the
Government should refuse conversations with the Italian
Government, or indeed with any other government which
shows any disposition to conversations with us for the betterment
of international understandings, yet we must be convinced
that the conditions in which these conversations take place are
such as to make for the likelihood, if not for the certainty, of
their success. I contend that these conditions do not exist
today.

I am compelled for a few moments, if the House will allow
me, to review the past with this situation as the background.
While I was privileged to be Foreign Secretary I was responsible for several attempts in the past eighteen months to better
our relations with Italy. They have all failed in the main,
though not wholly, because of the Spanish problem. In
January last year, after difficult negotiations, we signed the
Anglo-Italian Agreement, but within a very few days, indeed
almost simultaneously, the first considerable consignment of
Italians left for Spain. It may be held that this was not a breach
of the letter of our understanding, but no one, I think, surely
will contend that it did not run counter to its spirit. That same
agreement contained a clause—a specific clause—dealing with

the cessation of propaganda, yet propaganda was scarcely dimmed for an instant. Again, last summer my Right Honourable Friend the Prime Minister and Signor Mussolini exchanged letters, and after that in a few days the relations between our two countries took a marked turn for the better. Of that there can be no doubt. Then what happened? Then ensued the incidents in the Mediterranean, with which the House is familiar, and the glorification by the head of the Italian Government of the victories of Italian forces in Spain.

My submission is that we cannot risk a further repetition of these experiences. Therefore, it is my contention that before His Majesty's Government open official conversations in Rome with the Italian Government, conversations which have, and rightly have, as an objective not only an improvement of Anglo-Italian relations, but appeasement in the Mediterranean as a whole—before that can be done we must make further progress with the Spanish problem; we must agree not only on the need for withdrawal and on the conditions of withdrawal—we have had assurances of that in the past—but we must go further and show the world not only promise but achievement. The withdrawal must have begun in earnest before those conversations in Rome can be held on a really solid basis of goodwill, which is essential to success.

I think it likely that the House may wonder why I at this hour place so much emphasis on performance as opposed to promise, and even why I speak so much of the Spanish problem. It is only because it happens to be in this instance an example. We cannot consider this problem except in relation to the international situation as a whole. The conditions today are not the same as they were last July, nor even the same as they were last January. Recent months, recent weeks, recent days have seen the successive violation of international agreements and attempts to secure political decisions by forcible means. We are in the presence of the progressive deterioration of respect for international obligations. It is quite impossible to judge these things in a vacuum. In the light—my judgment may well be wrong—of the present international situation this is a moment for this country to stand firm, not to plunge into negotiations unprepared, with the full knowledge that the chief obstacle to their success has not been resolved.

The programme which I have outlined seems to me a not unreasonable programme. Indeed, if the desire of the two parties be to reach agreement on all subjects outstanding between them, including Spain, I am quite confident that it is the best method to pursue. It is the traditional method of diplomacy to prepare for conversations before they are formally opened. It is seldom right to depart from that traditional method, which has been tested by time and experience. It is certainly never right to do so because one party to the negotiations intimates that it is now or never. Agreements that are worth while are never made on the basis of a threat. Nor in the past has this country been willing to negotiate in such conditions. I repeat that if our objective is to promote a Mediterranean agreement, to promote lasting appeasement, then the method which I have described is not only the best, but the only possible one, and the only one consonant with our position in the world.

I may be told that by insisting that positive progress must be made with the Spanish question before formal conversations are opened between His Majesty's Government and the Italian Government in Rome, I am asking one party to the negotiations to yield in advance certain advantages that that party now enjoys. I shall not for one moment seek to argue whether those advantages, if indeed they be advantages, are legitimate ones. But it has never entered into my conception to suggest that the Italian forces should be withdrawn from Spain alone, but only that the Italian Government should agree and carry out with others a fair scheme for the proportionate withdrawal of all foreigners from Spain.

I am conscious—that is, of course, why I stand here—that my Right Honourable Friend the Prime Minister and my colleagues take another view. They believe in their policy, and they believe in their method, and they may be right. But, if they are right, their chances of success will certainly be enhanced if their policy is pursued by another Foreign Secretary, one who has complete conviction in the methods which he is being asked to employ. It may even be that my resignation will facilitate the course of these negotiations. If so, nobody will be more pleased than I.

I have spoken to the House of the immediate difference that

has divided me from my colleagues, but I should not be frank with the House if I were to pretend that it is an isolated issue as between my Right Honourable Friend the Prime Minister and myself. It is not. Within the last few weeks upon one most important decision of foreign policy which did not concern Italy at all, the difference was fundamental. My Right Honourable Friend is, I know, conscious of this. Moreover, it has recently become clear to me, and I think to him, that there is between us a real difference of outlook and method. It may be argued, perhaps I shall be told, that this is not a difference of fundamental principles. Well, in the sense that the objective of all foreign policy is the maintenance of peace, that is, of course, perfectly true. But in international affairs can anyone define where outlook and methods end and principles begin? If the Government of the country is to speak with undivided voice in international affairs, it is essential that the Prime Minister and the Foreign Secretary should have a similar outlook and wish to pursue similar methods. The more intense the interest which each one of them takes in the conduct of international affairs, the more imperative does this unity become.

My Right Honourable Friend has strong views on foreign policy, and I respect him for it; and I have strong views, too. Since we are, as I know, both of us conscious that those views have resulted in a divergence, not of aim, but of outlook and of approach, it is clearly in the national interest that unity should be restored at the earliest possible moment. Of late the conviction has steadily grown upon me that there has been too keen a desire on our part to make terms with others rather than that others should make terms with us. This never was the attitude of this country in the past. It should not, in the interests of peace, be our attitude today. The events of the last few days, which have dealt with one particular issue, have merely brought to a head other and more far-reaching differences, not, if you will, in objectives, but in outlook and approach. I do not believe that we can make progress in European appeasement, more particularly in the light of the events of the past few days —and those events must surely be present in all our minds—if we allow the impression to gain currency abroad that we yield to constant pressure. I am certain in my own mind that progress depends above all on the temper of the nation, and that temper must find expression in a firm spirit. That spirit, I am confident, is there. Not to give voice to it is, I believe, fair neither to this country nor to the world.

★

Some Press comment should be put on the record.

Differences in outlook and method there may well have been —differences, perhaps, of degree in their conceptions of what is or is not practicable in the way of appeasement under existing international conditions. Such differences, even with the utmost good will on both sides, must impair the effective administration of foreign policy in times like these, which demand that a Prime Minister and his Foreign Secretary shall work from day to day in the closest possible touch and with instructive mutual confidence. It may therefore be predicted with some assurance that nothing fundamental to British aims will be changed by Mr. Eden's resignation—which need not mean that there is no substance in the grounds upon which he has offered it—but that the attempt to prove the possibility or otherwise of building stable relations between democracies and dictatorships will be pursued with a confidence and conviction that Mr. Eden felt unable to give it. Public opinion, sympathetic as it is to this main aim, will be united in regret for this interruption of a brilliant public career.

The Times, 21 February 1938.

The man who will sacrifice a great position for his conviction deserves respect, if he cannot command agreement. It is evident that the Prime Minister, in accepting his Foreign Secretary's resignation, must have been equally convinced that his line of policy was not only right, but essential to the national interest. The decisive consideration has been the unwisdom of delay, if, as must be assumed, the Prime Minister had good reason to know that a mutually satisfactory agreement was desired by Italy. If it were done at all, it were best done quickly; and that consideration has rightly prevailed with the Cabinet, since at bottom no question of principle is at stake.

Daily Telegraph, 21 February 1938.

Mr. Chamberlain has come out stark and nakedly on the side of a system of power politics. In furtherance of that policy any concession, however ignoble and however humiliating, will be made to the forces of International Fascism in return for their promise to keep their hands off British interests. For, make no mistake about it, Mr. Eden has been sacrificed to Mussolini. But to secure Mussolini's friendship—or his promise of friendship—much more than a Foreign Secretary will have to be sacrificed. It is because he sees that, and because, although he has been in many ways a weak and vacillating Foreign Secretary, he does, to his credit, still hold fast to British integrity, that Mr. Eden is going. Public opinion will honour him for that decision.

Daily Herald, 21 February 1938.

The country will recognize the courage of Mr. Eden's action and will know that it is taken only on the strong ground of principle. For that reason it will be much regretted. In the public mind of this country Mr. Eden is associated with a genuine and active belief in the principles which the Government formally professes. Other countries know him as the British Minister who, in spite of all discouragements, kept his faith in the League and what it stood for. They will draw their inferences now. Germany and Italy will be glad, but it is a bad day for this country's reputation.

Manchester Guardian, 21 February 1938.

There will be a wide belief that Mr. Eden has been sacrificed by his colleagues under pressure from the two dictators. In almost the same way a French Foreign Minister, M. Delcassé, was practically forced to resign under Germany's virtual threat of war in June 1905.

Yorkshire Post, 21 February 1938.

Mr. Eden has declared that he does not consider the present time appropriate for the commencement of Anglo-Italian conversations. Mr. Chamberlain takes a contrary view. Hence Mr. Eden's resignation. But we do not fear that the ties binding Britain and France will be in any sense weakened. Mr. Chamberlain has forcibly underlined the reality of Franco-

British friendship, and we do not fear that that friendship will be lessened by the changes which have taken place within the British Cabinet.

Le Temps, 21 February 1938.

The totalitarian states can enter to the credit side of their account a weakening of British rule. We fear that, contrary to Mr. Chamberlain's expectations, these states will not become more conciliatory.

L'Echo de Paris, 21 February 1938.

Are we to return to those tragic prewar years, when the frowns of the Kaiser forced the French Foreign Minister Dalcassé to resign, and which Clemenceau described at the time as the greatest humiliation of the century?

Le Jour, 21 February 1938.

A new stage in European policy has been reached. With Mr. Eden's departure one period of principles is closed. His policy could only have succeeded if he had had the power and the will to use them. England was not yet ripe for this. His resignation is a great blow to democratic countries, and a success for the others.

Nieuwe Rotterdamsche Courant, 21 February 1938.

In the diplomatic struggle between Mr. Eden and Signor Mussolini the former has lost. The reasons of principle for which Mr. Eden has resigned are highly honourable to him, but the 'realist' policy of Mr. Chamberlain seems most likely to make possible a permanent understanding between Britain, Italy and Germany.

Journal de Genève, 21 February 1938.

The Italian Press, which was controlled by the Italian Government, was delighted at Eden's resignation, and accepted his resignation as the act of obeisance which Chamberlain had intended it to be. Of course the Italians read into this situation more than was warranted. They assumed that Chamberlain was a coward, when in fact he was only a ninny.

All the same it is a gain to see the Eden policy removed. In spite of the excitement in France, England is and remains the friend of France. Germany and Italy think and act commonly. The existence of these friendships will contribute to bringing the two axes together within a common frame for a new Europe. The task will not be easy. But the supporters of the League and the sanctionists merely pursued shadows.

Frankfurter Zeitung, 21 February 1938.

Mr. Eden's withdrawal from the British Cabinet may lead to a further clarification of the European situation. It can certainly be said by Mr. Eden that he was true to his principles. But it cannot be said that these principles served the cause of European understanding.

Diplomatisch-Politische Correspondenz, 21 February 1938.

With the facts so far as they are now known, it is impossible to challenge the correctitude of Eden's resignation. He was still being treated as 'the young man' with whom Baldwin had advised Hoare to 'settle direct'. It is often a misfortune in a man's career if he gets on too quickly. Though Eden had created for himself an international reputation and an enthusiastic, if unthinking, following among the British public, he did not carry great weight in the Cabinet. It is true that he had his friends and admirers within that body, Walter Elliot, Malcolm MacDonald, Oliver Stanley, Duff Cooper, De La Warr, but none of these able men mounted political cannon of the calibre disposed of by the inner Cabinet, Chamberlain, Halifax, Simon and Hoare. With the exception of Chamberlain, none of the quadrumvirate had much public backing in the country, and Simon and Hoare, rightly or wrongly, were actively distrusted. But all three of them had the confidence of the Prime Minister and easy access to him. Chamberlain had undisputed control of the Tory Party, which, because of its overwhelming majority in the House of Commons, was the effective governing instrument.

It followed that those who were known to enjoy Chamberlain's confidence were *ipso facto* men of power, while 'the young man', despite his blameless reputation, his charm and his glamour, counted for little. Of course they did not want to let him go. He was an emblem, a symbol, a mascot, an insurance policy. The quadrumvirate had profited much by exploiting this totem, and by manipulating 'the young man'. Eden was a disinfectant for the noisome intrigues, tergiversations, vacillations and indecisions of those who had the power. About this time, with the aid of his Parliamentary Under-Secretary, Lord Cranborne (now 5th Marquess of Salisbury), Eden perceived that he was to have no part in shaping policy but only in explaining away its repeated failures. He was right to escape from a position where he seemed to have all the responsibility but in fact had no power. It is droll that the weakness and unsuitability of his situation had not become apparent to him before.

It seems even more extraordinary (assuming that he did realize where power lay in the Cabinet) that he should have chosen this moment to absent himself. Was he, perhaps, too politically naïve to realize what was going on in the inner Cabinet and among the Cliveden set? Perhaps. He certainly knew far more about what was going on in Europe than did the inner Cabinet or the Cliveden set. He must have sniffed that something was going on in Austria. Surely this was a time in the interests of Europe, of Britain and of himself when he should have been on deck. If, however, there was a compulsive need for him to go to the Riviera, would it not have been sensible for him to have secured his communications, and made sure that he was promptly and accurately informed of all that was going on?

> The heights by great men reached and kept
> Were not attained by sudden flight,
> But they, while their companions slept,
> Were toiling upward in the night.

In the weeks following on his resignation Eden on a number of occasions gave accounts of the issues as he saw them to a number of intimate friends, some of whom made full records at the time. The account which follows is based on a collation of these contemporary records and can be accepted as an accurate, if not in all respects complete, account of Eden's story at the time.

Two days after Roosevelt's telegram was received in London the Prime Minister agreed to the suggestion of Sir Alexander Cadogan that the Foreign Secretary should be recalled. Cadogan telephoned on January 14 to Eden, who said that he would be back the next day.

The Foreign Office bag containing the Roosevelt-Chamberlain telegrams missed him at Marseilles, since there was a bad storm and no planes were flying, and the first detailed information that he received was at Folkestone,* where he was met in the early afternoon by Cadogan. That night Eden and Cranborne dined together. During dinner a telegram came from the British Ambassador in Washington indicating that Roosevelt might be prepared to give the British Cabinet some extra time for consideration. A telephone call was put through to Lindsay, who stated that he feared that the President was disappointed. Eden telegraphed the same night to the Ambassador giving him some material designed to keep the President sweet for the moment.

The next day there was a meeting of the Foreign Policy Committee of the Cabinet. Eden did not like the telegram which it was proposed to send. The Foreign Policy Committee met again on the afternoon of February 20. Various draft telegrams were considered and Malcolm MacDonald and Oliver Stanley were set the task of combining them.

The Foreign Policy Committee met again the following morning but found themselves unable to accept the draft produced by MacDonald and Stanley, who were instructed to try again. In the afternoon the final draft was approved with Eden's acquiescence. Two days later the Ambassador telegraphed to say that the telegrams were 'well received by Sumner Welles, at least' and that he was 'confident' that the

---

* Not at Dover, as stated by Sir Winston Churchill.

President 'would be pleased with them'. On February 10 there came a message from the President agreeing to put off his plans 'for days, not weeks' in the hope that the German situation might clear.

It was on February 16 that Eden wished to see Grandi and that Grandi avoided a meeting. The following day Sir Philip Sassoon, who was at the time Under-Secretary of State for Air, gave one of his regular weekly luncheon parties at 25 Park Lane for Cabinet Ministers and senior officials. Among those present were Chamberlain, Eden, Simon, Swinton, Hankey (Secretary of the Cabinet), Cadogan and David Margesson (the Chief Whip). During the course of this luncheon Eden suggested that Cadogan should put forward his own ideas against Chamberlain's project of seeing Grandi. This plainly embarrassed Cadogan, since he did not feel as passionately on this issue as his chief. However, he loyally made a strong case.

The next day Chamberlain and Eden jointly received Count Grandi at Downing Street. After all the lengthy approach march to this meeting, Grandi had very little to say. He conveyed a message in general terms from the Italian Foreign Minister, Count Ciano, expressing the desire of the Italian Government for conversations. There was some talk about Spain, but, as Chamberlain had rightly anticipated, Grandi did not wish to discuss Hitler's machinations against Austria. None the less, the matter seems to have been raised, presumably by Eden; for Chamberlain tells us in his diary quoted by Keith Feiling in *The Life of Neville Chamberlain* that 'He [Grandi] denied emphatically that any agreement concerning Austria had been made between Hitler and Mussolini, but . . . how could he move troops to the Brenner as he did before, if he felt that Great Britain was a potential enemy?'

Grandi's main point was that an announcement should be made that day that Anglo-Italian conversations had been opened. He was invited to come back in the afternoon. After Grandi had left there was a rather rough conversation between Chamberlain and Eden, the latter sticking to his point that negotiations should not be opened until there had been substantial withdrawals of Italian troops from Spain, while Chamberlain pressed that the conversations should be opened immediately. When Grandi returned in the afternoon, Eden had persuaded Chamberlain that no decision should be made without a full meeting of the Cabinet on the following day, Saturday, February 19. Grandi was accordingly told that he would not get his answer till Monday.

At the Cabinet meeting on the Saturday Eden found little support for his view, even when he made it plain that he was prepared to resign. During the Saturday night and Sunday several of Eden's colleagues sought to prevail on him to change his mind; but he was inflexible, and his resignation was accepted and announced on the Sunday evening.

It is true, in one sense, that Eden resigned on a point of principle; but in another his position was made untenable and he was pushed out. At a succession of Cabinet meetings Eden was asked in different forms the question: 'What is the Foreign Office doing to make peace with the dictators and why are they not getting a move on'? Eden's most active critics were Simon, Swinton and Kingsley Wood, the last of whom on one occasion said that we ought to open up negotiations in Berlin at once. Eden became despondent at the lack of imagination and breadth of mind of some of his colleagues. After he had resigned he told some of his intimate friends that Kingsley Wood 'had the mind of an election agent'. Kingsley Wood told Eden that he was very sorry that he had decided to go, and that he thought that he had made a great mistake. Eden replied: 'You ought to be delighted. Now you will be able to run our foreign policy as you like.' Kingsley Wood blushed.

In the days following Eden's resignation Simon several times asked Eden to come and see him. Eden was not over-fond of Simon, but after three or four invitations he went to see him at the Treasury. After a few complimentary remarks Simon said: 'You look terribly tired. Quite done up in

fact. You ought to take a good rest.' Eden, in fact, was tired
after his ordeal and admitted this, but when, subsequently,
Simon put it around that Eden had been obliged to resign
because he was on the brink of a breakdown, Eden told his
friends that he was convinced that Simon had only asked
him to go round to the Treasury for the purpose of extracting
from him an admission that he was tired, in order to use it
against him afterwards.

Immediately after his resignation, Eden sought the advice
of his old political chief Stanley Baldwin. Baldwin told Eden
that if his resignation should create a political crisis involving
Chamberlain's position and he were consulted by the King
as to whom he should invite to form a Government, he would
recommend Eden. Baldwin and Eden saw each other
frequently at this period and went so far as to draw up a list
of names for an alternative Government.

If Eden had remained in England, if he had made, as he
had a right and, indeed, a duty, to make, his friends in the
Cabinet privy to his plans and difficulties, if he had been
present and competent to argue these matters out in Cabinet,
if, in short, he had been a bigger man than he was, he might
have prevailed and have imposed his will, with the backing of
the outer Cabinet, upon the inner Cabinet. Whether or not
this would have changed the course of history is anybody's
guess. The irony of Eden's destiny is that, having allowed
himself to be outmanœuvred, outplayed, thwarted in his
policy, and having allowed the 'skids to be put under him',
he was unwittingly, but inevitably, enhanced in his own
career.

★

The drama of Eden's resignation, his 'broken career',
purged him of all the malfeasance of the MacDonald-
Baldwin decade, for which he was every bit as responsible
as MacDonald, Baldwin, Hoare, Simon and Halifax. When,
in later years, 'appeasement' (first used by Eden as a term
of diplomatic art) reared its head as a dirty word, Eden was

in public estimation sacrosanct, because of his act of resignation. Though he certainly did not plan it this way, it was his resignation which ultimately led, with disastrous consequences, to his becoming Prime Minister of Great Britain. During the war the word 'Munich' as well as the word 'appeasement' became terms of unthinking abuse. Eden was not incriminated by either. This was due to his timely resignation. The Tory Party, who are not as stupid as some people suppose, realized that in Eden, whom fundamentally they distrusted and disliked even more than they did Churchill, there resided a valuable electoral asset. Indeed, they could not see, after the electoral disaster of 1945, how they could hope to win without his magic aura. Eden had disinfected himself. He could be used to greater advantage even than Churchill (who was after all, 'only an adventurer') to disinfect them.

CHAPTER TEN

Vienna, Munich, Prague

WHILE all this comical charade was being played out in London in an atmosphere of high drama, serious events were taking place on the Continent. On 11 March 1938 Hitler's troops crossed the Austrian frontier, notwithstanding that Schuschnigg had not only agreed to the terms which Hitler had dictated to him at Berchtesgaden on February 12, but had also agreed to abandon his ingenious idea for a national plebiscite on the question whether Austria was to be united with Germany or not.

Another massive lurch downhill towards war or slavery for France and Britain had been achieved while the politicians of Britain, who should have been striving in unison to prevent this, were disputing among themselves the precise conditions under which they were prepared to open discussions with Mussolini—discussions which the Prime Minister had ordained should not include any talk about Austria. In the nostrils of Chamberlain, Simon, Halifax and Hoare, Austria had a dirty smell. Chamberlain was urgent in his desire to have talks with Mussolini. The threatened rape of Austria was more directly menacing to Mussolini than it was to Britain. If Austria were to be an undiscussable topic, one is prompted to inquire what did Chamberlain wish to talk about? In due course we shall see.

Nothing in these pages is intended to single out any one political figure as a sole scapegoat for the follies of the nation. In the thirties British political leaders were fatally hampered by the fecklessness and imbecility of the British public. MacDonald, Baldwin, Halifax, Hoare, Simon and Eden were the chosen representatives of the British public, and it is reasonable to assume that at all times, except perhaps at the moment of Hoare-Laval, they had a majority of the British electorate behind them. Of course those who wish to exercise the power in the State have a special measure of responsibility; and it is right that they should fall under the chastisement of the nation if they have had power and have misused it, more especially if they have wilfully deceived the public as to what was going on.

A democracy has at all times an overriding duty to be informed and to exercise its rights with discretion and sense. If, however, it is wilfully misled as it was in the thirties, though it should blame itself for its choice of leaders it has some right to feel aggrieved and to punish those who have led it into misfortune. But a democracy has no justification for punishing it improvident servants unless it is itself prepared to learn the lessons for which it has paid in blood, treasure and prestige. There are few signs that the British people have learnt the lessons of these tormented years. In these pages is set down a melancholy catalogue of the follies of MacDonald, Baldwin, Halifax, Simon, Hoare and Eden. It would all be a wasted effort if the reader were to conclude that all our misfortunes arose solely through the folly of these high-minded and patriotic men and were to forget that it was he who chose them, he who voted for them, he who applauded what they had done.

Kipling wrote in 1902:

> No doubt but ye are the People—absolute, strong and wise;
> Whatever your heart has desired ye have not withheld from your eyes.
> On your own heads, in your own hands the sin and the saving lies.

★

In the debate on Austria in the House of Commons on March 14, Winston Churchill said:

> Why should we assume that time is on our side? I know of nothing to convince me that if the evil forces now at work are suffered to feed upon their successes and upon their victims

our task will be easier when finally we are all united. Not only do we need a clear declaration of the Government's policy, but we require to set to work to rally the whole country behind that declared policy, in order that there may not be shifts and changes, as well as that there may not be any doubt or hesitation. It will certainly be no easier for us to face the problems with which we are confronted a year hence than it is today. Indeed, we might easily delay resistance to a point where continued resistance and true collective security would become impossible.

The gravity of the event of the 11th of March cannot be exaggerated. Europe is confronted with a programme of aggression, nicely calculated and timed, unfolding stage by stage, and there is only one choice open, not only to us, but to other countries who are unfortunately concerned—either to submit, like Austria, or else to take effective measures while time remains to ward off the danger and, if it cannot be warded off, to cope with it. Resistance will be hard, yet I am persuaded—and the Prime Minister's speech confirms me—that it is to this conclusion of resistance to overweening encroachment that His Majesty's Government will come, and the House of Commons will certainly sustain them in playing a great part in the effort to preserve the peace of Europe, and, if it cannot be preserved, to preserve the freedom of the nations of Europe. If we were to delay, if we were to go on waiting upon events for a considerable period, how much should we throw away of resources which are now available for our security and for the maintenance of peace? How many friends would be alienated, how many potential allies should we see go, one by one, down the grisly gulf, how many times would bluff succeed, until behind bluff ever-gathering forces had accumulated reality? Where shall we be two years hence, for instance, when the German Army will certainly be much larger than the French Army, and when all the small nations will have fled from Geneva to pay homage to the ever-waxing power of the Nazi system, and to make the best terms they can for themselves?

He concluded:

If a number of states were assembled around Great Britain and France in a solemn treaty for mutual defence against aggression; if they had their staff arrangements concerted; if all this rested, as it can honourably rest, upon the Covenant of the League of Nations, in pursuance of all the purposes and ideals of the League of Nations; if that were sustained, as it would be, by the moral sense of the world; and if it were done in the year 1938—and, believe me, it may be the last chance there will be for doing it—then I say that you might even now arrest this approaching war. Then perhaps the curse which overhangs Europe would pass away.

Eden did not choose to intervene in the debate. It was strange that with all his knowledge and concern he did not feel in a position at this time to give any guidance to the House of Commons and the nation.

★

As has already been indicated, Eden, after his resignation, fell increasingly under the advice of Baldwin, who particularly enjoined upon him the folly of becoming involved with Churchill. Eden soon allied himself with an influential body of Conservative M.P.s who held regular weekly meetings in great secrecy and who were known as 'the Group'. The chairman of 'the Group' was Sir Sidney Herbert and its vice-chairman Mr. Leo Amery. The other members were Harold Macmillan, Duncan Sandys, Richard Cartland, Ronald Tree, Lord Cranborne, Richard Law, Louis Spears, C. G. Lancaster, Paul Evans, Anthony Crossley, Mark Patrick and Derek Gunston. Eden's Parliamentary Private Secretary, J. P. L. Thomas (now Lord Cilcennin), also joined 'the Group' at the same time as did Eden. 'The Group' received another valuable recruit when Duff Cooper resigned from the Government on the issue of Munich. These members concerned themselves mainly with foreign affairs and national defence. As war came steadily nearer, they became increasingly out of sympathy with the Chamberlain Administration, and it was their concerted action on 10 May 1940 which, more than anything else, led to the fall of the Government and to Chamberlain's resignation.

While these complicated realignments were proceeding on the English domestic front, Hitler was getting on with the job. Having gobbled up Austria, 'his last territorial ambition', he was ready to devour Czechoslovakia. This small, civilized, highly armed country, possessing a strong mountain frontier line and the Skoda works, was an obviously desirable feast. And as Hitler had shrewdly realized that as France and Britain were too scared to stand up to Mussolini they would be even more frightened of opposing him, he was able to play the hand in his own way with complete confidence of success. It is strange that an ignorant, illiterate, jumped-up Austrian who could not even speak the German language correctly should have had the measure of educated, civilized Englishmen such as Baldwin, Simon, Hoare, Halifax and Eden, while Baldwin, Simon, Hoare, Halifax and Eden, with all their advantages of superior education and tradition, misunderstood what Hitler had in mind.

There is no space to chronicle in these pages the full and melancholy catalogue of the ghastly miscalculations of the statesmen in whom the British public chose to confide their destinies in these 'Nine Troubled Years'. But if anyone is still interested in how the second world war came upon us and how, although we won, we lost, they should read the books, not merely those of Sir Winston Churchill. Read also with diligence the apologias of Halifax, Simon and Hoare; and await with a lively interest the explanations of Sir Anthony Eden.

*

Having procured the resignation of his Foreign Secretary by methods more worthy of his father's caucus manager in Birmingham, Mr. Schnadhorst, than of a man who had risen from the squalor of Birmingham municipal politics to preside over the destinies of the British Empire, Chamberlain proceeded rapidly to open the negotiations he so ardently desired with the Italian Government. They were speedily completed, which was not surprising since the agreement

achieved amounted to nothing save an acceptance of what
Mussolini had done in Spain and Abyssinia and a promise
that we would not fortify Cyprus without consulting Mussolini; in return for which we were promised a cessation of
hostile propaganda in the Mediterranean. It is a strange fact
that Neville Chamberlain and Ramsay MacDonald, who
could not have been more different in character and temperament, had one thing in common—they seem to have
believed that conferences and agreements were good things
in themselves, irrespective of the realities of the situation or
the outcome.

At this time Churchill wrote to Eden:

> The Italian pact is, of course, a complete triumph for
> Mussolini, who gains our cordial acceptance for his fortification
> of the Mediterranean against us, for his conquest of Abyssinia,
> and for his violence in Spain. The fact that we are not to fortify
> Cyprus without 'previous consultation' is highly detrimental.
> The rest of it is to my mind only padding.
>
> Nevertheless I feel that considerable caution is necessary in
> opposing the agreement bluntly. It is a done thing. It is called
> a move towards peace. It undoubtedly makes it less likely that
> sparks from the Mediterranean should light a European con-
> flagration. France will have to follow suit for her own protec-
> tion, in order not to be divided from Britain. Finally, there is
> the possibility that Mussolini may be drawn by his interests to
> discourage German interference in the Danube basin.
>
> Before making up my mind, I should like to know your
> views and intentions. I think the Anglo-Italian pact is only the
> first step, and that the second will be an attempt to patch up
> something even more specious with Germany, which will lull
> the British public while letting the German armed strength
> grow and German designs in the East of Europe develop.
>
> Chamberlain last week told the Executive of the National
> Union [of Conservative Associations] in secret that he 'had not
> abandoned hopes of similar arrangements with Germany'.
> They took this rather coldly.
>
> Meanwhile our progress in the air is increasingly disappoint-
> ing. . . .

Eden replied:

    ... With regard to the Italian pact, I agree with what you write. Mussolini gives us nothing more than the repetition of promises previously made and broken by him, except for the withdrawal of troops from Libya, troops which were probably originally sent there for their nuisance value. It has now become clear that, as I expected, Mussolini continued his intervention in Spain after the conversations in Rome had opened. He must be an optimist indeed who believes that Mussolini will cease increasing that intervention now, should it be required to secure Franco's victory.

    As a diplomatic instrument the pact embodies a machinery which is likely to be found very troublesome to work. It is not to come into force until after the Italians leave Spain. It is almost certain, however, that many months will elapse before that occurs, and since what is important is not the presence of Italian infantry, but the assertions of their experts and the Germans, it will be difficult to establish with certainty that the withdrawal has taken place. But maybe some do not mind much about that.

    Then there is the Italian position in Abyssinia, which, from what I hear, so far from improving grows steadily worse. I am afraid that the moment we are choosing for its recognition will not benefit our authority among the many millions of the King's coloured subjects.

    None the less I equally agree as to the need for caution in any attitude taken up towards the agreement. After all it is not an agreement yet, and it would be wrong certainly for me to say anything which could be considered as making its fruition more difficult. After all, this is precisely what I promised I would not do in my resignation speech and at Leamington.

    The most anxious feature of the international situation, as I see it, is that temporary relaxation of tension may be taken as a pretext for the relaxation of national effort, which is already inadequate to the gravity of the times. ...

★

During the summer Hitler started stepping up his claims against Czechoslovakia and stirring up the German minorities in that country. It was apparent that he meant to march

in and 'liberate' the Sudeten Germans. It was in the hope
of preventing this that Chamberlain made his three disastrous journeys to Germany—first to Berchtesgaden, then
to Godesberg, and ultimately to Munich, where he and
Hitler were joined by Mussolini and Daladier. This was big-
Power policy with a vengeance. The Czechs, whose future
was after all somewhat involved in these transactions, were
of course not invited. They were subsequently, in the middle
of the night, shamefully bullied into acquiescence by the
British and French Ambassadors in Prague, the latter
representing a country which was the formal ally of
Czechoslovakia.

On this issue Duff Cooper quitted the Cabinet, making a
most moving resignation speech in the House of Commons.
During the crisis he had very strongly pressed his colleagues
to mobilize the British fleet. This, after many days, was done.
It is very characteristic of Lord Templewood that in his
memoirs he goes to a lot of trouble to deny all credit for this
action to Duff Cooper, who was First Lord of the Admiralty
at the time.

The Press commented on the Munich agreement:

> The volume of applause for Mr. Chamberlain, which con-
> tinues to grow throughout the globe, registers a popular judg-
> ment that neither politicians nor historians are likely to reverse.
> One fundamental truth that Mr. Chamberlain's daring diplo-
> macy brought into the light was this—that even in a totalitarian
> State the people will have their influence in the last resort upon
> the party. The man who has arrested universal destruction by
> appealing to that truth need not fear that in his own country
> the cavillings of party will outweigh the people's gratitude.
> But, even if there is the inevitable reaction, there must be no
> retrograde step. Relief from intolerable strain cannot be
> followed by mere relapse into inertia. The lessons of the crisis
> are plain and urgent. The policy of international appeasement
> must be pressed forward. There must be appeasement not only
> of the strong but of the weak—of the State that has allowed
> itself to be weakened for the common good. Czechoslovakia has
> deserved well of humanity, and it should be a first international

responsibility not only to guarantee the contracted frontiers, but also to assist in solving the new problems that the settlement has imposed upon her. As between the greater Powers the field for necessary appeasement is wide.

The Times, 3 October 1938.

Peace, for its own sake, is a gain immense indeed. Nevertheless, the satisfaction that hails it is not by any means undivided. There are many who believe that the price which has been paid for it is not only high, but unnecessarily high. But there can be no one, however much he may be persuaded that Mr. Chamberlain did all that was possible in the circumstances, who will escape a feeling of profound anxiety alike as to the course of events already enacted and as to the future which hereafter confronts us. To Great Britain the moral of the crisis is clear. Failing an immediate agreement for disarmament we must redouble the energy of our defensive effort, especially in the air. It has been proved that when sufficiently provoked our nation will rise as one man to make ready its defences. But improvisation at the last moment is utterly inadequate to the need. Within an hour or two of a declaration of war—if indeed this formality is observed at all—we shall all be exposed to a crashing attack. That is a contingency which we must be prepared to meet with resources far more extensive and efficient than are at present available.

Daily Telegraph, 3 October 1938.

Heavy has been the price of peace. 'The Prime Ministers who after the Munich Conference went to their homes were welcomed as the saviours of peace. All that Prague and the Czechoslovak nation received was a crown of thorns.' That is the voice of Czechoslovakia. It is a voice which must ring in the ears and hearts of all men and women who hold that the obligations of honour and justice are not lightly to be set aside. Czechoslovakia has been sacrificed to the ambitions of German Fascism. War has been averted. But has peace been secured? ... Two things are necessary to secure peace. One is that there shall be a firm collective resistance to aggression. The second is a removal of the causes of war by a readiness to examine all claims for the peaceful revision of treaties, for a settlement of minority disputes, and for the proper distribution of raw materials, and where such claims are proved legitimate, to meet them.

Daily Herald, 3 October 1938.

The pacificators of Munich . . . have done something that has hardly ever before happened in history—the snatching of the world at the eleventh hour from a universal calamity, from a return to barbarism, from untold cruelty and misery. The instinct of the peoples today to praise the peace-makers is sound. And whatever view we take about the policies that led up to the crisis and the character of the settlement we cannot help sharing the common thankfulness. None of us can disguise from himself that even had a European war been fought on the deeper issues, and Germany been overcome, the boundaries of Czechoslovakia could not have remained intact. Great as are the injustices that Czechoslovakia suffers under the Munich agreement, and they are for her calamitous, they cannot be measured against the horrors that might have extinguished not only Czechoslovakia but the whole of Western civilization. . . . No one in this country who examines carefully the terms under which Hitler's troops begin their march into Czechoslovakia can feel other than unhappy. Certainly the Czechs will hardly appreciate Mr. Chamberlain's phrase that it is 'peace with honour'.

Manchester Guardian, 3 October 1938.

It was necessary for us to choose between a badly prepared war on unfavourable territory or a solution of resignation and reason. Everything cannot yet be said. Many things will be known only little by little when everything is restored to order. We are paying dear—it would be vain to hide it—for the calm regained for a limited time.

Echo de Paris, 3 October 1938.

The Munich agreement has done better than put aside war. It has brought back into the hearts of all the love of peace and has shown in a striking fashion that the most difficult problems can henceforward be resolved round a table.

L'Oeuvre, 3 October 1938.

The agreement is simple and relatively easy to apply. . . . It really could not have been otherwise, since the task of the conference was merely to work out the means whereby certain Czechoslovak territories, already decided on with the resigned consent of the Prague Government, would be transferred to the Reich. This first direct contact between the heads of the four Governments has had the effect of entirely modifying the political atmosphere, and may well create a new spirit in Europe. . . . It is evident that the changes brought about in the situation of Central Europe by the Munich agreement necessitate the revision of a number of doctrines which have hitherto prevailed. In particular, these changes remove a great part of the practical value of the Franco-Polish alliance and of the Franco-Soviet pact of mutual assistance.

Le Temps, 3 October 1938.

Nothing is so disruptive as a common setback. The Anglo-German declaration signed between Herr Hitler and Mr. Chamberlain echoes like a warning. If, as has been declared by the army chiefs, we were a match for the German Army, our yielding, given the formidable stakes, is incomprehensible.

L'Ordre, 3 October 1938.

We must recognize that the juridical and administrative conception of the international policy which was symbolized by the League of Nations, the guardian of treaties, now belongs to the past. The first lesson to be drawn is: We must carefully re-examine on the map, and not in the dust of Chancelleries, the nature and extent of all our obligations. We must estimate the credit and the debit, and distinguish between those which contain mutual and effective guarantees and those which represent only risks. We must strengthen and clarify the first and denounce the second. Finally, instead of dispersing erratic efforts on all points of the globe, we must decide on the zones of vital interests for our country and apply our strength there with grim determination. France will have to introduce industrial mobilization and labour camps if she wishes to assure peace and her own security.

Paris-Soir, 3 October 1938.

The Germans gained a great success. They are annexing a numerous population which, German as it may be, would still never have belonged to the Empire created by Bismarck. They are being enriched by a territory abundantly provided and marvellously equipped. The people of France will show themselves equal to the test which menaces their country. French policy must now be worthy of it.

Le Figaro, 3 October 1938.

The peace of Munich has left us less strong than we were yesterday, since we have lost an ally, and more than thirty divisions will be available to be turned against us. If we were incapable of resisting the formidable German menace in the past when we were stronger, how will we resist the next time when we will be less strong?

L'Epoque, 3 October 1938.

The most dangerous illusion from which we could suffer would be to think that now our security has been established for ever and that it will suffice in future for a few statesmen to meet to prevent all wars. The peaceful method, which has just been employed, has succeeded this time, but do not let us forget that those who used it represented strong and resolute peoples.

L'Intransigeant, 3 October 1938.

The solution, whatever its imperfections, is fundamentally workable and stable, and is capable, by intelligent direction, of being converted into a really constructive settlement. To say that it may mean the opening of a new day for Europe is not at all far-fetched.

Washington Post, 3 October 1938.

Let no man say too high a price has been paid for peace in Europe until he has searched his soul and found himself willing to risk in war the lives of those who are nearest and dearest to him. But no man who is honest will attempt to pretend to himself that a high price has not been paid. It is a price which enables a dictator who would willingly destroy the last vestige of democracy in Europe to claim with justice that he scored over the democracies of Europe the greatest diplomatic

triumph of modern times, that he accomplished by a mere
ultimatum what Bismarck failed to accomplish with armies.

New York Times, 3 October 1938.

What the world would like to know is whether Herr Hitler's
success will embolden him to further aggression in the conviction that he can do what he wants without fear of actual pre-
ventative measures by Britain and France? If he was bluffing,
there is hope for Europe, despite his success this time. If, on the
other hand, he is, like the madman he seems to be, ready to
plunge the world into war if that is the only manner wherein
he can have his own way, Europe, and the world, should realize
that grave dangers lie ahead.

New York Herald Tribune, 3 October 1938.

It becomes difficult to understand what Chamberlain and
Daladier were contending for if they were willing to concede so
much. There is little now to prevent Hitler from dominating
and organizing Middle and Eastern Europe.

Chicago Tribune, 3 October 1938.

For three and a half millions of Sudeten Germans the Munich
agreement means freedom. Their freedom coincided with the
political realization of Greater Germany. We thank our Führer
not only for an act which has made the German people happier,
more powerful and greater, but also for the way in which it was
executed, without a sword blow. We do not know if this sort of
eternal peace is realizable, but we know that the Führer, and the
statesmen gathered together in Munich, have given practical
proof that a national aim can be achieved by peaceful means.

Völkischer Beobachter, 3 October 1938.

The event at Munich is a turning-point in European history.
The boldness and genius of the Führer are to be thanked that
the crisis was overcome and a solution found which set up a
condition of justice. There is now hope of better fundamental
understanding and co-operation between the nations. Herr
Hitler and Mr. Chamberlain have given expression to the
wish of both countries never again to make war against each
other.

Berliner Borsen Zeitung, 3 October 1938.

The Nobel Prize should be awarded to Mr. Chamberlain. The whole world agrees that nobody ever did more for peace. The prize was created for men like him.

Tidens Tegn (Norway), 3 October 1938.

★

The general jubilation because war had been at least temporarily avoided wore off quite soon. When Chamberlain arrived back at Downing Street from Heston airport, a deliriously happy crowd cheered him to the echo when he said that, like Disraeli, he had brought back peace with honour. A small group of Foreign Office officials were standing on the roof of their office opposite 10 Downing Street to witness the occasion. As they turned to go downstairs, Sir Orme Sargent, at that time deputy Permanent Under-Secretary of State, turned to a recently joined member of the Foreign Office staff and remarked: 'You might suppose they were celebrating the gaining of a major victory instead of merely the betrayal of a minor Power.' This mood was, in the next few months, to communicate itself to ever-widening circles in all classes and all parties in Britain.

In the debate, Eden said:

This is a time for stocktaking; it may also seem to some of us, as I confess it seems to me, to be a respite during which a great national effort is called for by our people. There is throughout the world at this time an immense sense of relief and thankfulness that war has been averted. Perhaps the most striking and most encouraging event of all during these recent weeks was the warmth of the spontaneous reception accorded in Germany to the Prime Minister. It was clearly a manifestation of the deep desire of the German people for peace. Nobody in this House has ever doubted that desire, but the fact that it has at last found expression may be a real signpost on the road to peace. . . .

No one, I suppose, would wish to contend that those proposals are just. War has been averted, for which the world is immeasurably grateful; but let it be remembered that war has been averted, not at our expense or that of any other great Power, but at the cost of grave injustice to a small and friendly nation. Czechoslovakia was not even heard in her own defence. . . .

There can be few of us who, whatever our sense of relief, did not feel also a sense of humiliation when we read those proposals. . . .

It is impossible for anyone who has studied these matters in the past, and I feel sure the Prime Minister must share this feeling himself, not to feel grave anxiety for the future of this State when we look at these strangely contoured concessions. Is its economic life possible, is its continued political existence possible, in this reduced, and in this still unknown reduced, form? That is why I cannot but feel considerable anxiety about our guarantee. Under such conditions it must have specially grave significance. Let no one have a doubt as to the importance of this departure from our traditional policy. We have never done such a thing before, I think, in all our history, as guarantee frontiers, and in this case frontiers that do not exist. My anxiety is this, and I would like some information on the point. The Prime Minister hoped that the guarantee would be effective in steadying the situation. Only twenty-four hours after the Munich proposals, another Power issued another ultimatum, and another concession was made. The question is, when does that guarantee come into operation? Is it the case that it does not come into operation before all the frontiers are finally delimited; or does it come into operation now? It is important that we should know, so that the country may be aware what its responsibility is. I should have thought that on moral grounds at least the guarantee had to come into force from the moment when the Czechoslovak State accepted the proposals pressed upon it. . . .

This is not perhaps the moment at which to put forward detailed proposals, but three conclusions from recent events seem to me to be quite inescapable. The first is that the speed of our rearmament has been, and is, too slow. It should be accelerated by every means in our power. The second is that the scope and character of our rearmament needs re-examination in the light of the events of the last few weeks. And the third is that the nation on its civil side should be encouraged so to organize itself as to enable it to meet any future challenge in conditions fairer to our own people than those that exist today.

Surely the House will be agreed that foreign affairs cannot indefinitely be continued on the basis of 'stand and deliver!'. Successive surrenders bring only successive humiliation, and they, in their turn, more humiliating demands. We have lately—let there be no doubt about it—run into grave dangers.

However the immediate issues have been resolved, no Member of the House can doubt the menacing dangers that must confront us for some time. These cannot be conjured by words of goodwill; they cannot be met even by negotiations, however sincerely meant and well pursued. If they are to be met and overcome it can only be by the revival of our national spirit, by a determined effort to conduct a foreign policy upon which the nation can unite—I am convinced that such a policy can be found—and by a national effort in the sphere of defence very much greater than anything that has been attempted hitherto. If there ever were a time for a call for a united effort by a united nation, it is my conviction that that time is now. If such an effort were made I believe we could not only save peace for this month and the next, but save it for our generation.

The true lessons of Munich were expressed in a speech of a singularly prophetic character by Winston Churchill:

We really must not waste time after all this long debate upon the difference between the positions reached at Berchtesgaden, at Godesberg, and at Munich. They can be very simply epitomized, if the House will permit me to vary the metaphor. £1 was demanded at the pistol's point. When it was given, £2 were demanded at the pistol's point. Finally the Dictator consented to take £1 17s. 6d. and the rest in promises of goodwill for the future.

No one has been a more resolute and uncompromising struggler for peace than the Prime Minister. Everyone knows that. Never has there been such intense and undaunted determination to maintain and secure peace. Nevertheless, I am not quite clear why there was so much danger of Great Britain or France being involved in a war with Germany at this juncture if in fact they were ready all along to sacrifice Czechoslovakia. The terms which the Prime Minister brought back with him could easily have been agreed, I believe, through the ordinary diplomatic channels at any time during the summer. And I will say this, that I believe the Czechs, left to themselves, and told they were going to get no help from the Western Powers, would have been able to make better terms than they have got after all this tremendous perturbation. They could hardly have had worse.

All is over. Silent, mournful, abandoned, broken, Czechoslovakia recedes into the darkness. She has suffered in every respect by her association with France under whose guidance and policy she has been actuated for so long. . . .

I find unendurable the sense of our country falling into the power, into the orbit and influence of Nazi Germany, and of our existence becoming dependent upon their goodwill or pleasure. It is to prevent that that I have tried my best to urge the maintenance of every bulwark of defence—first, the timely creation of an Air Force superior to anything within striking distance of our shores; secondly, the gathering together of the collective strength of many nations; and thirdly the making of alliances and military conventions, all within the Covenant, in order to gather together forces at any rate to restrain the onward movement of this power. It has all been in vain. Every position has been successively undermined and abandoned on specious and plausible excuses.

I do not grudge our loyal, brave people, who were ready to do their duty no matter what the cost, who never flinched under the strain of last week, the natural, spontaneous outburst of joy and relief when they learned that the hard ordeal would no longer be required of them at the moment; but they should know the truth. They should know that there has been gross neglect and deficiency in our defences; they should know that we have sustained a defeat without a war, the consequences of which will travel far with us along our road; they should know that we have passed an awful milestone in our history, when the whole equilibrium of Europe has been deranged, and that the terrible words have for the time being been pronounced against the Western democracies: 'Thou art weighed in the balance and found wanting.' And do not suppose that this is the end. This is only the beginning of the reckoning. This is only the first sip, the first foretaste of a bitter cup which will be proffered to us year by year unless, by a supreme recovery of moral health and martial vigour, we arise again and take our stand for freedom as in the olden time.

★

At the end of the three-day debate, there were two divisions. The first was on the Opposition amendment to the Government resolution. In this division some twenty Government supporters demonstratively abstained. Among them were Churchill, Eden, Duff Cooper, Cranborne, Wolmer, J. P. L. Thomas, Harold Nicolson, Richard Law, Sir Sidney Herbert, Sir Roger Keyes, Louis Spears, Harold Macmillan, Derek Gunston, Hubert Duggan, Duncan Sandys, Brendan Bracken, Vyvyan Adams and Anthony Crossley. After the Opposition amendment had been defeated by 369 votes to 150, a majority of 219, a vote was taken on the Government resolution which read: 'That this House approves the policy of H.M. Government by which war was averted in the recent crisis, and supports their efforts to secure a lasting peace.' On this vote Leo Amery and Robert Boothby, who had voted against the Opposition amendment, joined the ranks of the abstainers. The motion was carried by 366 votes to 144, a majority of 222.

Hitler greatly aided the disillusionment of those British and French who had fecklessly endorsed the Munich agreement. At the beginning of November a Polish Jew who had been expelled from Germany assassinated Herr von Rath, a diplomat who was serving on the staff of the German Embassy in Paris. Hitler took advantage of this to let loose the most savage pogrom which Germany had yet seen. Hundreds of Jews were assassinated. The shops and homes of scores of thousands of others were looted and destroyed and a reign of terror which lasted several weeks made life hellish, not only in the large urban centres, but even in hundreds of small provincial towns.

A revulsion of public opinion swept over the free world. By Christmas Munich had lost its glamour and was fast on the way to becoming a dirty word. Even Hitler's staunchest

apologists in Printing House Square, including Mr. Geoffrey
Dawson, Editor of *The Times*, and his deputy and successor,
Mr. R. M. Barrington-Ward, began to find their task
increasingly difficult and less tasteful.

★

In the early months of 1939 there seemed, outwardly,
to be a lull in international affairs. Sir Samuel Hoare was
moved to speak of the possibilities of 'a golden age'. *Punch*
published a cartoon showing John Bull awaking from a
nightmare, reassured to find his fears of war disappearing
through the window. The same day Hitler struck again.
The German Army entered Prague and incorporated in the
Reich all of Czechoslovakia except the eastern part, which
was grabbed by Poland. Now at last the scales fell from the
obstinate, blinkered eyes of Neville Chamberlain. He felt that
he had been personally cheated by Hitler. Chamberlain's
first reaction, it is true, was to belittle what had happened.
He sought to convince the House that the Czechoslovak
State had merely disintegrated, as the traditional skivvy tells
her mistress that 'it fell to pieces in me 'and'. He 'bitterly
regretted' what had happened but made no proposals for
retrieving the situation, and expressed no word of sympathy
for the Czechs, who had been enslaved in consequence of
taking his advice.

Chamberlain, however, soon discovered that he was wholly
out of touch with the mood of the British public. All classes
and all parties were outraged by Hitler's action and
Chamberlain was quickly compelled to recognize that his
policy had wholly failed and that new measures were
urgently needed.

Speaking two days later at Birmingham, he began by
apologizing for his statement to the House of Commons,
which he attributed to the fact that the Government were
not fully informed and were therefore unable to make a
considered opinion. He told his Birmingham audience that the
policy of appeasement had been founded on the assurances

that he had received from Hitler at Munich that the Sudetenland was Hitler's last territorial ambition in Europe. Chamberlain concluded by asking: 'Is this the end of an old adventure or is it the beginning of a new? Is this the last attack upon a small State or is it to be followed by others? Is this, in fact, a step in the direction of an attempt to dominate the world by force?' These were questions to which a British Prime Minister might have been expected to know the answers.

In the debate in the House, Eden had suggested that the times were so grave that the Government should be broadened to include men of all parties. This suggestion was impracticable since no one in the Labour Party would have been prepared to serve under Chamberlain. Another suggestion made in the debate was that negotiations should be initiated with Russia with a view to forming a defensive alliance. This was acted upon, and all through the summer talks proceeded in Moscow.

Meanwhile, a British guarantee of the integrity of Poland was announced. Subsequently, following upon the Italian invasion of Albania, similar guarantees were extended to Greece and Roumania. It became clear that any further move by Hitler would automatically mean war. In his apologia for what was done at Munich, Lord Templewood tells us in his *Nine Troubled Years* :

> I must insist that, after the fall of Austria, Czechoslovakia was militarily indefensible against a swift act of aggression. The trouble was not so much Czech policy as Czech geography. If it had not been for the country's geographical position, its future might have been assured. Not, however, for the first time in history the hard facts of geography destroyed the carefully arranged plans of statesmen and peoples. When military protection is lacking in support of a weak geographical position the temptation to aggression is not only almost inevitable but often irresistible.

The three states which Britain now guaranteed were all of them far less defensible from German attack than had been Czechoslovakia, but Templewood appears to notice no inconsistency between the policy he supported in regard to Czechoslovakia and the wholly contrary one to which he was now a party in Eastern Europe and the Balkans.

The situation seemed so menacing even to Chamberlain, Hoare, Simon and Halifax that the Cabinet soon became convinced of the need of some limited form of conscription. The Secretary of State for War, Mr. Hore-Belisha, had to argue for many weeks to gain his point, and, before he did, he had to fortify his arguments with the threat of resignation. Sir Winston Churchill in his war memoirs records:

> On April 27 the Prime Minister took the serious decision to introduce conscription, although repeated pledges had been given by him against such a step. To Mr. Hore-Belisha, the Secretary of State for War, belongs the credit of forcing this belated awakening. He certainly took his political life in his hands, and several of his interviews with his chief were of a formidable character. I saw something of him in this ordeal, and he was never sure that each day in office would not be his last.

Templewood in a three-page account of the discussions which culminated in this important decision, with his usual ungraciousness towards former colleagues, does not even mention Hore-Belisha's name. With war on the horizon, the Labour and Liberal oppositions of course voted against this tardy, tentative step.

★

Since his resignation Eden had usefully consolidated his position in the House of Commons and had made a number of journeys abroad. He visited the United States in December 1938 and made a number of speeches in Paris in the early summer of 1939. As the situation darkened, Eden set a good example to the nation by offering his services to the War Office, who gazetted him a Major in a Territorial unit which was affiliated to his old regiment, the King's Royal Rifle Corps.

On August 24 came the news that Ribbentrop had arrived in Moscow and had signed the non-aggression pact with Molotov, by which Hitler secured himself from the danger of war on two fronts. All the time that Mr. William Strang of the Foreign Office had been negotiating with the Russians, they had been conducting parallel talks with the Germans. Britain was not prepared to scupper the Baltic States and she had no means of compelling Poland to agree that in the event of war with Germany, the Red Army should have the right of transit across Polish territory. Britain was rightly not prepared to agree. War was now certain. The world awaited for the most part with calm the opening salvoes. They did not have to wait long. In September Hitler launched a massive attack on Poland. Two days later Britain declared war on Germany, and a few hours later France, having frantically but vainly cast about for some means of extricating herself, followed suit.

CHAPTER ELEVEN

War

THE Government was immediately reconstructed. The two principal recruits to the Government were Churchill and Eden. Churchill went to the Admiralty, with a seat in the War Cabinet, which consisted of Chamberlain, the Prime Minister, Simon, Chancellor of the Exchequer, Halifax, Foreign Secretary, Lord Chatfield, Minister for Defence Co-ordination, Hore-Belisha, Secretary for War, Kingsley Wood, Secretary for Air, Hoare, Lord Privy Seal, and Lord Hankey, Minister without Portfolio, and Churchill. Eden went to the Dominions Office.

It is not the intention of the author to tell the story of the second world war. That would be disproportionate to the scale of this book. We propose to confine ourselves to chronicling the more important features of Eden's activities during this period.

Eden was well cast for his role. His diplomatic training and his easy charm with statesmen overseas made this a singularly happy appointment. Early in the war there was a meeting in London of representatives of all the Dominions, and Eden accompanied them on a tour of the Allied front in France. He naturally concerned himself closely with the welfare of Dominion troops. He met the first contingent of the Canadian Army when they arrived in Britain and he flew out to Suez early in 1940 to meet the first Australian contingents which were arriving in Egypt.

When Churchill succeeded Chamberlain on May 10, he moved Eden from the Dominions Office to the War Office in the place of Oliver Stanley, who had been appointed in January when Chamberlain dismissed Hore-Belisha. His tenure of the War Office lasted no more than six months.

It was marked by the foundation of the Local Defence
Volunteers, or L.D.V., as they were inevitably called, until
Churchill gave them the more dignified appellation of
'Home Guard'.

On July 26 Churchill minuted:

> I don't think very much of the name 'Local Defence Volun-
> teers' for your very large new force. The word 'local' is unin-
> spiring. Mr. Herbert Morrison suggested to me today the title
> 'Civic Guard', but I think 'Home Guard' would be better.
> Don't hesitate to change on account of already having made
> armlets, etc., if it is thought the title of Home Guard would be
> more compulsive.

★

In October the Prime Minister asked Eden to go out to
Cairo to investigate the condition of the armed forces in the
Middle East. After some preliminary talks in Cairo with
General Wavell, Eden flew down to Khartoum for a meeting
with General Smuts to concert plans for the dispatch to
the Libyan Desert of a considerable South African army.
While in Khartoum news came of the Italian attack on
Greece.

The Prime Minister instantly ordered Eden to return to
Cairo to cope with the Greek situation and to urge upon the
Middle East Command some other policy in the Western
Desert than awaiting a set-piece battle at Mersa Matruh when
the Italians attacked, as they were expected to do.

This is one of the best periods in Eden's story. He established most intimate relations with both Wavell and Wilson,
Commander of the Desert Army, with the latter of whom
he had a natural affinity, since they were both Green Jackets.
The telegram which Eden sent to the Prime Minister
admirably demonstrated his mastery of the military
situation:

> We cannot from Middle East forces send sufficient air or land
> reinforcements to have any decisive influence upon the course
> of fighting in Greece. To send such forces from here, or to
> divert reinforcements now on their way or approved, would

imperil our whole position in the Middle East and jeopardize plans for an offensive operation now being laid in more than one theatre. After much painful effort and at the cost of grave risks we have, so far as our land forces are concerned, now built up a reasonably adequate defensive force here. We should presently be in a position to undertake certain offensive operations which if successful may have far-reaching effects on the course of the war as a whole. It would surely be bad strategy to allow ourselves to be diverted from this task, and unwise to employ our forces in fragments in a theatre of war where they cannot be decisive. . . . The best way in which we can help Greece is by striking at Italy, and we can do that most effectively from areas where our strength has been developed and where our plans are laid. I am anxious to put before you in detail at the earliest date the disposition and plans which have been worked out here, and propose . . . to return home by the shortest route, leaving on the 3rd.

When Eden arrived in London on November 8 with the news of the details of the proposed offensive in the desert, he was greeted with jubilation by his colleagues in the Cabinet.

Within a week of Eden's return to London, Wavell and Wilson launched their campaign in the desert. In rapid succession Sidi Barrani, Mersa Matruh, Tobruk and Benghazi were taken. This brilliant victory greatly enhanced Eden's standing with the Prime Minister. He had himself most effectively handled the situation in Cairo and had procured, what the War Cabinet desired above all else, a British victory. All this must have been very much in the Prime Minister's mind when, on December 12, the British Embassy in Washington fell vacant on the untimely death of Lord Lothian. In the closing weeks of his life he had rendered memorable service to his country by his negotiation with President Roosevelt of the Lend-Lease agreement. He was one of the two or three most successful ambassadors that Britain has ever sent to the United States, and his death was widely mourned on both sides of the Atlantic, not merely by his many friends, but by all who knew and appreciated the value of the unique work he had done.

It was obvious that he must be replaced by a man of equal calibre. The Prime Minister considered the idea of sending Mr. Lloyd George, but he, though flattered by the proposal, excused himself from this undertaking. Instead, the Prime Minister suggested to the Foreign Secretary, Lord Halifax, that he should step into the breach with all the authority which an ambassador would have who had just left the Foreign Office. Halifax did not like the idea at all, but in wartime nearly everyone is prepared to subordinate his own inclinations to the common interest. Halifax accepted the appointment and made a brilliant success of his embassy. The way was thus open for the Prime Minister to bring Eden back to the Foreign Office. His account of these transactions must be put on record here:

> I next turned to Lord Halifax, whose prestige in the Conservative Party stood high, and was enhanced by his being at the Foreign Office. For a Foreign Secretary to become an Ambassador marks in a unique manner the importance of the mission. His high character was everywhere respected, yet at the same time his record in the years before the war and the way in which events had moved left him exposed to much disapprobation and even hostility from the Labour side of our National Coalition. I knew that he was conscious of this himself.
>
> When I made him this proposal, which was certainly not a personal advancement, he contended himself with saying in a simple and dignified manner that he would serve wherever he was thought to be most useful. In order to emphasize still further the importance of his duties, I arranged that he should resume his function as a member of the War Cabinet whenever he came home on leave. This arrangement worked without the slightest inconvenience, owing to the qualities and experience of the personalities involved, and for six years thereafter, both under the National Coalition and the Labour-Socialist Government, Halifax discharged the work of Ambassador to the United States with conspicuous and ever-growing influence and success.
>
> President Roosevelt, Mr. Hull, and other high personalities

in Washington were extremely pleased with the selection of
Lord Halifax. Indeed it was at once apparent to me that the
President greatly preferred it to my first proposal [Lloyd
George]. The appointment of the new Ambassador was
received with marked approval both in America and at home,
and was judged in every way adequate and appropriate to the
scale of events.

I had no doubt who should fill the vacancy at the Foreign
Office. On all the great issues of the past four years I had, as
these pages have shown, dwelt in close agreement with Anthony
Eden. I have described my anxieties and emotions when he
parted company with Mr. Chamberlain in the spring of 1938.
Together we had abstained from the vote on Munich. Together
we had resisted the party pressures brought to bear upon us in
our constituencies during the winter of that melancholy year.
We had been united in thought and sentiment at the outbreak
of the war and as colleagues during its progress. The greater part
of Eden's public life had been devoted to the study of foreign
affairs. He had held the splendid office of Foreign Secretary
with distinction, and had resigned it when only forty-two years
of age for reasons which are in retrospect, and at this time,
viewed with the approval of all parties in the State.

He had played a fine part as Secretary of State for War
during this terrific year, and his conduct of Army affairs had
brought us very close together. We thought alike, even without
consultation, on a very great number of practical issues as they
arose from day to day. I looked forward to an agreeable and
harmonious comradeship between the Prime Minister and the
Foreign Secretary, and this hope was certainly fulfilled during
the four and a half years of war and policy which lay before us.
Eden was sorry to leave the War Office, in all the stresses and
excitements of which he was absorbed; but he returned to the
Foreign Office like a man going home.

This was, of course, a decisive event in Eden's career.
It would have been a notable event if he had returned to the
Foreign Office as a result of the death of the incumbent;
but to have the office cleared for him by sending the incumbent, who was sixteen years older than himself, against his will,
to America, underlined the significance of the appointment

in a striking fashion. Apart from the fact that the Prime Minister, as he implies in the passage quoted above, found that he could work more easily and intimately with Eden than he could with Halifax, there was doubtless present, at least in the back of his mind, the issue of Munich. He naturally found it more agreeable to work with those whose minds had been in harmony with his in the difficult days of peace when the war could still have been prevented, rather than with those who had been the long-term architects of the national misfortune. Eden, it is true, bore a heavy responsibility for the mismanagement of our affairs, but he had not, to his credit, been involved in the culminating shame and disaster of Munich.

Those few who resisted the dire processes of the Baldwin-MacDonald decade, though they were ready to forgive and wished to unite everyone in the war effort, never felt comfortable in the presence of the men of Munich. The Prime Minister seems to have felt it in his bones that those who had worked, to a greater or lesser degree, with him in trying to stop the war ought to play leading roles in trying to win it. Thus it was that men like Duff Cooper, Cranborne (later Lord Salisbury), Lord Wolmer (later Lord Selborne), Richard Law (later Lord Coleraine), Harold Macmillan, Duncan Sandys, Brendan Bracken (later Lord Bracken), and Leo Amery rightly and naturally obtained advancement in this period, and it was altogether seemly that the men of Munich like Halifax and Hoare—though very able men in their own way—should suffer some interruption in their political careers and work their passages back abroad. Thus it was that Lord Simon the other leading survivor of the Munich period, had talents which justified, when Churchill became Prime Minister, his vacating the Treasury and going to the Woolsack, but played little part in the conduct of the war. Mr. R. A. Butler, the Under-Secretary of State at the Foreign Office, received advancement and became President of the Board of Education, that office, like that of Lord Chancellor, being a backwater in time of war.

Very soon after Eden had once more taken over the
Foreign Office, a congenial field for him, events required
that some member of the War Cabinet should visit the
Middle East. Eden, in view of the success of his previous
tour, was the obvious choice. Mussolini had got himself
entangled to great disadvantage in Greece and it seemed
that he would shortly need Hitler to come to his rescue.
Yugoslavia, as well as Greece, might well be involved.
Eden, with the laurels of the Libyan victory and as a member
of the War Cabinet, returned to the Middle East on this
mission with far wider powers than he had exercised the
year before. He was especially authorized by the Prime
Minister and the War Cabinet, in what was obviously going
to be a critical, violent and quickly moving situation, himself
to take decisions on the spot if he judged it necessary,
without reference to the War Cabinet.

Accordingly Eden arrived in Cairo early in March 1941.
He was accompanied by Sir John Dill, Chief of the Imperial
General Staff. Events were to protract his visit for a good deal
longer than had originally been planned.* The impending
German attack on Yugoslavia and Greece, both of which
countries he visited, was to prolong his stay in the Mediterranean.

On 22 June 1941 Hitler, having decided some months
before that he could not undertake the invasion of Britain,
launched his attack on Soviet Russia. British policy, which
had for a few weeks created a Balkan front, and for the
creation of which Eden deserves much praise, produced an
unexpected and unplanned benefit. Hitler's Balkan campaign
caused him to postpone his Russian campaign by five or six

* The author arrived at Ismailia in No. 8 Commando, and had the good
fortune to pass several agreeable hours with the Foreign Secretary in the
British Embassy at Cairo. Eden concluded a telegram to the Prime Minister
with the words, 'have seen Randolph, who has just arrived. He sends his love.
He is looking fit and well and has the light of battle in his eye'. It has been
said (the author has not verified the tale, though) that either owing to a corrup-
tion in transmission or to a lively sense of mischief on the part of a Foreign
Office official, this telegram was delivered in London with the 'a' in battle
replaced by an 'o'.

weeks. If he had had five or six more weeks of good campaigning weather, which he would have had if he had attacked
Russia around May 10 instead of June 22, he might well
have captured Leningrad, Moscow and Stalingrad and
rendered further resistance by the Russians impossible
except on a guerrilla basis.

From the outset Britain did all in her power to assist the
Russians, who by accident, had become our allies. Eden was
the first British statesman to visit Moscow during the war.
Conversations opened in Moscow on December 16. When
Eden returned to England at the end of December he gave a
broadcast on his visit. He said:

> Mr. Molotov and other representatives of the Soviet
> Government met us on our arrival late at night in Moscow,
> the city Hitler had hoped to capture long ago. The next day
> we began our series of talks with Mr. Stalin and Mr. Molotov
> in the Kremlin. These talks went further than any political or
> military discussions that have taken place at any time between
> our two countries since the last war.

When the Prime Minister flew to the United States in
June 1942 for another meeting with President Roosevelt.
there took place an episode which was unique in our constitutional history and which, though it was not publicly
known at the time, confirmed in a formal way the fact,
already established when Eden replaced Halifax at the Foreign
Office six months before, that a successor to the Tory Party
leadership had emerged. At the request of King George VI
the Prime Minister offered formal advice as to who the King
should send for in the event of his death.

Churchill sent the King the following letter:

> In case of my death on this journey I am about to under-
> take, I avail myself of Your Majesty's gracious permission to
> advise that you should entrust the formation of a new Govern-
> ment to Mr. Anthony Eden, the Secretary of State for Foreign
> Affairs, who is in my mind the outstanding Minister in the
> largest political party in the House of Commons and in the
> National Government over which I have the honour to pre-

side, and who, I am sure, will be found capable of conducting Your Majesty's affairs with the resolution, experience and capacity which these grievous times require.

In October of this year Eden made another visit to Moscow. His mission was complicated by the fact that while he was in Moscow the Prime Minister had felt it necessary to adopt the unusual diplomatic course for an ally of refusing to accept a cable which had come through the newly appointed Russian Ambassador, M. Gousev. The scene is admirably described by Sir Winston Churchill in his war memoirs:

On the same day I asked the Soviet Ambassador to come to see me. As this was the first occasion on which I had met M. Gousev, who had succeeded Maisky, he gave me the greetings of Marshal Stalin and M. Molotov, and I told him of the good reputation he had made for himself with us in Canada. After these compliments we had a short discussion about the Moscow Conference and the Second Front. I explained to him that this kind of operation could not be undertaken on impulse, and that I was always ready to arrange for a meeting between British and Russian military experts, who would go into the facts and figures, upon which everything depended, and without which discussion was futile. I spoke to him earnestly about the great desire we had to work with Russia and to be friends with her, how we saw that she should have a great place in the world after the war, that we should welcome this, and that we would do our best also to make good relations between her and the United States. I further said how much I was looking forward to a meeting with Marshal Stalin if it could be arranged, and how important this meeting of the heads of the British, American, and Soviet Governments was to the future of the world.

I then turned to Stalin's telegram about the convoys.* I said very briefly that I did not think this message would help the situation, that it had caused me a good deal of pain, that I

* Earlier in the year it had been necessary, because of heavy losses, to postpone some of the convoys which were carrying supplies from Britain to Russia. It was now proposed to resume them, but the Russians had been difficult about the conditions affecting British seamen and personnel in Russian ports.

feared any reply which I could send would only make things worse, that the Foreign Secretary was in Moscow and I had left it to him to settle the matter on the spot and that therefore I did not wish to receive the message. I then handed back to the Ambassador an envelope. Gousev opened the envelope to see what was inside it, and, recognizing the message, said he had been instructed to deliver it to me. I then said, 'I am not prepared to receive it,' and got up to indicate in a friendly manner that our conversation was at an end. I moved to the door and opened it. We had a little talk in the doorway about his coming to luncheon in the near future and discussing with Mrs. Churchill some questions connected with her Russian fund, which I told him had now reached four million pounds. I did not give M. Gousev a chance of recurring to the question of the convoys or of trying to hand me back the envelope, and bowed him out.

Churchill wired to Eden, defining his task:

I feel so much for you in the bleak Conference, and wish I were with you. You may have full confidence in the strength of the British position on all these questions, and I have every hope that you will make them feel at once our desire for their friendship and our will-power on essentials. All good luck.

On his return from Moscow to London Eden joined Churchill in Cairo to take part in conferences held in November and December in Cairo and in Teheran. At the end of the conferences the Prime Minister stayed on for a few days to have talks with General Eisenhower, and it fell to Eden just before the end of the year to explain to the House of Commons so far as wartime secrecy allowed what had been the fruits of these important discussions:

Now let me describe our work. It fell into three main, easily defined chapters. First, the first Cairo Conference for the prosecution of the war against Japan, next the Teheran Conference for the prosecution of the war against Germany, and then the second Cairo Conference for discussions with the President and the Foreign Secretary of Turkey. I propose to say something about each, and also about a number of sub-sidiary and important matters which were discussed and

dealt with in both Cairo and Teheran. The greater part of the
time of the first two Conferences in Cairo about the Far East,
and in Teheran about the war against Germany, was taken
up with military matters. It was possible for us to bring these
matters to a state of complete and collective preparation far
exceeding anything that had hitherto been realized in this war.
The thought is, I think, quite well expressed in two sentences of
the Teheran communiqué, to which I draw the attention of
the House because they are, I think, the most important of all.
It states:

> 'Our military staffs have joined in our round table discus-
> sions and we have concerted our plans for the destruction of
> the German forces. We have reached complete agreement as
> to the scope and timing of the operations which will be under-
> taken from the East, West and South.'

The latter part of 1944, following upon the Allied invasion,
was to be an exceptionally busy time for Eden and much
travel was required of him. In September he joined the Prime
Minister in Quebec for another meeting with President
Roosevelt and the Canadian Prime Minister, Mr. Mackenzie
King. In October he accompanied the Prime Minister to
Moscow (this was Mr. Eden's third wartime visit). While
Mr. Churchill returned to London, Mr. Eden came back via
Cairo, Athens and Italy.

In all these travels and conferences Eden was gaining
in experience and authority, and was daily growing in
stature among his colleagues in the Cabinet. Since November
1941 he had been discharging the onerous duties of Leader of
the House as well as those of Foreign Secretary. He had
succeeded in establishing himself with all parties as a parlia-
mentarian of greater stature than he had been before.

Eden flew with Churchill to Paris for the Armistice cele-
brations on November 11 and on Christmas Day they flew
together to Athens where, in the teeth of the opposition of
the Labour Party, practically the whole of the British and
American Press and of President Roosevelt, they succeeded in
saving Greece from falling into the hands of the Communists.

February 1945 found Eden participating in the conference at Yalta. On April 12 came the news of President Roosevelt's sudden death. Eden flew to Washington to represent the British Government at his funeral. From Washington Eden flew on to San Francisco for the conference which was drawing up the Charter of the United Nations. There, he suffered from a duodenal ulcer which was to keep him in bed during most of the election. While Eden was ill, he received confirmation of the death of his son, Simon, who had been serving with the R.A.F. in Burma.

A month later Germany surrendered and the war in Europe was over. It was found impossible to maintain the Coalition Government for the purpose of concluding the war in the Far East. The Government broke up and after a brief period of 'caretaker' Government in which Eden continued to serve as Foreign Secretary, Parliament was dissolved and a general election was held on July 5.

There was a three weeks' delay in counting the votes so that the services' ballot papers could be brought back from overseas. Meanwhile Eden had been with Churchill at the Potsdam Conference from which they flew home to learn the melancholy tidings on July 26 that the Government and the Tory Party had suffered a staggering electoral disaster.

The final figures were Labour 392 seats, Conservative and Unionist 198 seats, Liberal National and National 15, Independents 14, Liberal 12, I.L.P. 3, Communist 2 and other Labour allies 3. The Labour Party had a clear majority over all other parties combined of 147. Eden himself had his usual magnificent majority at Warwick and Leamington of 17,634 compared with 24,816 in 1935.

The Prime Minister immediately resigned and Eden and the Tories were back in opposition.

CHAPTER TWELVE

Opposition; Back to the Foreign Office

IT took a long time and much spadework to rebuild the fortunes of the Tory Party. These six years of opposition were difficult ones for Eden and did not serve to increase his stature. He had never had much taste, or, indeed, opportunity, for the hurly-burly of partisan politics in the House of Commons. The important work in rebuilding the party was undertaken by Lord Woolton and the reshaping of Tory policy by Mr. R. A. Butler. These were not fields in which Eden had ever specialized. Although of course he had made many speeches in the House and in the country on a wide variety of topics other than foreign affairs, he definitely suffered from the fact that all his official life, with the exception of two short periods, one at the Dominions Office, the other at the War Office, had been spent at the Foreign Office, and that in consequence he had very little experience of domestic affairs.

None the less, he was so firmly entrenched as Churchill's eventual successor and was so much better known and more popular in the country than any possible rival that his position remained unchallenged and was, in fact, unchallengeable. At the end of 1945 it became known that Churchill was going to spend a three months holiday in the United States. Eden was deputed to act as Leader of the Opposition in his absence.

In June 1946 Eden visited Bermuda to take part in the deliberations of the Empire Parliamentary Association and took the opportunity on his way home of visiting Canada and the United States. In October he made an important speech at the Tory Conference at Blackpool. Here it was that he proclaimed the slogan of a nation-wide property-owning democracy. He said:

> Long experience has taught us that to offer to the people any single panacea as the Socialists offer nationalization would be merely to delude ourselves and them. Life is not as simple as that. For the manifold and diverse problems that face us, manifold and diverse solutions must of necessity be required. But this I believe we can say, that there is one single principle that will unite all the solutions that we shall seek and propound. There is one principle underlying our approach to all these problems, a principle on which we stand in fundamental opposition to Socialism. The objective of Socialism is state ownership of all the means of production, distribution and exchange. Our objective is a nation-wide, property-owning democracy. These objectives are fundamentally opposed. Whereas the Socialist purpose is the concentration of owner-ship in the hands of the State, ours is the distribution of owner-ship over the widest practicable number of individuals.

During the summer of 1947 he made a number of speeches in the country and attracted exceptionally large crowds. At the end of the year he made a tour of the Middle East and inspected the Anglo-Persian oilfields. He also paid a visit to King Ibn Saud of Saudi Arabia, who presented him with a sword encrusted with pearls.

Shortly after his return he found himself once more in ill health and had an operation for appendicitis. He had a good recovery and during the summer he made a large number of speeches, attending the Tory Conference at Llandudno later in the year and making a speech on foreign affairs.

Early in 1949 he embarked on a considerable tour which took him to Canada, Australia, New Zealand, Malaya, India and Pakistan. In the following year he revisited Canada and the United States. Shortly after his return there took place the General Election of October 1950. Under the Redistribution Bill, Stratford on Avon, which had been part of the Warwick and Leamington division, was cut off and joined to a considerable rural area which had

up till then been part of the Rugby division. Eden had the
choice of standing for the newly created constituency which
was overwhelmingly Tory or of standing by Warwick and
Leamington, which had become considerably industrialized
and was likely not to be quite such a safe seat as Stratford
on Avon. Eden loyally decided to stand by Warwick and
Leamington.

In the event it looked as if there was not much to choose.
Eden's majority at Warwick and Leamington was 8,814;
that of Major Profumo, who fought the seat of Stratford on
Avon, was 9,349.

At the General Election the Tories registered considerable
gains, and when the new Parliament met the Socialists'
massive majority of 147 in 1945 had been cut to the narrow
margin of six.

Few people believed that the Labour Party would be
able to stay in office with a majority as small as this. In fact
their parliamentary difficulties proved less than might have
been expected and it was not the smallness of their majority
but rather the impending economic disaster they saw ahead
which impelled them suddenly to dissolve Parliament
eighteen months later and go to the country in October 1951.
Whereas in the previous Parliament the Tories had been in a
minority of six, in the new Parliament which met on October
31 they had a majority of sixteen. After a long uphill fight for
six years Churchill was once more back in Downing Street.
In his new Government Eden returned once more to the
Foreign Office.

★

Within a week of becoming Foreign Secretary he flew
to Paris to attend the disarmament proposals under discussion at the United Nations Assembly. In December he
was once more in Paris with the Prime Minister to meet
the French leaders, M. Pleven and M. Schuman. They saw
General Eisenhower at the headquarters of NATO. At the
end of the month they left by sea for America.

The whole range of political and military problems was discussed with President Truman at the conference which opened in Washington early in January. At its conclusion Churchill and Truman issued a joint communiqué: 'We will remain in close consultation on the developments which might increase danger to the maintenance of world peace. We do not believe that war is inevitable.'

Eden went on to Columbia University and delivered a speech on the international situation:

> For twenty-five years I have been concerned with international problems. I have taken some part in the search for peace in responsible years of office, as well as in those of greater freedom and less responsibility in Opposition. In the twentieth century peace has been precarious and elusive.

In reference to the Middle East he said:

> Let me make it clear where my country stands in that area of the world. We have no imperialist ambitions. We neither added, nor sought to add, one square inch to our territories as a result of the war, in which we played a not unworthy part. We are not seeking selfish ends. Our policy in Egypt today bears this out. The Suez Canal is an international waterway whose free passage is of world concern. We do not guard the Canal for ourselves alone. The approach which we have recently made to Egypt is a joint one with the U.S.A., France, and Turkey. It offers Egypt a full and equal partnership with us all. We seek in effect a joint arrangement to ensure the freedom of this international highway and the security of the Middle East as a whole.

★

On February 6 King George VI died. Dr. Adenauer came to London to attend his funeral and had a special interview with Eden ten days later. During the next three days tripartite talks about the European Defence Community were held between the British, French and American Foreign Secretaries. The French, having originated the plan, were to play the leading role in sabotaging it. EDC was eventually rejected in 1954 by a free vote of the French Assembly. This promoted a serious European crisis, a solution to which was found by the enterprise and resource of Eden. One of the reasons for the French rejection had been that Britain had refused to play a part. Eden realized that no agreement could be found unless Britain were to co-operate. He made a quick tour of European capitals, Brussels, Bonn, Rome and Paris. Then, at the end of September 1954, he called a meeting in London of the Foreign Ministers of France, Germany, Italy, Belgium, Holland, Luxembourg, Britain, Canada and the United States. To this important gathering he made the dramatic declaration that the four British divisions in Germany and the Tactical Air Force would not be withdrawn against the wishes of the majority of the Brussels Treaty Powers. The results of this conference were held as a great triumph for Eden, and in October 1954 the Queen gave him the highest honour in her power, the Garter.

★

In August 1952 Anthony Eden was married to Clarissa Churchill, the niece of Sir Winston Churchill. The wedding reception took place at 10 Downing Street, soon to be their home. The honeymoon was spent in Portugal.

During the whole of 1952 Eden was concerned with the war in Korea, the Persian oil dispute, and the tussle between Tito and Italy over Trieste. The war in Korea was turning into a stalemate, but the negotiations at Panmunjom were still unsuccessful. Dr. Mossadeq and Persian resistance were weakening but were not yet broken. In the autumn, Eden discussed Trieste with Signor de Gasperi, Prime Minister of Italy, at Strasbourg, and with President Tito at Belgrade. Tito returned the compliment with a visit to London in the spring of 1953.

In February, Eden and Butler went to America to discuss trade and monetary policy. The *New York Times*, quoting a London expert on economics, said that the British plan was so complex that 'Mr. Eden understands ten per cent of it,

Mr. Butler about forty per cent, and their advisers about ninety per cent.' On March 5 came the news of the death of Stalin. Eden immediately visited the newly elected President, General Eisenhower, and the new Secretary of State, Mr. Dulles.

Eden had been due to visit Italy, Greece and Turkey in April, but on March 30 it was announced that he would have to undergo an operation. (During his absence Lord Salisbury was put in charge of the Foreign Office.) Two unsuccessful operations were performed in London in April. An American specialist, Dr. Richard Cattell, offered to operate, though he could only do so in America. Eden agreed to fly to Boston, and an obstruction to the bile duct was successfully removed. After three months of convalescence in America and the Mediterranean, he returned to Westminster.

While Eden was still in the Boston clinic the Prime Minister had a serious stroke. It is probable that, if Eden had been in England and in good health, he would have resigned and Eden would have become Prime Minister. As it was, the general view was held in high governing circles that it would be wrong if Eden, who had waited so long to be Prime Minister, should forfeit his reversionary rights by the strange misfortune that he and the Prime Minister were ill at the same time. Various expedients were debated, including that of a 'caretaker' Government under Lord Salisbury, to hold the fort till Eden should be recovered. Friends wrote and told Lady Eden that her husband's interests were being constantly borne in mind and that he should think of nothing save getting well.

Quite soon, however, the difficulties resolved themselves, owing to Sir Winston's fantastic powers of resilience and recuperation. He fought his way back to health with a Roman mastery of mind over the flesh and within a few weeks was back on deck again.

★

May, June and most of July of the following year, 1954, were occupied with a conference at Geneva which sought to find some way of bringing to an end the war in which France had long been engaged in Vietnam. In the course of these discussions there were numerous misunderstandings between Eden and the American Secretary of State, Foster Dulles. Eventually Dulles packed his bags and went home, and it was left to Eden and the new French Prime Minister Mendès-France to settle the matter between themselves. The solution, though not heroic, avoided what was otherwise certain, that the flower of the French Army would have been slaughtered, imprisoned or pushed into the sea. Whatever one's views on the outcome of this tragic affair, the conduct of the negotiations was a triumph for Eden and his talent for negotiation was never seen to better advantage.

We must now revert once more to Egypt, which seems to run as the dominant thread through the tapestry of Eden's career. For many years, under Socialist and Tory Governments alike, there had been persistent negotiations to make a revision of the Anglo-Egyptian Treaty which Eden had negotiated with Nahas Pasha in 1936 and which was due to expire in 1956.

As early as April 1952 Eden had summoned Sir Ralph Stevenson, the British Ambassador to Egypt, and the Governor of the Sudan, Sir Robert Howe, to talks in London. He had called a conference in June at which eleven Middle East countries were represented. A month later General Neguib had carried out his bloodless *coup* in Cairo which had forced King Farouk into exile. He was superseded in February 1954 by Colonel Nasser.

Withdrawal from the Canal Zone was Eden's policy, and it was he who signed the new Anglo-Egyptian agreement on 19 October 1954. Having decided to leave, it would have been better to have gone without haggling. Mr. Head, then Secretary of State for War, defended the evacuation by saying that military ideas which had been sound a year ago were already 'utterly obsolete' owing to the advent of nuclear weapons. In the debate Eden said that if troops remained in the Canal Zone they would be 'a beleaguered garrison'; what was vital to any army was mobility. He argued that the compensation for leaving the Canal Zone was that the eighty thousand troops who were now a 'beleaguered garrison' would become a mobile strategic reserve.

A strategic reserve is useless if it lacks a convenient base and mobility. Since the British Government failed to build a deep-water harbour in Cyprus or to provide the R.A.F. with a sufficiency of transport aircraft, the loss of the Suez base was to prove almost fatal to our position in the Near and Middle East. But of this more later—but not much later; the sky was very soon to be darkened by the wings of the chickens coming home to roost.

★

Eden was now fully restored to health and was awaiting the retirement of Sir Winston Churchill and his own entry to 10 Downing Street. His friends were loud-mouthed in calling for Churchill's departure and suggested that if Eden's succession were to be long delayed he might become so frustrated that he would have passed the peak of his powers by the time that he entered into the joy of his inheritance. It was curious that Eden was so impatient. In the spring of 1955 Eden was fifty-eight years old. Churchill had not become Prime Minister until he was sixty-five and thereby qualified to draw the old-age pension. All, however, was now arranged and on April 5 Sir Winston tendered his resignation.

Some people had supposed that Sir Winston might defer his resignation, which had been long agitated, until the ending of the strike of all the national newspapers which had been proceeding for some time, since he might not wish his passing from the scene to be unrecorded. These conceptions were wide of the mark. Sir Winston's fame and glory were not likely to depend on the ephemeral comments of the national newspapers on the day of his departure. None the less it may be of interest to preserve from oblivion a contemporary account by the author of this book of the change of guard which took place and which was published in the *Manchester Guardian* on 6 April 1955:

> An hour before Sir Winston Churchill arrived at the Palace to tender his resignation to the Queen, there was a crowd of perhaps a thousand people, but as there were no newspapers to speculate rightly or wrongly about the hour of his arrival, they gradually melted away. When he arrived at 4.30 p.m. not more than three hundred or four hundred people stood at the gates. The *Manchester Guardian*, one of the few great English papers which is still being published, yesterday quoted an anonymous politician as saying: 'The absence of newspapers diminishes the size of events.' It evidently diminishes crowds still more.
>
> Speculation in Fleet Street about when Sir Winston's successor would be summoned to the Palace was rife, but because of the strike was inevitably muted. Everyone had expected that Sir Anthony Eden would be sent for within an hour or two of Sir Winston's resignation. As the hours passed, it became apparent that though it is certain as tomorrow's sunrise that the Queen's choice will fall on Sir Anthony, he will not, in fact, receive his summons to the Palace until tomorrow.
>
> The delay which has bewildered many people is constitutional and not political. It is not generally realized that under the traditions of the British Constitution the Sovereign is under no obligation to consult a retiring Prime Minister about his successor, and it would be unseemly for him to volunteer advice.
>
> When Mr. Gladstone resigned in 1894, the present Queen's great-great-grandmother, Queen Victoria, did not ask for any advice. The choice seemed to lie between Sir William Harcourt and Lord Rosebery, and it was to the latter that the Queen entrusted the task of forming a new Government. As a matter of fact, if the Queen had consulted Mr. Gladstone, he had

intended to recommend Lord Spencer. It may have been because the Queen knew this that she did not ask his advice.

With the exception of certain court appointments and the awarding of certain honours, the Garter, the Thistle and the Order of Merit, the choice of a Prime Minister is the only part of the royal prerogative which a modern British Sovereign can exercise without Ministerial advice. The reason for this is obvious. The resignation of the Prime Minister involves the resignation of all other Ministers. Therefore, at the moment when a new Prime Minister is chosen, there are no Ministers for the Sovereign to consult. This is one of those moments. One of the greatest strengths of the British Constitution is that, being unwritten, it is extremely flexible, and all constitutional authorities attach the highest importance to preserving this part of the royal prerogative intact in the Sovereign's hands.

The timing of today's change of guard was obviously intended to underline this constitutional feature. Though Sir Winston placed his resignation in the Queen's hands at 4.30 this afternoon, it will not be until tomorrow that the Queen will send for his successor.

In choosing a Prime Minister, the main consideration in the Sovereign's mind must be to find a man who can command a majority in the House of Commons. Since the Conservative party at the moment has a majority over all other parties of nineteen, he must plainly, on this occasion, be a Conservative. Sir Anthony Eden stands out as the obvious choice, acceptable to the overwhelming body of Conservative opinion alike in the House of Commons and in the country. For the last three and a half years he has been Deputy Prime Minister,* and though the office has no actual validity in the Constitution it none the less has helped to mark him out for the succession.

Sir Winston has several times over the last seven or eight years referred to him as 'my eventual successor'. But of course, he did not mean as Prime Minister. That would have been an invasion of the royal prerogative. Sir Winston has only said this at meetings of the Conservative party and only when he was, of course, referring to the leadership of the party and not to the office of Prime Minister.

It is open to the Sovereign to consult anyone she likes about

* This appellation has now been abandoned.

the choice of Prime Minister and in cases of doubt, as when Mr. Baldwin was preferred to Lord Curzon in 1923 after the resignation of Mr. Bonar Law, the Sovereign is likely to consult some elder statesmen. In 1923, King George V sent for the late Lord Balfour, and his private secretary, Lord Stamfordham, also consulted the late Lord Salisbury. This time the choice is so obvious that the Queen will almost certainly rely upon her own judgment.

When Sir Anthony, or whoever else the Queen may designate, has kissed hands and accepted the invitation to form a Government, the next step will be for the two Chief Whips, Mr. Buchan-Hepburn, in the House of Commons, and Lord Fortescue, in the House of Lords, to summon a party meeting which will be informed of the resignation by Sir Winston of the party leadership and will be invited to carry a resolution appointing the new Prime Minister leader in his stead. A full party meeting of this character is only called for the purpose of selecting a new leader. The resolution will almost certainly be carried unanimously.

Those summoned will be the 320 Conservative members of the House of Commons, about 280 peers who take the Conservative whip, the 250 officially adopted parliamentary candidates and the 150 members of the Executive Committee of the Conservative and Unionist Association. The last time there was a party meeting was in 1940, when Neville Chamberlain resigned the leadership and Winston Churchill was chosen.

Meanwhile, the first big decision of the new Prime Minister will concern the date of the general election. Most people think that he will decide for an early election and that the likely date will be May 26. If this is his decision he will probably make very few changes in the Government until after the election. If he should decide as a temporary arrangement to keep the Foreign Office in his own hands no changes will be necessary at all.

If, on the other hand, he vacates the Foreign Office, it is likely that Mr. Harold Macmillan will move in from the Ministry of Defence and a number of consequential changes will be necessary. If the decision is for an autumn election, a great number of changes may be expected immediately.

Ministers who will probably be omitted from the new

Government, whether now or after the election, include Lord Woolton, Chancellor of the Duchy of Lancaster, Mr. Crookshank, the Lord Privy Seal and Leader of the House of Commons, and Sir Walter Monckton, the Minister of Labour.

Power cannot be handed over on a plate in England any more than it can be in Russia. And though no one anticipates that the new Prime Minister will have so short a premiership as Mr. Malenkov, it is obvious that a great deal of the immense political power which Sir Winston has amassed through his record, experience, and ingenuity has already vanished with his departure from Downing Street. It seems certain that the power which remains will be more widely distributed than it has been during the last three and a half years. Power will probably be distributed in the new Government between a quadrumvirate consisting of Sir Anthony Eden, Mr. R. A. Butler, Mr. Harold Macmillan, and Lord Salisbury: and the new Prime Minister, to begin with at any rate, may only be first among equals.

Some who were saddened by Sir Winston's departure consoled themselves with the fact that Lady Eden is a Churchill and were saying, happily or ironically: 'There will always be a Churchill in Downing Street.'

CHAPTER THIRTEEN

Prime Minister

Sir Anthony Eden succeeded Sir Winston Churchill as Prime Minister on 6 April 1955. He came into a fair heritage which he had awaited with increasingly ill-concealed impatience. His long career of public service, his widespread popularity at home and abroad, and his knowledge and supposed understanding of men and affairs misled nearly everyone into supposing that he was likely to be a successful Prime Minister.

At the time of the change-over, as we have seen, there was a strike of all the national newspapers. In consequence valedictory comment on Sir Winston's departure and appraisal of Sir Anthony were at first confined to the provincial, weekly and foreign Press. A few samples deserve to be put on the record:

> It is fortunate for Britain that there exists to succeed Sir Winston a leader who is a world statesman in his own right. . . . The prestige and fortunes of Britain remain in safe hands.
>
> *Yorkshire Post*, 6 April 1955.

And again on the following day:

> Because of his outstanding success as Foreign Secretary, some people have asked whether he has the gifts of a good Prime Minister. Such questionings are unintelligent. . . . He will command respect in the Cabinet room, in the House and in the country.
>
> *Yorkshire Post*, 7 April 1955.

> The friendship between Great Britain and the United States is secure in his hands.
>
> *New York Herald Tribune*, 8 April 1955.

> There are two kinds of Prime Minister, the colossal individual genius like Churchill who is not really a party Prime Minister

at all and the true party Prime Minister whose task is to enable his party to govern as competently as it may. Eden will belong to the second company and his past political record suggests that he may well stand among the greatest of them. The first essential quality of a successful party Prime Minister is that he should be able to hold his party together. Eden can do this. He has an instinctive understanding of his party, of its personality, its myth, its moods and its impulses.

Henry Fairlie, *Spectator*.

As soon as the national newspapers were rid of their strike, some of them tardily added their praises to the paean:

Training, knowledge and courage are in high degree the unquestionable assets of our new Prime Minister. He incarnates as well as any man the new Conservatism.

Colin R. Coote, *Daily Telegraph*, 21 April 1955.

Sir Anthony is no doubt a much lesser man than Sir Winston. But he may, despite, or even because of that, very likely prove a better Prime Minister for this day and age. . . . Above all, Sir Anthony possesses the quality that Sir Winston lacks—that of making the diplomacy and actions of his country cease to be objects of hatred and suspicion among Asians, Arabs, and Africans.

Alistair Forbes, *Sunday Dispatch*, 24 April 1955.

Few there were, even among those who had already detected the fundamental defects in his character, who can have surmised the catastrophe in which his carefully nurtured and ordered career was soon to be engulfed. Eden certainly meant to be master in his own house. But he made the elementary mistake of not refurnishing it to his own liking when he moved in; he merely shifted some furniture around as the consequential process of his arrival. He should have called for the resignation of all his colleagues, and re-fashioned the Government in accordance with his own taste. Instead of sending some of the more massive pieces to a handy junk-shop, he merely discommoded himself of some bric-à-brac which he thought was no longer fashionable. Only two of Sir Winston's Ministers failed to find a place in

Eden's first Administration—Viscount Swinton, who was created an earl, and Earl De La Warr, who could hardly have expected to become a marquess for his services as Postmaster-General; he received no leaving present.

When Eden did reorganize his Government eight months later, in December, the changes he made were still little more than consequential. Lord Woolton, Captain Harry Crookshank, Mr. Osbert Peake and Lord de Lisle and Dudley all left the Government. Eden got himself a new Chief Whip, Mr. Edward Heath, thus making Mr. Patrick Buchan-Hepburn free to accept a place in the Cabinet. Like Noah in his ark, Eden wanted his Cabinet animals to enter two by two. His changes gave him two Foreign Secretaries (Mr. Macmillan and Mr. Lloyd), two Chancellors (Mr. Butler and Mr. Macmillan), two Ministers of Labour (Sir Walter Monckton and Mr. Iain Macleod), and now two Chief Whips in the Cabinet (Mr. Buchan-Hepburn and Mr. James Stuart) as well as one outside, his newly-appointed, the true Chief Whip, Mr. Edward Heath. But Eden dropped his old friend Mr. Henry Hopkinson, whom in opposition he had promised: 'I will make you Minister of State for European Affairs when we come to power.' Hopkinson, who was unsuited to political life, allowed himself to be fobbed off with a barony, and now sits in the Upper House as Lord Colyton of Farway and of Taunton.

Eden also dispensed with Mr. Geoffrey Lloyd; but Lloyd, despite his deceptively boyish charm, is not and was not so malleable. He rejected with disdain the idea that he should be 'kicked upstairs'. Eden was astounded when Lloyd refused the proffered barony and explained to Eden's incredulous inquiry as to his future plans that he had been a Minister for so long that he now looked forward to comparative ease and freedom of life on the back benches. By one of his neatest political strokes, the present Prime Minister, Mr. Harold Macmillan, to the astonishment of everyone, particularly Geoffrey Lloyd, was to rehabilitate this discarded Minister after he himself moved into No. 10; indeed, he promoted him and brought him into the Cabinet as Minister of Education. The Prime Minister is quite a tease and this was quite a good tease on Sir Anthony. Mr. Macmillan was suavely demonstrating that he, unlike his predecessor, knew how to be master in his own house.

Within a week of becoming Prime Minister Eden an-announced that Parliament would be dissolved on May 6 and that the General Election would be held on May 26. The election campaign was quiet and orderly and, from the point of view of Eden and the Tory Party, highly satisfactory. Sir Winston's slender majority of nineteen over Labour and Liberal combined was increased to a far more workable sixty-one.

The *Annual Register* records: 'The general character of the election was respectability. What it lacked in excitement it made up in decorum. Neither side indulged in scandalous insinuations.' *

Apart from the Khaki Election in 1900 (when the Tories under Lord Salisbury succeeded in increasing their majority from 130 to 134) this was the first time for ninety years that a Government was returned with a majority larger than that which it had had at the previous election.† In these circum-stances Eden and his Government got off to a good start and the prospects were favourable for a successful term of office.

★

Within two days of his triumph at the polls the political skies were darkened by a railway strike which led to the declaration of a state of emergency. The strike was caused by the refusal of the railway footplatemen to accept the wage award offered by the State-owned British Transport Commission. The footplatemen demanded the recognition

* Some journalists, however, were not as fortunate as the politicians. And scandalous observations were made by the *People* against the journalist who reported the election for the *Evening Standard*. This resulted in a libel action. See *What I Said About the Press*, by Randolph Churchill (Weidenfeld and Nicolson, 1957).

† Eden's own majority at Warwick and Leamington increased from 9,803 in 1951 to 13,466, a remarkable net gain of 3,663.

and restoration of their differential wage rates as compared
with other railway staff, which they claimed had been
largely obliterated by the flat-rate all-round increases that
had been awarded since the war. The nationalized undertakings, already in a poor financial position, had for some
time been trying to escape their inherited obligation (or
custom) of paying these differentials. The inflationary effect
of rising wages was imposing a severe strain on their internal
finance. The strike lasted only seventeen days, but caused
severe damage to the nation's economy. It ended when the
British Transport Commission, on the advice of the Government, yielded to the railwaymen's demands. The leading
part in the negotiations on the Government's side was taken
by the Minister of Labour, Sir Walter Monckton. As in
nearly every other industrial dispute during his period of
responsibility, he gave in—thus earning himself the reputation of being a successful Minister of Labour. In the classical
words of Mr. Stanley Holloway:

> The manager wanted no trouble,
> He pulled out his purse right away.
> 'How much to settle the matter?'
> And Pa said: 'What do you usually pay?'

This pattern established by Sir Walter Monckton has happily
not been followed by his successor, Mr. Iain Macleod.

★

For several years Sir Winston Churchill had been calling for a
'parley at the Summit'. And shortly before he quitted office, the
Russians showed fewer signs of being obdurate about this proposal. On March 29 Sir Winston told the House of Commons:

> Things certainly seem to have taken a friendly turn lately.
> I have never departed in any way from my view that a top-
> level meeting without agenda might be a hopeful manner of
> approaching the solution to world problems. It might be
> helpful to have the wish and the will expressed from the
> Summit, and the agreement of Heads of Governments recorded
> in broad and simple terms, if any can be reached. These can
> then be studied and implemented on the official level.

Seven weeks before, Malenkov had been displaced from power in the Kremlin by Krushchev and it was this change of régime which made possible a more pliant attitude on the part of the Soviet Government. Late in April the Western Powers were starting official discussions among themselves as to the attitude that should be adopted at the Summit talks. On May 10, just a month after Eden had become Prime Minister, Britain, the United States and France made fresh proposals to Moscow, and these were accepted by the Russians on May 26, the day that the British electorate went to the polls.

It was soon agreed that the meeting should be held in Geneva on July 18, and that the participating Powers should be Russia, France, Britain and the United States. Dr. Adenauer, who had visited London and Washington for consultations, accepted the fact that he should not himself be present in return for an undertaking by the other Western Powers that the reunification of Germany should be the main objective of the West at the conference.

It was the insistence of the West on the reunification of Germany which more than anything else led to the failure of the Summit talks. The author was one of the few observers of the Geneva talks who never saw how the reunification of Germany would be to the long-term interest of France, Britain or the United States. Shortly after the first world war M. Clemenceau was credited with the remark that the danger to the future of European peace was inherent in the fact that there were twenty million too many people living in Europe—and that the tragedy was that all of them were Germans. It was the gross disparity between the populations of Germany and France (seventy million against forty million) which was the prime factor in the almost inevitable rise of Hitler and the outbreak of the second world war.

The Russian partitioning of Germany was an odious crime against humanity and it contained within itself the seeds of a future war between Germany and Russia. None the less it is only just to recognize that it was not an unmixed curse, for it has made unlikely for many generations another German-French war. These long-term considerations await the verdict of history. But even in the shorter-term view it is difficult to comprehend why the statesmen of the West, when after a laborious approach-march they reached the Summit, should have placed such fatiguing emphasis on this issue, since anyone could see that it was the one issue on which Russian agreement could not possibly be gained. In fact, three of the five days of the talks were consumed on this palpably intractable problem. Apologists of the West explained at the time that Western insistence and over-insistence in the cause of German reunification were essential lest Western Germany should make a deal with the Kremlin. This fear was a further absurd aberration of Western thought, but again invites the verdict of history.

The excessive preoccupation with the German problem left the conference only time to discuss President Eisenhower's proposals for disarmament and mutual aerial inspection—an egg destined for addledom before it was laid—and such fascinating minor problems as the promotion of 'cultural exchanges' between East and West, and tourism!

The convivial dinner parties, at which President Eisenhower had the opportunity of seeing once more his wartime colleague Marshal Zhukov; the obvious delight of Mr. Krushchev in visiting a civilized country for the first time; the boating expeditions on Lake Geneva of Mrs. Eisenhower, Lady Eden, Lady Dorothy Macmillan, Mrs. Foster Dulles and Mme Faure (alas, the Russians brought no wives!)—all these junketings were transmitted to the Western world by the popular Press, and produced a sense of reassurance, a mood of relaxation. They also tempted Sir Anthony Eden to invite Messrs. Bulganin and Krushchev to visit London for an Anglo-Russian parley at an early date.

This was one of the few positive steps that Sir Anthony was able to take. Inevitably, a conference of this nature, held under the searching gaze of world publicity, gave little encouragement to original thought or speech. Only on the subject of East-West contacts was the British Prime Minister in a position to take a fresh and independent line:

> We should be glad if closer relationships could be established between professional, scientific and artistic groups of all kinds. We should welcome exchanges of visits by students as well as teachers. We think that more could be done to encourage the exchange of books, learned journals and documentary films. All these are things which can best be arranged between individual countries of East and West. We have recently established a special committee to further these aims.

Despite the deterioration in the relations between East and West that was soon to take place, some improvement in cultural contacts and tourist facilities was effected. But such easement as has occurred might well have been achieved on a less grandiose level than the Summit.

In retrospect, one can see that the only valuable part of the conference was the recognition by the representatives of the four governments that a major war was, in prospect, so dreadful that it had, by that very fact, become impossible. This thought found expression in an interview given by the British Foreign Secretary, Mr. Harold Macmillan, in which he declared: 'There ain't gonna be no war.' This phrase was thought a trifle crude at the time, but its validity would scarcely be challenged today, now that we have survived two crises in the Middle East and one in the Far East without the dire and baleful results which are apprehended by cowardly people and which could only befall us if the Russian Communists believed that the defeatists in the West were more numerous than they are.

Cyprus was now to raise its head in an increasingly ugly and murderous shape. Early in July preparations were made for a conference to be held in London at the end of August between the British, Greek and Turkish Foreign Ministers and their defence advisers, to discuss political and defence questions affecting the Eastern Mediterranean including Cyprus. But it became evident by mid-July that the Greek and Turkish delegations might as well have saved themselves a journey. For by then Archbishop Makarios had been to Athens and had made clear to the Greek Government what his views were on the London conference. 'It is a trap,' he pronounced, 'aimed at torpedoing recourse to the United Nations. The people of Cyprus will never accept any decisions of the London conference which do not accord with their rights and aspirations, even if those decisions are endorsed by the Greek Government.' With a Greek Government unable, or unwilling, to curb the machinations of the Cypriot ethnarchy, there was little hope that the London talks could end otherwise than in breakdown. Terrorism, which had begun in December 1954, now reached its most serious stage to date. Even before the talks were finally abandoned after nine days, the terror had reached such a pitch, and the smuggling of arms had reached such proportions, that the ten-point constitutional proposal put forward by Britain after the conference was little more than a diplomatic formality.

From that time onward it became clear that only stern measures would prevent the island from becoming a bloody battleground for racial and political agitators. Though the terrorist organization Eoka was banned on September 15, its strength and influence grew, and with it the list of British servicemen who were its victims. In an effort to throttle the terrorist organization, Eden asked the retiring Chief of the Imperial General Staff, Sir John Harding, to become Governor and Commander-in-Chief of Cyprus at the end of September. Harding, who had been looking forward to his retirement, accepted this ungrateful task out of an inborn sense of duty and as a personal gesture to Sir. Anthony. That violence and terror never got out of hand was largely due to his resolute leadership. That he never completely conquered it was due to the spiritual and financial backing that the Eoka movement continued to receive from Makarios and the ethnarchy. It says much for Harding's self-restraint and good will that he continued to treat with Makarios, although he well knew of the priest's complicity in the crimes which had killed his own soldiers. And it was not until all attempts at negotiation had failed that, for the security of the island, Makarios was exiled to the Seychelles in March 1956.

★

Meanwhile a gradual deterioration had taken place in the economic affairs of the nation. The Budget which the Chancellor, Mr. Butler, had introduced two weeks after Sir Anthony became Prime Minister was an 'election Budget'. The purchase tax on cotton and linen textiles was halved, and the standard rate of income tax was reduced by sixpence in the £. It is doubtful whether these measures could have been justified on economic and financial grounds alone. By the end of July it was plain that difficult times lay ahead. Credit restrictions were announced; there was a cut in Government overseas investment; a slowing down of expenditure and capital investment by nationalized industries; and deposits on hire purchase agreements were doubled. In September interest rates were raised on local authority loans and on October 26 the Chancellor was put to the necessity of introducing a supplementary Budget. Its main features were increasing the purchase tax and undistributed profits tax, higher postal charges, cuts in housing subsidies and Government building, and central control over local government borrowing.

At the end of 1955 Eden made the changes in the Government which have already been briefly alluded to earlier in this chapter. Mr. Butler, who had been subjected to an increasingly gruelling time at the Treasury for upwards of four years, while trying to cope with the deteriorating economic situation, had been voicing to the Prime Minister his desire to be moved to some less strenuous office. He had for many months endured with sympathy and courage the spectacle of his dearly loved wife dying by inches in agony. Only one of his colleagues, the Foreign Secretary, Mr. Macmillan, had the stature or capacity to occupy the Treasury in a time of such growing difficulties. Macmillan did not wish to leave the Foreign Office but felt bound to accede to the Prime Minister's wishes. It was suggested at the time that Eden was glad consequentially to have the opportunity of bringing Mr. Selwyn Lloyd, a much more malleable type, to the Foreign Office, a department in which all Prime Ministers have a duty and a right to take particular interest, and that Eden by virtue of his long service there felt himself particularly well equipped to supervise. Eden knew all about the Foreign Office and nothing about the Treasury. It was therefore inevitable that he should send his ablest colleague to the Treasury.

When Macmillan reached the Treasury he found himself compelled to introduce further anti-inflationary measures. In February 1956 he increased the bank rate from 4½ to 5½ per cent, increased hire purchase deposits, cut food subsidies and suspended industrial investment allowances. Restrictions were imposed on capital issues, and the banks were instructed to tighten their squeeze on their customers. Two months later, on April 17, in Macmillan's first and only Budget, the duty on tobacco was increased, as was the tax on company profits. All this was most vexatious to Sir Anthony. Both at home and abroad a blight seemed to have settled upon his Government, and the first fresh bloom was wearing off.

The general *malaise* which seemed to have fallen on the Government by the turn of the year led to severe criticism of Sir Anthony and his colleagues, and most of the blame was put on Sir Anthony. The criticism was not confined to Opposition newspapers, and even began to creep into the gossip columns of the *Daily Telegraph*, an organ which has traditionally given faithful and unwavering support to all Conservative leaders. On 3 January 1956, the *Daily Telegraph* sniping was reinforced by a magisterial article from the pen of the deputy editor, Mr. Donald McLachlan, in which he wrote:

> There is a favourite gesture of the Prime Minister's...To emphasize a point he will clench one fist to smack the open palm of the other hand—but the smack is seldom heard. Most Conservatives, and almost certainly some of the wiser trade union leaders, are waiting to feel the smack of firm government...

What are the actual criticisms that are heard wherever
politics are discussed?

They fall under three heads: changes of mind by the Government; half measures; and the postponement of decisions . . .

In his new position [Lord Privy Seal], Mr. Butler should
have more time to help with the captaincy; but the spirit and
the strategy can be created only by the Prime Minister himself.

The *Daily Mail* also joined in: 'Too many events are
wrapped up in uncertainty and indecisiveness. . . . There are
few hard-and-fast decisions. The Government's trouble
seems to be not paralysis so much as a lack of will.'

These criticisms naturally encouraged a state of considerable over-excitement in opposition and uncommitted
newspapers. Rumours began to circulate that the Prime
Minister intended to resign and make way for Mr. Butler.
Such a commotion arose that Eden thought it necessary to
take the unprecedented step for a Prime Minister who had
only been in office for nine months of issuing a *démenti* from
Downing Street: 'The report is false and without any
foundation whatever.'

Mr. Butler issued a statement on the same day; in it he
denied any knowledge of the resignation rumours. None the
less, he expressed his determination 'to support the Prime
Minister in all his difficulties'.

The Prime Minister was due to make an important policy
speech at Bradford eleven days later. In view of the *démenti*
and the forthcoming speech most of the critics held their
fire, but the Bradford speech was not considered a success.
Sir Anthony had the misfortune of having his microphone
stolen from him by Miss Leslie Greene, organizing secretary
of the Empire Loyalists. She had the opportunity of saying
a number of insolent things before she was removed by Mr.
Donald Kaberry, a vice-chairman of the party. Eden showed
that he had been nettled by the attacks made on him in some
sections of the Press, but following the technique of the
Archbishop of Canterbury failed to specify which newspapers
he had in mind. Sir Anthony said in part:

I do not have to advise this great Yorkshire audience not to believe everything they read in certain London newspapers. I know that one or two of these cantankerous newspapers claimed that they were reflecting public feeling. They were doing nothing of the sort. What they were doing was to try to make you think and feel what they wanted you to. I am sure you will always be on your guard against such methods. That way lies the denial of democracy. Yorkshire will never let Britain forget that the first duty of a citizen of a free country is to think for his or her self.

I would not even mention these matters tonight except for one reason. I must be concerned for our party when baseless reports of disunity are spread abroad. I want everyone, therefore, to understand this. Our party is united, and the Government is more than ever determined to do what it believes to be right for our country, whatever anyone says. This country is not on its way down, and this Government is not on its way out. As to the Government, we were elected not for six or eight months but for five years. It is on our record at the end of those years that we are prepared to be judged, and I intend—if God wills—to be there on that day. In the Cabinet we have a good team and a loyal one, and they are in the right places in the field. Under my instructions plans are being prepared which will be unfolded as our term of office continues.

*

Several accounts have appeared in the newspapers suggesting that the mounting criticism of Sir Anthony in the *Daily Telegraph* arose in the first instance from a quarrel between Lady Pamela Berry, the wife of the Editor-in-Chief-for-Life of the *Daily Telegraph*, Mr. Michael Berry, and Lady Eden. It is better that the social and personal squabbles between women who are friends and who play an important part in public life should not be needlessly aired; unfortunately the author is not in a position to deny the authenticity of some of the stories which were current at this time. It seems, from irrefutable evidence, that Mr. Joseph Alsop, the distinguished American political commentator, was in London just before Christmas 1953 and was entertained to luncheon by Lady Pamela Berry at 3 Barton Street. He sat on her left hand, while the Italian Ambassador, Signor Manlia Brosio sat on her right. Mr. Alsop had been touring Europe, and had stopped in London briefly on his way home for Christmas. Eden had recently been ill and Alsop inquired of his hostess as to his state of health. She replied that it was very bad and she was quite certain that he could never become Prime Minister.*

Shortly after this luncheon in Barton Street Mr. Alsop was entertained to dinner in Connaught Square by Mr. Raimund and Lady Elizabeth von Hofmannsthal.† Among those present were Mr. and Mrs. Eden and Lord Norwich. In the course of dinner Lord Norwich trotted out one of his favourite hobby-horses about the inherent dangers and bestialities of the German race and attacked Eden in lively and severe terms for his European policy which sought to embrace Western if not all of Germany in an United Europe. Eden defended himself and the Government's policy with vigour and spirit, and was far from worsted in the disputation. Shortly after dinner he excused himself on the ground that he had to return to the Foreign Office where work awaited him. Alsop remarked to the whole company after the Edens had left how glad he was that he had been present there and had seen the Foreign Secretary in action, as otherwise he might have carried back to Washington an entirely inaccurate account of the Foreign Secretary's health, based on what he had gathered a short time before in Barton Street.

Lord and Lady Norwich spent Christmas at Vaynol with Sir Michael and Lady Caroline Duff.‡ At the end of the year

---

* Lady Pamela's opinion was widely shared at the time. Sir Anthony had for many years been dogged by persistent ill health but he was courageous and resilient. He had his good days and his bad days. Consequently his friends' views on his health were apt to vary.

† Mr. Raimund von Hofmannsthal, the son of the distinguished Austrian poet and playwright, is the London representative of Time Inc., the holding company which controls Mr. Henry Robinson Luce's newspaper properties, *Time, Life, Fortune*, the *Architectural Forum* and *Sports Illustrated*.

‡ Lady Caroline is a niece of Lady Norwich: the latter, since her husband's death, has reverted to her former style of Lady Diana Cooper.

the Norwiches sailed for Madeira. Lord Norwich some months before had had a severe illness and this voyage was intended as an opportunity for him to recuperate. Alas, it was not to be; he died on January 1 while the ship was still at sea. The next day Mrs. Eden woke up in Carlton Gardens to read in *The Times* of the death of her friend. A few hours later she received what must have seemed like a voice from the grave. Before he left England Lord Norwich had written her a valedictory letter in which he warned her to be on her guard in the new responsibilities she had accepted by her marriage against people who were not truly her friends. He also told her what Mr. Alsop had told him of his luncheon at Barton Street and of his dinner in Connaught Square. Lady Eden is a woman of somewhat inflexible habit of mind; Lady Pamela Berry has a tongue and pen both of which are fluent and vivacious. In the event it is not surprising that a rift was caused between these two old friends, all the more regrettable because Lady Pamela, unlike those society hostesses who had only taken up Miss Clarissa Churchill after her marriage to the Foreign Secretary, had long before befriended Clarissa when she was an impecunious Bloomsbury career girl.

It has been suggested that the hostility shown by the *Daily Telegraph* towards Sir Anthony Eden two years later had its origin in this quarrel. Those who have the advantage of having known at first hand the strong character and sense of justice of Mr. Michael Berry will not accept these stories. He was not in England when Mr. Donald McLachlan's article was published, and all responsibility for policy must presumably be accepted as editorial responsibility. None the less, the ill feeling which is reported to have arisen between Lady Eden and Lady Pamela Berry left a trail of unhappiness and misunderstanding, particularly since so many people ascribed to it the attitude towards Sir Anthony in the columns of the *Daily Telegraph*.

CHAPTER FOURTEEN

A Russian Interlude

APRIL 1956 was marked by the visit to London of Marshal Bulganin and Mr. Krushchev in response to the invitation extended to them the previous year at Geneva by Sir Anthony Eden. When, some months before, Mr. Malenkov had made a tour of British industrial areas the public, whipped up by television and the popular press, allowed themselves to be stampeded into a grotesque delirium of unthinking delight. Some parents even had the indelicacy to allow this murderer to paw and fondle their innocent young children. Bulganin and Krushchev were greeted with rather more reserve than had been Malenkov. This was due to a number of reasons. The Soviet leaders made the mistake of sending in advance of themselves the head of the Russian secret police, General Serov, a particularly ruthless and bloodthirsty murderer. He came to London to concert the security arrangements with Commander Burt, head of the Special Branch of Scotland Yard. Serov's visit caused a public outcry and his masters thought it better public relations to dispense with his services when they themselves came to London. Then, before they had left Moscow, Bulganin and Krushchev, in a statement released by Tass, complained of the time-table which had been made for their visit. It seems that they were hoping that, like Malenkov, they would have repeated opportunities of basking in the good will of the British proletariat, and complained that the proposed tour condemned them to too much confabulation with the British Government and too little contact with the British masses. Some old-fashioned people thought it an unusual diplomatic innovation for guests to complain in advance of the hospitality that was being prepared for them; but in the century of the common man and the commoner woman much must be endured.

Highlights of the Russian visit to Britain were a sightseeing tour of London, dinner at 10 Downing Street, where the Russian leaders met Sir Winston Churchill, luncheon at the Mansion House, a visit to Harwell, a rowdy reception by the undergraduates at Oxford and tea with the Queen at Windsor Castle. During their visit to Harwell a keen-eyed scientist had an opportunity of looking inside Mr. Krushchev's hat, a broad-brimmed velveteen affair which had excited much public curiosity. It was found, as some London hatters had already suspected, that it was the *dernier cri* from East Berlin. During their visit to Windsor a number of interesting gifts were, in accordance with oriental tradition, presented to members of the Royal Family. There was a sable wrap for the Queen, a horse for the Duke of Edinburgh, a pony for Prince Charles and a small bear called Nikki for Princess Anne. Since there was no accommodation for bears in the castle Nikki had to be confined in the Zoo in Regent's Park. Two years later he was joined in captivity by the Red Chinese panda, Chi Chi, which had been denied an entry permit to the United States on account of its country of origin.

A regrettable incident of the visit and one which attracted world attention was a dinner party which the Russians attended in a private room in the House of Commons, at which the host was Mr. Hugh Gaitskell, the Leader of the Socialist Party and of Her Majesty's Opposition. It transpired after the dinner that Mr. George Brown raised some embarrassing questions as to the well-being and whereabouts of a number of Social Democratic leaders in the Iron Curtain countries. These questions were not at all to the liking of the Communist leaders and prompted Mr. Krushchev later to observe that if he lived in England he would be a member of the Conservative Party. This unusual social and political occasion served once more to expose the deep divisions in the Socialist Party. The Right Wing was delighted that Mr. Brown had spoken up for freedom and had thereby disinfected the Labour Party from any Communist ideological contagion, while the crypto-Communists in the party were naturally distressed that their foreign masters should have been exposed to embarrassment. Shortly before the departure of the Russian statesmen Mr. Gaitskell called upon them at Claridge's Hotel in an endeavour to smooth their hairy heels which some of his colleagues had rubbed up the wrong way.

This somewhat farcical and abortive conference ended with a communiqué of so flatulent a character and so studded with clichés that many people supposed at the time that Sir Anthony himself must have taken a large part in its preparation. It was adorned with such phrases as:

> . . . expressed their determination to take all possible measures to facilitate the strengthening of mutual confidence and the improvement of relations between states.

In the Middle East the communiqué could do no better than confirm that the two countries would:

> do everything in their power to facilitate the maintenance of peace and security . . . the governments of the two countries express the strong hope that their states will also do everything possible to help the United Nations in bringing about a peaceful solution of the dispute between the Arab states and Israel.

Etcetera, etcetera.

The only interesting part of this routine communiqué concerned Anglo-Soviet trade. The Russians said that, if there were no restrictions, they could increase their purchases from Britain to as much as £1,000,000,000 in the next five years. They handed over a shopping list which was promptly rejected by the British representatives on the grounds that many of the items on it were covered by the strategic embargo.*

* At around the half-way mark, two and a half years later on 30 September 1958, the total value of British exports and re-exports to the Soviet Union since 1 January 1956, was £147,792,182, compared with about £51,000,000 in the preceding two and a half years.

An addendum to the communiqué about furthering cultural contacts between the two countries and exchanging information and ideas was never taken seriously by the public or, indeed, by the governments concerned; for Russian jamming of Western broadcasts had continued unhampered by these professions of good will.

On the night of April 20, Marshal Bulganin and Mr. Krushchev, together with their large retinues, were entertained to a dinner in the Painted Hall at Greenwich. The First Lord of the Admiralty, Lord Cilcennin, presided. The Secretary of State for War, Mr. Antony Head, and the Air Minister, Mr. Nigel Birch, sat at either end of the table. The Cabinet was represented by Mr. Selwyn Lloyd, the Foreign Secretary, and the Earl of Home, Secretary for Commonwealth Relations. Elaborate security precautions had been taken for the conveyance of the Russian visitors in the Port of London Authority's launch *Nore* from Westminster to Greenwich. A twenty-four-hour police guard was mounted on the vessel, and as she moved down the Thames at eight knots she was escorted by no fewer than eighteen police launches, who cleared all traffic from the river for the forty-five-minute trip.

In the great Painted Hall the company sat down to a dinner of turtle soup, Dover sole fillets stuffed with lobster, with white wine sauce, braised duck with olives, and raspberry bagatelle. The speeches came round with the port which was beginning to exercise a mellowing influence when Mr. Krushchev got up to propose a toast 'to friendship and to peaceful coexistence'. He spoke about the arms race:

> We, for our part, are trying to get new weapons, new technical means of warfare in the same way that the fox tries to catch its own tail. Because at the present rate that which is first-rate this year might be out of date next year. . . .
>
> Our cruiser, for instance, on which we came: I don't want to cause any bad feelings among our sailors, because they like that cruiser and it is a handsome cruiser. It is a very up-to-date cruiser.

But under modern conditions the best that that cruiser can be used for is to carry guests to a friendly country. The cruiser carries five guns to fire salutes as we near Portsmouth. But who would ever think of fighting a sea duel with those guns?*

On April 29, two days after the Russians had left Britain, the Admiralty issued a communiqué which stated that Commander Lionel Crabb, a frogman of the Royal Naval Volunteer Reserve, was missing, presumed dead, after making a dive in Stokes Bay, near Portsmouth Harbour, on April 19. The communiqué added that Crabb had been 'engaged in the testing of new frogmen's equipment, for which he had been specially employed'. Five days later, on May 4, there arrived at the Foreign Office a note from Moscow. This asserted that at seven-thirty on the morning of April 19 sailors on the Russian ships had seen a frogman floating on the surface and then diving again. According to the Russian note, Rear-Admiral Kotov drew attention to the incident in the course of conversation with Rear-Admiral Burnett, Chief of Staff, Portsmouth, who apparently rejected the possibility of frogmen near the Russian ships on the grounds that 'at the time there were no operations in the port involving the use of frogmen'. In view of the Admiralty announcement on April 29 the Russians, 'attaching great importance to such an unusual event as the carrying out of secret frogmen tests alongside Soviet ships on a friendly visit', asked the Foreign Office for an explanation.

Now, a full fortnight after the dinner in the Painted Hall, the significance of Mr. Krushchev's remarks was revealed, but at the time his pleasantries about the Russian cruiser fell flat. None of the English guests or hosts knew anything about the frogman. The First Lord was considerably mystified when, after the proceedings had broken up, Marshal

---

* Mr. Krushchev was being unduly modest about the capabilities of his vessel. The twenty-two Sverdlov Class cruisers, to which the *Ordzhonikidze* in which he arrived belongs, carry twelve six-inch guns in four triple turrets, twelve 3·9-inch guns in six twin mountings, thirty-two 37 mm. anti-aircraft guns, ten twenty-one-inch torpedo tubes in quintuple mountings, and fittings for laying 140 to 240 mines.

Bulganin offered his apologies for his colleague's 'rudeness'.*
It was not until April 27 that the First Lord received any
official report about Commander Crabb's activities in
Portsmouth Harbour. And by then the Russian guests were
already embarked on the *Ordzhonikidze* and on their way
home. Even then his information did not come at first hand.
The junior members of the British Secret Service who had
instigated the affair had by that time lost their nerve. They
reported the facts to Earl Mountbatten, the First Sea Lord,
who had returned on April 27 from a lengthy overseas
tour. It was not until then that the First Lord and consequently the Prime Minister were informed, and two days
later the Admiralty communiqué was issued.

Soon the newspapers got to hear of the activities of the
Chief Constable of Portsmouth, Mr. A. C. West. On April 21
he had instructed Detective-Superintendent Lamport to
visit the Sallyport Hotel in Portsmouth and there to rip from
the hotel register a number of pages. It was alleged that these
pages noted the arrival on April 17 of Commander Crabb
and his friend, 'Mr. Smith'. Further investigation showed
that after spending two nights in the hotel Crabb and 'Mr.
Smith' left early on April 19, the day after the Russian
warships bringing the visitors had anchored in Portsmouth
Harbour. Later that day 'Mr. Smith' returned to the hotel
alone—to pay the bill.

Of all these events the Admiralty and apparently the
entire Cabinet were to remain in complete ignorance for
many days. But when the full extent of this piece of cloak-
and-dagger folly became known heads began to roll. Lower
down in the Secret Service there were dismissals. The chief
of the Secret Service might well have lost his job too, had
he not been due to retire anyway within a few days. Though
it must be accepted that the Navy knew nothing beforehand
about Commander Crabb's enterprise, it is strange that it

* Bulganin evidently thought that Greenwich was the personal palace of
the First Lord, for he added: 'When you come to Moscow and visit my house,
I promise you you will not be subjected to such rudeness.'

spotted nothing while he was carrying it out. The Russians were vigilant enough to see Commander Crabb. Is it credible that the naval authorities at Portsmouth are so unmindful of the security of Her Majesty's ships at anchor in Britain's greatest naval port as to allow an unauthorized and unidentified frogman to swan around in the harbour? And how was it possible that the Admiralty was not informed of the Russian admiral's remarks to the Chief of Staff, Portsmouth? Clearly no blame attached to the Chief of Staff, for he was to remain at his post until he retired in the normal way the following year. Communications must have broken down somewhere between Portsmouth and London. Perhaps that is also the explanation for the Chief Constable's apparent failure to inform the Home Office of the extraordinary action he was taking to ensure that no trace of the stay at the Sallyport Hotel of Commander Crabb and 'Mr. Smith' remained in the hotel register. It is scarcely possible that the Home Secretary, Major Gwilym Lloyd George (now Lord Tenby), knew about this but neglected to inform the Prime Minister. And yet no blame appears to be attached to the Chief Constable, for two years later he was to receive promotion and was appointed head of the British Transport Commission's police, the second largest police force in the country.

It took the Prime Minister some time to assemble and assimilate all these facts. Indeed, when he received the Russian note on May 4 (the Foreign Secretary was away, ill), Sir Anthony spent five days cogitating upon his reply. Then he admitted the truth of the Soviet allegations, declared that Crabb had acted without any permission and expressed the Government's apologies. On the same day, May 9, Sir Anthony answered questions in the House of Commons about the incident, but forbore to mention that he had received a note from the Russians, and that a reply was on its way. Eden's statement to Parliament was as follows:

It would not be in the public interest to disclose the circumstances in which Commander Crabb is presumed to have met his death. While it is the practice for Ministers to accept responsibility, I think it is necessary, in the special circumstances of this case, to make it clear that what was done was done without the authority or the knowledge of Her Majesty's Ministers. Appropriate disciplinary steps are being taken.

This was, up to a point, a proper and dignified answer for a Prime Minister who is at all times responsible for the operations of the British Secret Service. But it contained unnecessary and feckless inconsistencies. Why was it necessary for the British Government to apologize for acts which it had not initiated, for which it had no responsibility, and of which it claimed to have no knowledge either before or after the action of which the note complained?

The Opposition were not satisfied, and on May 14 a full-scale debate was held to discuss this curious affair. No more details were elicited from the Government, but the Prime Minister took the opportunity to elaborate on 'the exceptional course of making it plain that what was done was without the authority of Her Majesty's Ministers—and that of course includes all Ministers and all aspects of the affair':

> In this instance there were special circumstances which I judged compelled me to state [this]. At that time my colleagues and I had been conducting important discussions with the Soviet leaders. *We were completely unaware of any episode of this kind.* Had I not made this clear publicly, doubts would inevitably have been thrown on the sincerity of our position during these discussions. That is a very serious and a very exceptional situation. But it explains to the House why on that account I thought it right to take the very unusual course of making that statement. . . .
>
> All I care for is that the outcome of our discussions with the Soviet leaders should prove to be the beginning of a beginning. I intend to safeguard that possibility at all costs. I believe that is also in the minds of the Soviet leaders. For that reason I deplore this debate and will say no more.

Sir Anthony's motives in making this statement were no doubt admirable. They were none the less sadly misguided.

Of all the Ministers, there was one who ought to have known of the Crabb affair all along. And if he did not know, his ignorance did not absolve him from responsibility. Rather it was a dereliction of duty and responsibility not to know. That Minister was the Prime Minister, to whom alone the Secret Service is ultimately responsible. In view of what Sir Anthony later said, it is inconceivable that the chief of the Secret Service knew about the plans for the operations in Portsmouth Harbour before April 19 without informing the Prime Minister. But when he did know, and he should have known by the time the Chief Constable gave his order to remove the pages from the hotel register on April 21, was Sir Anthony still kept in ignorance? If, as he asserts, he was, it reflects as little credit on the Prime Minister's grasp of everyday affairs as it does on the Secret Service itself. Naturally, no Prime Minister can be expected to involve himself in all the *minutiae* of Secret Service work. But the whole point of making the Secret Service responsible to the Prime Minister is to allow some political control to be exercised over its activities. It is to prevent precisely such political blunders as the Crabb affair that the Prime Minister assumes responsibility. To remain in ignorance of the facts for so long that the Prime Minister is driven to make a virtue of his ignorance shows that all was not well with the relationship, which should be almost a daily drill, between the Secret Service and Downing Street. Then to shrug off responsibility for the events in so unprecedented a manner shows, at best, neglect on the Prime Minister's part of his duties in relation to the Secret Service.

CHAPTER FIFTEEN

The Dismissal of General Glubb

DURING the period of the Suez crisis, and indeed in the months preceding it, the author had a mobile front-seat view of what was going on. At the end of January 1956 he sailed on the same ship as Sir Anthony Eden and his Foreign Secretary, Mr. Selwyn Lloyd, from Southampton to New York, and was present in Washington throughout the three-day Anglo-American conference.

Apart from a general exchange of views, the main purpose of the conference, certainly in British eyes, was to hammer out an agreed Anglo-American policy for the Middle East. But, as was reported in the *Evening Standard* on 2 February 1956:

> The Washington conference has failed to produce any result which could not have been procured through normal diplomatic channels.
>
> This was made abundantly plain by a pompous declaration and uninformative communiqué.
>
> When the statesmen and politicians can't think of anything else to say they always drag in God. Last night's declaration did it twice over, both in preamble and in peroration.
>
> It was obvious from the start of the conference . . . that as no planning had been done by either side, no joint plan could be produced.
>
> The declaration and the communiqué were full of pious platitudes and impeccable opinions.'

Early in the afternoon of 1 March 1956, General John Bagot Glubb was dismissed by the twenty-year-old King Hussein from his post as Chief of Staff of the Arab Legion and told to leave Jordan with his family within two hours. He had served the Hashemite Kingdom of Trans-Jordan for a quarter of a century and for more than fifteen years had commanded the finest Arab fighting force in the Middle East. With his summary dismissal, confirmed later that night after a seven-hour meeting of the Jordan Cabinet, British policy in the Middle East lay in ruins.

The reasons that prompted King Hussein to dismiss Glubb were largely personal, but he had been subjected for some time to pressure from Arab nationalists in his own country, who had been increasingly animated by Cairo. None the less, it was the personal aspect that prompted the King at this time. Hussein is a soldier by temperament and by training—after Harrow he went to the Royal Military College, Sandhurst. He had a clear view—and one that differed from Glubb Pasha—as to how Jordan should be defended if she were attacked. Perhaps his irritation with Glubb was aggravated by repeated comments in the British Press to the effect that Glubb, not Hussein, was the real ruler of Jordan, which had been the theme of a recent article in the British weekly *Illustrated*,* a copy of which came into the King's hands. Perhaps, too, King Hussein was unduly influenced by Colonel Ali Abu-Nuwar, who had served the King dutifully on gay visits to Paris during his Sandhurst days.

In London the Government seemed slow to react to the news. This was strange, since British policy, arms and money had long been directed to preserving the alliance with Jordan, which was regarded as an indispensable *place d'armes*, particularly after Britain had evacuated her bases in the area of the Suez Canal. Only four months before Britain had augmented her stake in Jordan by bringing the annual subsidy up to £12,000,000, three-quarters of which went to the Arab Legion. With this attitude Sir Anthony had himself been intimately identified. His repeated warnings to Israel against attacking Jordan, his espousal of Jordan's case before the United Nations and his refusal to send arms to Israel while stepping up supplies to Jordan

* An organ, now defunct, of Odhams Press.

had all been prominent features of his recent Middle East policy.

Only three months before, in December 1955, the Government had given a striking demonstration of the importance of Jordan in the British structure of defence in the Middle East, when Field-Marshal Sir Gerald Templer, the newly appointed Chief of the Imperial General Staff, was dispatched to Amman to try to persuade Jordan to join the Baghdad Pact. Templer's dramatic attempt ended in failure, when the four Palestinian members of the Jordan Cabinet resigned rather than support the rest of the Cabinet in adhering to the Pact. This brought the Jordan Government down, and its successor later stated that Jordan would not join the Pact. Field-Marshal Templer only narrowly failed to attain his objective, but the consequences of his failure were serious. For it demonstrated to the world Britain's lack of influence over her Jordanian ally. And it must have come as a particular disappointment to Sir Anthony Eden.

Now, however, the Prime Minister was strangely inactive. On March 2 Sir Anthony did indeed meet his Service Ministers and the Minister of Defence, Sir Walter Monckton. But no more meetings between them or, indeed, between the Chiefs of Staff were recorded over the next three days. The American Ambassador, Mr. Winthrop Aldrich, went to see Sir Anthony on March 3. That afternoon the Prime Minister went to Chequers for the week-end.

Mr. Selwyn Lloyd was meanwhile on his way to a meeting of the South-East Asia Treaty Organization in Karachi, his first big overseas tour since he had become Foreign Secretary the previous December. By one of those fortuitous and unhappy coincidences that were to be a feature of this period, Mr. Lloyd was dining with Colonel Nasser in Cairo on the night of Glubb's dismissal. We shall see the way in which Sir Anthony Eden was surprised at his dinner table with King Feisal by the news of the grabbing of the Suez Canal, and have already described how Mr. Krushchev was able to pull the legs of the Board of Admiralty in the Painted Hall about the Crabb affair. Now the Foreign Secretary had the mortification of receiving his first intelligence of this deadly blow from a casual remark by his host during dinner.*

But Mr. Lloyd did not allow the fact that he had been put at this awkward diplomatic and social disadvantage to interfere with his long-planned itinerary. Doggedly he resumed his tour the following day, and arrived in the British Protectorate of Bahrein, where he suffered the further misfortune of being stoned—fortunately, unlike Stephen the protomartyr, not to death.

That Sunday, March 4, Glubb, who had flown in to London from Cyprus the previous evening, went to see Mr. Anthony Nutting, the Minister of State,† at the Foreign Office before going to Chequers to have luncheon and to spend the afternoon with the Prime Minister. What views he conveyed may be deduced from a letter by Glubb that appeared in *The Times* four days later:

> It would be a serious political error to 'get tough' with Jordan at this stage. Armed coercion is out of the question, and suddenly to cut off the [British] subsidy would either destroy Jordan or force the King into the arms of friends who would almost certainly ruin him. I feel strongly that such irrevocable action should not be taken under the influence of resentment.

Britain's treaty with Jordan gave her a right, among other things, to move troops to the area in case of emergency. It had been confidently expected that the Government would take some such action, and that it would react strongly to the challenge of Glubb's dismissal by some action. But it became clear that week-end that this action to protect British interests and prestige in the Middle East was not materializing.

* Another example, from an even unhappier period, occurred in 1937, when Ribbentrop was lunching with Neville Chamberlain as news of Hitler's invasion of Austria arrived.

† Subsequently to resign over Suez.

Mr. Julian Amery, son-in-law of Mr. Macmillan, the Chancellor, and at that time a back-bench M.P., was staying in Suffolk with the author that Sunday. Both were appalled by the supine inattention of the Government, and astounded to discover that no Cabinet meeting had been arranged. At lunch-time they descended on Mr. Butler, the Lord Privy Seal, at his home at Halstead, Essex, and pressed him to seek an early Cabinet meeting. Mr. Butler seemed surprised by their urgency, for he had no doubt been lulled by the Sunday newspapers into believing that nothing much was at stake, an impression assiduously fostered by the Foreign Office. Nevertheless, he got in touch with Mr. Macmillan, and the following morning Sir Anthony Eden presided over his first meeting of the Cabinet since Glubb's dismissal four days before.

The following morning there appeared two letters in *The Times* which gave clear warning to Sir Anthony and his colleagues of the strong feelings and serious misgivings of Tory back-benchers. Mr. Julian Amery wrote:

> The dismissal of General Glubb from the command of the British-paid Arab Legion and the stoning of the Foreign Secretary in the British Protectorate of Bahrein attest the bankruptcy of the policy of appeasement in the Middle East. These are the ineluctable consequences of the retreats from Palestine, Abadan, the Sudan, and the Suez Canal Zone.
>
> We are now very close to the final disaster. The challenge to our influence in Jordan and on the Persian Gulf, if left unchecked, must lead to the break-up of the Baghdad Pact. Our oil supplies, without which we cannot live, would then be in immediate danger; our communications with other Commonwealth countries would be threatened; and all Africa would be opened to Communist advance.
>
> In the glare of these dangers only a complete abandonment of appeasement can save the situation. . . .
>
> In recent months the Government have been charged with failing to give leadership. They now have the chance, as they have the duty, to confound their critics and promote a rescue operation to save Britain from disaster in the Middle East.

Another Tory member, Captain Charles Waterhouse, wrote:

> The time for concession is past. We must accept this
> challenge while the Communist position there is still uncon-
> solidated and show the world that there are points beyond
> which we will not be driven.*

That day Mr. Aldrich saw Sir Anthony for half an hour,
before the Cabinet meeting. Then Eden consulted Butler
and Nutting separately and alone. The following day the
Cabinet met again, and both Ministers of State, Mr. Nutting
and Lord Reading, the Minister of Fuel, Mr. Jones, and the
Minister of Transport, Mr. Harold Watkinson, were called
in. That day Sir Anthony was Lord Mountbatten's guest at
luncheon. At last, it seemed, things were beginning to move,
and all those horrid things about the Prime Minister in the
Evening Standard were to be proved wrong. Or so nearly
everyone thought.

It only needed a good speech from the Prime Minister
in the debate on March 7 to scotch the rumours that he did
not have a grasp of the situation. Never since he became
Prime Minister was so much good will towards him stored
up among Tory back-benchers as when Sir Anthony rose to
reply to the debate. Earlier Mr. Gaitskell had made a good,
clear speech, sharply outlining the new dangers that the
Middle East faced as the result of the Jordan crisis. Captain
Waterhouse had expressed the Suez rebel view when he said:

> Britain is still powerful and on occasion our strength must
> be used.

Now when so much depended on his performance Sir
Anthony hesitated and stumbled:

> I must tell the House bluntly that I am not in a position to
> announce tonight, in respect of immediate policy for Jordan,
> definite lines of policy which are inevitably to be followed,

---

* The author added his voice to the growing criticism of the Government in
an article on the same day (March 5) in the *Evening Standard* entitled 'Britain
is in Danger'—'I was told . . . that the Prime Minister was doing his best. I do
not doubt it, and that is why I am sure there has got to be, and quickly, a
change in the occupancy of 10 Downing Street.'

because I am sure that to attempt to do so now, with such information as we have,* would be not only premature but probably dangerous to our own interests—more perhaps than those of Jordan.

Ian Waller in his syndicated provincial newspaper commentary from Westminster describes the scene.

His performance can be summed up in one word! Deplorable. It was inept and inconclusive. Even if Sir Anthony had restated his old policies with firmness and conviction he might have held the House.

Instead, he met an outburst of barracking and contemptuous roars of disapproval and disgust such as a Premier has not been subjected to for many years. Sir Anthony, looking ill and exhausted, was quite incapable of overcoming it, and had to be rescued at one stage by the Speaker restoring order.

It was a shocking scene, and it was hard to believe that Sir Anthony who has, on foreign affairs, always held the House, was the centre of it. The Government won the vote, but Sir Anthony suffered a blow to his prestige that was clearly reflected in the silent, devastated ranks on the Conservative benches behind him.

Inevitably, these episodes start one asking the question: 'How long can Eden go on for?' . . . Events may save Sir Anthony, but it is hard to avoid the feeling that the cards are mounting and that, if the year goes on as it has begun, it will not be Sir Anthony Eden but Mr. Harold Macmillan who reigns in Downing Street in 1957.†

Mr. Ian Trethowan, political commentator of the *News Chronicle*, added the following harrowing description (12 March 1953):

Towards the end of last week's debate Mr. Robens suggested that Sir Anthony might be frightened of the Churchill pen.

---

* Not for the first or last time Eden had to make a parade of his lack of information. When he had made his first statement in Parliament about Glubb on March 6, he took pride in emphasizing that both Glubb and the British Ambassador had no suspicion of King Hussein's intentions.

† Mr. Waller was the first political commentator who went on record as believing that when Sir Anthony left office it would be Mr. Macmillan, not Mr. Butler, who would succeed him.

'Frightened? Frightened?'—Sir Anthony's voice shot through octaves of indignation. His flushed face showed that Mr. Robens had brought the Eden temper to the boil.

Angry with Mr. Robens, angry with the Americans for not giving him some agreement, tired from days of non-stop negotiation (shouldn't we have recalled Mr. Selwyn Lloyd?), his nerves taut as a banjo string, Sir Anthony was then ripe for fiasco.

Politically the debate revealed that Britain had lost this round to the hotheads of Arab nationalism. As far as Sir Anthony was concerned the debate marked the beginning of the disintegration of the personality and character that the public thought him to possess.

CHAPTER SIXTEEN

The Suez Grab

O N 26 July 1956, Colonel Nasser announced that Egypt intended to nationalize the Suez Canal. The shareholders would be paid according to the last prices on the Paris Bourse.* And then the Canal would be Egypt's—and its annual hundred-million-dollar revenue would be used for building the great Aswan Dam. He told a deliriously excited crowd in Alexandria:

> We shall build the High Dam on the skulls of 120,000 Egyptian workmen who died in building the Suez Canal.† We shall industrialize Egypt and compete with the West. . . . With the revenue from the Company we shall not look to Britain and U.S.A. for their $70,000,000 grant. . . . Egypt will build the Aswan Dam without pressure from any nation.‡

The Prime Minister was giving a dinner party at 10 Downing Street in honour of King Feisal of Iraq when this disagreeable piece of news arrived. Among the guests were Ministers, military leaders, and two representatives of the Opposition, Mr. Hugh Gaitskell and Sir Hartley Shawcross. Sir Anthony had every reason to be in a good mood, for just before he received his guests he had returned from a meeting of the 1922 Committee of Tory back-benchers, which he had expected to be rowdy and critical of defence and Middle East policy, but which ended in his being thanked 'for the way in which he is carrying out his heavy

---

* This would have cost Nasser £56 million.

† The actual figure was 1,394. No doubt Nasser obtained his figure from the works of Herodotus who was describing the building of another canal in Egypt—in 630 B.C.

‡ So far as the building of the Dam was concerned, this boast proved unrealistic, and despite the help in building the foundations on the alleged 120,000 skulls, no work had started at the time when this book went to press.

responsibilities'. It was towards the end of the meal that news of Nasser's speech in Alexandria was brought in.

As soon as the guests had left, Eden asked four of the five Cabinet Ministers who were present at the dinner, Lord Kilmuir, Lord Salisbury, Lord Home and Mr. Selwyn Lloyd, to remain behind for urgent discussions. The Chief of the Air Staff, Air Marshal Sir Dermot Boyle, was already there, and he was later joined by Lord Mountbatten, the First Sea Lord, and Field-Marshal Sir Gerald Templer, the C.I.G.S. Later still the French Ambassador, M. Chauvel, and the American Chargé d'Affaires, Mr. Andrew Foster, were invited to call. These talks went on until after two o'clock in the morning, and it is believed that M. Mollet, the French Prime Minister, telephoned Eden in those early hours.

*

For many years there had been a project to build a High Dam at Aswan* in order to conserve the waters of the Nile and to add to the fertility of the Nile Delta. Many experts have suggested that Aswan is not the right place to build a dam. However, there was a sort of obsession in the minds of the Egyptian political leaders and among the readers of the Press throughout the world that this would be a good and magnificent thing to do. Americans who were at that time prepared to spend a lot of money round the world in order to pre-empt against the Russians were keen to play a leading part in this enterprise. On 18 December 1955, America and Britain made their offer to contribute loans towards the Aswan Dam—America $56,000,000, Britain $15,000,000 and the World Bank conditional upon these two loans being made, $200,000,000. A total of $271,000,000, with Egypt left to contribute the balance of approximately $700,000,000.

This arrangement was utterly unrealistic, because as anyone should have seen, most of all the World Bank,

---

* The adjective refers not to the height of the proposed dam but to its distance up the Nile.

Egypt was not in a position to meet its side of the bargain. By April 1956 it became clear that the Egyptian leaders were going in the opposite direction. It was announced they had mortgaged $200,000,000 worth of unplanted cotton for Czech-produced MIGs and for Stalin tanks, and on July 9 their budget for the coming year showed a rise in military expenditure from 18 per cent to 25 per cent of the total, and the Egyptian Government's intention to spend £E54,000,000 on arms and only £E2,900,000 on the Dam. These financial considerations must have weighed with the Americans as well as Nasser's purchase of arms from Russia and the Iron Curtain countries, which enabled the Soviet Union to obtain a foothold in the Middle East; for the object of the American loan was to keep Egypt on the side of the West. Internally also there were pressures on the American Secretary of State to abandon his proposed loan to Egypt. Congress was making its annual demands for a cut in foreign aid, and early in July the Senate Appropriations Committee actually asked Dulles to abandon the Dam project. The Cotton Lobby of the Senate also approached the Secretary of State, pointing out that the Dam would bring under cultivation an additional two million acres of Egyptian soil which might force down world cotton prices.

In April Ahmed Hussein, the Egyptian Ambassador to the United States, returned to Washington and announced that Egypt definitely wanted Western aid for the Dam. Previously Egypt had been toying with the idea of getting Russia interested. Now, however, they were making it quite clear that they relied upon the United States for support. That also was the day when the Senate Cotton Lobby made its representations to Mr. Dulles. It is believed that it was on the following day that Dulles informed Eden of his intention to withdraw the offer. On July 19 Dulles, in the course of a long conversation in the late afternoon with the Egyptian Ambassador, informed him of his decision to withdraw assistance for the Dam. In fact, news of this decision had already got around in Cairo just as Nasser was leaving Yugoslavia after an eight-day visit to Tito. He arrived in Cairo shortly after midnight on July 20 accompanied by Nehru. What should have been a crowning triumph for Nasser, after consorting for two weeks with the two leading neutralists, Nehru and Tito, must have been a moment of exasperation, if not of humiliation.

Whether or not Britain was consulted beforehand by the American Government, it was obvious that the British Government had no serious objections to the American decision, for early on the following day Britain also withdrew her offer on the Aswan Dam. Sir Harold Caccia, then Deputy Under-Secretary of State at the Foreign Office, informed the Egyptian Ambassador of this decision at the Foreign Office. That day, President Eisenhower and Mr. Dulles flew to Panama for an official visit. A Cabinet meeting was held in London, and Mr. Menzies,* the Australian Prime Minister, also had an opportunity of having a few words with the Prime Minister when he went to say goodbye to him at No. 10 before leaving for Australia. July 20 was a Moslem holiday, so there was no immediate reaction from Cairo to the Anglo-American decision.

*

The Aswan decision marked a drastic change in American policy towards Egypt. When Dulles became Secretary of State three years before, one of his first actions was to make an extended tour of the Middle East and of Southern Asia. Accompanied by Mr. Harold Stassen, Director of the Mutual Security Agency, Mr. Dulles set out on 10 May 1953 on a twenty-day fact-finding mission. It was the first visit of its kind to be undertaken by an American Secretary of State. In Cairo, where Anglo-Egyptian negotiations about the withdrawal from the Suez Canal had just broken down, Dulles met the leaders of the new Egyptian military régime which had seized power ten months before by forcing the

* Mr. Menzies had been in Britain and stayed some time after the Conference of Commonwealth Prime Ministers held earlier in the month.

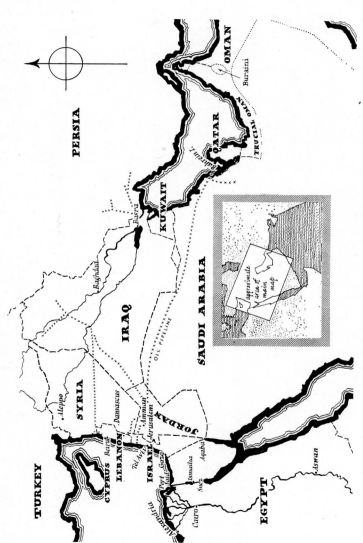

Strategic map of the Suez area and the principal oil pipelines.
Scale: approximately 300 miles to one inch.

abdication of King Farouk. From Cairo Dulles informed the
world that the American people regarded General Neguib
as 'one of the outstanding Free World leaders of the postwar
period', and that they admired the courage with which he
had approached the many problems besetting Egypt.
Understanding of the Egyptian viewpoint, he said, had
been enhanced to such an extent as a result of discussions
with the Egyptian leaders that he was able to give the
opinion that the problem of the British military bases in the
Suez Canal area should be met by 'a solution consistent
with full Egyptian sovereignty, with a phased withdrawal of
foreign troops'. As a further mark of esteem Mr. Dulles
presented General Neguib with a silver-plated Colt revolver
inscribed: 'To General Neguib from his friend Dwight D.
Eisenhower.' 'This,' said Mr. Dulles, 'is not for shooting.
It is to defend yourself.'

The Secretary of State's visits to other parts of the Middle
East, including his conversations with officials of the
Arabian-American Oil Company (Aramco) in Saudi
Arabia as well as his talks with Mr. Nehru in Delhi, all
served to confirm him in his views that friendship with
Egypt and the Arab States had to be an essential part of his
foreign policy. On his return to Washington he emphasized
that the United States had to discard the appearance of
giving any support to colonialism in the Middle East, that
the United States' policy had become unnecessarily
ambiguous in not making it clear that America had no
intention of defending the old colonial interests of France
and Britain, and that, most regrettably, the deep suspicions
of the colonial Powers in that area also extended to the
United States because of her association with France and
Britain in the Atlantic alliance. This was the basis of the
Middle East policy that Dulles was to pursue for two and a
half years. In the execution of that policy he was aided by
Mr. George Allen, head of the Middle East section of the
State Department, whose dislike of colonialism was well
known, and by the American Ambassador in Cairo, Mr.

Charles Byroade, who was an avowed personal admirer of Colonel Nasser's. This was a policy that did not greatly endear Mr. Dulles to the British Government; but the Middle East was not a subject on which Dulles frequently consulted his English friends. It was not until September 1955 that Dulles thought it necessary to join with Britain in making a statement on Middle East policy, and then it was the subject of Russian arms for Egypt that impelled him to do this.

The entry of the Soviet Union into the Middle East as suppliers of arms to Nasser made Dulles angry. If the Egyptians wanted arms they could obtain them from Washington—and silver-plated ones at that. Nevertheless, old ideas died hard and in a final effort to go one better than the Russians he announced in December 1955 America's willingness to make a loan towards the building of the Aswan Dam. But the continued ingratitude that Nasser was now showing in inviting the Russians into Egypt (and apart from arms there was a stream of technical advisers, and the staff of the Russian Embassy in Cairo increased from 40 to 150) irked Mr. Dulles, and he began to think of changing his policy entirely. News of the Czech arms deal in April finally decided him, and his first action was to move to other posts Mr. Allen and Mr. Byroade. With their disappearance from the Middle Eastern councils of the State Department, the way was open for a complete reversal of the policies with which they had been associated, and for Mr. Dulles to withdraw the offer for the Dam.

The fear that the Russians would take advantage of this decision and finance the Dam project themselves proved baseless. Mr. Dulles had clearly weighed up this consideration and decided that this was just a Russian bluff. And very quickly on July 21 Mr. Shepilov, the Russian Foreign Minister, announced that his country had no immediate intention of financing the Dam.* The truth is that the

* It was not until more than two years later, on 23 October 1958, that the Russians made their first move by offering a loan of 400 million roubles for the Dam. But as this amounted to barely eight per cent of the total cost, it was unlikely to get the Dam builders very far.

Russians did not have enough money, or equipment, or skill and manpower available for the High Dam. Many strategists in the West would, indeed, have preferred the Russians to build a dam at Aswan rather than a dam on the Dnieper. Wisely, however, the Russians decided they could not afford both—and settled for the Dnieper. They had learned from Britain and the United States that the reward for pouring money into the countries of the Middle East was often the hostility of the native populations.

To the Egyptians, who had been growing accustomed to being bun-fed by the Americans, the decision not to help with the Aswan Dam came as a dreadful shock. Nasser, however, set about his revenge coolly and purposefully, and the detailed planning for the take-over of the Canal by Egyptians was skilful and comprehensive. Such were the main events which led up to Nasser's seizure of the Canal.

★

Sir Anthony Eden acted swiftly and resolutely when confronted with Nasser's challenge. Only a few hours after his late-night talks with Ministers and Service chiefs, he was on the telephone again to Paris, and after Lord Home had seen the High Commissioners for the Commonwealth countries, Sir Anthony went to the House of Commons to make a statement:

> The unilateral decision of the Egyptian Government to expropriate the Suez Canal Company, without notice and in breach of the concession agreements, affects the rights and interests of many Nations. Her Majesty's Government are consulting other governments immediately concerned, with regard to the serious situation thus created. The consultations will cover both the effect of this arbitrary action upon the operation of the Suez Canal and also the wider questions which arise. . . .
>
> We got in touch, and are in touch, with the United States Government and the French Government, and we are in touch this morning with a number of governments, I hope all,

of the Commonwealth. I would ask the House not to press me to say more than this at the moment. The situation must be handled with both firmness and care, I think. I undertake to give the fullest information to the House at every stage.

Mr. Gaitskell, for the Labour Party, identified himself with many of the Prime Minister's remarks, and 'deeply deplored the high-handed and totally unjustifiable step by the Egyptian Government'. Mr. Clement Davies for the Liberal Party described the nationalization as a 'deplorable action'. But it was left to Mr. R. T. Paget, Labour Member of Parliament for Northampton, to steal the thunder, when he compared Colonel Nasser's technique with that of Hitler, and asked the Prime Minister whether he was 'aware of the consequences of not answering force with force until it is too late'.

After leaving the House Eden had a long talk with Mr. Selwyn Lloyd. This was followed by a Cabinet meeting, at which all members were present with the exception of Mr. R. A. Butler, the Lord Privy Seal, who was indisposed. Mr. Aubrey Jones, the Fuel Minister, was called in, and so were the Chiefs of Staff. After the Cabinet Sir Anthony had further talks with Sir Walter Monckton, the Defence Minister, while Mr. Selwyn Lloyd saw, in succession, M. Chauvel and Mr. Andrew Foster. That afternoon Sir Harold Caccia, Deputy Under-Secretary of State at the Foreign Office and who was later to become Ambassador in Washington, handed to the Egyptian Ambassador a sharp note, condemning the seizure of the Canal as an unjustified and unjustifiable act. Before the day ended, Sir Anthony Eden once again had discussions with Mr. Selwyn Lloyd and Lord Home, and the High Commissioners for the Commonwealth countries were again kept informed.

The sentiments expressed in the House of Commons during the short time of questioning were reflected throughout the country, and both on July 27 and July 28 the newspapers were almost unanimous in their condemnation of Nasser's action.

It is a clear affront and threat to Western interests, besides being a breach of undertakings which Egypt has freely given and renewed in recent years. . . . The time has arrived for a much more decisive policy.

The Times, 27 July 1956.

The Canal is an oil pipeline, an economic lifeline.
Nasser must be shown that he cuts it at his peril.
And the unanimity of the House today, the swift consultation with other Powers, the Premier's promise of firmness—these are signs this flamboyant Colonel with ex-Corporal Hitler's technique would do well to heed.

The Star, 27 July 1956.

The seizure is an act of international brigandage. . . . Colonel Nasser's Government has such a bad record in international dealings that it can be relied upon to use its control of the Canal as an instrument of blackmail even if it does not violate the international convention forthwith.

The Times, 28 July 1956.

This reckless defiance of those international decencies. . . . The British Government will be fully justified in taking retaliatory action.
If Egypt's evil example is followed all hope of friendly co-operation between the Western and Arab worlds will be lost. For their benefit no less than ours, Britain, France and the United States must ensure that Colonel Nasser does not tear up treaties with impunity.

News Chronicle, 28 July 1956.

These, of course, are newspapers which are not normally friendly to the Government. The more Conservative newspapers were still more definite and vehement in their condemnation of Nasser.

Is Britain going to tolerate this new arrogance?
With each act of surrender to Nasser the task of resistance has become harder, but the need for resistance has become more insistent.

Daily Express, 27 July 1956.

To insensate ambition Colonel Nasser now adds, as we suspected he would, the dictator's technique. . . . All the more reason why the British reaction should be prompt and firm.

Daily Telegraph, 27 July 1956.

Nasser must not get away with this. He must be stopped before he sets the Middle East aflame. . . . Our troops are in Cyprus, and intend to remain there, said Sir Anthony Eden, to safeguard our oil supplies in the Middle East. If need be they must reoccupy the Suez Canal to fulfil that very purpose. It will be better, however, to act in concert with America—if the U.S. will rally to us as quickly as we rallied to her in Korea. Her firmness over the Aswan Dam encourages us to think that she might be as forthright now. If not, then Britain must 'go it alone'.

Daily Mail, 27 July 1956.

This time the British Government can prove that its legs are not completely palsied by getting up on them and raising hell.

Daily Sketch, 27 July 1956.

Firmness is the right recipe for Britain and other interested countries, but it must be applied quickly.

Daily Telegraph, 28 July 1956.

The time for appeasement is over. We must cry 'Halt!' to Nasser as we should have cried 'Halt!' to Hitler. Before he sets the Middle East aflame, as Hitler did Europe.

Daily Mail, 28 July 1956.

The *Manchester Guardian* alone struck a note of disagreement in that week-end's comments.

The West can hardly use military power as the means of guaranteeing the oil supply. (That is why the Government's case on Cyprus looks so poor. The argument there has been that a military base in Cyprus is essential for safeguarding arms supplies. But now that an emergency has arisen, it is clear that military force is not the best way for overcoming it.) Any retaliatory measures by the West which led to the closing of the Canal would defeat the very end which Western policy should aim at securing. It is just silly to talk of withdrawing the Canal's technicians.

Manchester Guardian, 28 July 1956.

★

When on Sunday, 29 July 1956, the representatives of Britain (Sir Anthony Eden), France (M. Pineau, the Foreign Minister) and the United States (Mr. Robert Murphy of the State Department) met in London to discuss the Egyptian crisis, the British and the French Governments were assured of the almost universal support of the peoples of their countries for any steps taken to check Nasser. Public opinion was no longer prepared to accept the tardy and ineffective way in which the British Government had been reacting to increasingly dynamic challenges in the Middle East. Many people still retained fresh in their memories the complete failure of the British Government to accept the challenge of Glubb Pasha's dismissal from the Arab Legion in the previous March. There were some, indeed, who held that Britain's failure to act firmly then was at least in part to blame for the insolent challenge that Nasser had now thrown down.

In Parliament the Government continued to receive almost unanimous support. Mr. Gaitskell made a speech in the Commons debate on August 2 condemning Nasser's action in forceful terms:

> We cannot forget that Colonel Nasser has repeatedly boasted of his intention to create an Arab Empire from the Atlantic to the Persian Gulf. He has made a number of inflammatory speeches against us, has continually attempted subversion in Jordan and other Arab states, and has persistently threatened Israel and made it plain that it is his purpose and intention to destroy Israel if he possibly can. Here, if ever there was, is clear enough notice of aggression . . . .
>
> I have no doubt that . . . Colonel Nasser . . . wanted to raise his prestige in the rest of the Middle East. . . . That is all terribly familiar. It is exactly the same as we encountered with Mussolini and Hitler in the years before the war. And we must

not underestimate the danger of the effects this may have on the other Arab states. . . .

Obviously there are circumstances in which we might be compelled to use force, in self-defence or as part of some collective defence measures. I do not object to the precautionary steps which the Prime Minister has announced. Any Government would have to do that, as we had to do it during the Persian crisis. . . .

I think we were right to react sharply to this move. If nothing were done it would have serious consequences for all of us, and especially for the Western Powers.

All the Labour back-benchers who spoke in the debate, with the exception of Mr. William Warbey, supported the Government's actions with all the eloquence that they could command. Mr. Herbert Morrison, who had had some experience of these matters when he was Foreign Secretary at the time of the Abadan crisis, went even farther:

This pocket dictator in Cairo does not consult his Parliament. I am not sure that he is permitting his Parliament to function in any effective way, if at all. . . . There is no discussion with us or the other countries who are parties to the Convention. . . . One night he decides to go out and make a speech on the hustings and towards the end whacks out his decree. . . . Colonel Nasser is to be condemned because he has acted contrary to the law of nations and to international good faith. This action is morally wrong. It is utterly unjustifiable, and I refuse to speak a single syllable in justification of what Colonel Nasser has done. . . . Now and again our American friends do rather try our patience. About this Middle Eastern business the Americans have been pretty unsatisfactory, and it is time they took a clear line. I hope . . . that the world may know that Britain, France and the U.S.A. stand together. If the U.S.A. will not stand with us, we may have to stand without them.

The day before this debate, August 1, a *Times* leader entitled 'Resisting the Aggressor' said: 'Quibbling over whether Nasser was legally entitled to make the grab will delight the finicky and comfort the faint-hearted, but entirely misses the real issues.' When Parliament adjourned for the summer recess on August 2, Sir Anthony Eden must have felt that whatever steps he was going to take and whatever the success of his policy, at any rate he had so far been carrying the nation with him.

But during the August Bank Holiday weekend left-wing Socialists began to make themselves heard. They made representations to Mr. Gaitskell and wrote letters to *The Times* regretting their Leader's speech on August 2. Gleefully they pointed to the final remarks in Mr. Gaitskell's speech which referred to the use of force only under United Nations auspices. As news of troop movements became more widely known, Mr. Gaitskell appeared alarmed at the position in which his speech, which had so generously supported the Prime Minister's policy, was placing him. Together with Mr. Alfred Robens, the Shadow Cabinet's spokesman on Foreign Affairs, and Mr. James Griffiths, deputy leader of the Labour Party, Mr. Gaitskell called on the Prime Minister on August 11 to explain their newly adopted attitude about referring to the United Nations before using force. They asked Eden to give an undertaking that he was not preparing to use force unless in accordance with the United Nations Charter. This the Prime Minister refused to do, and from that moment the Labour Party opposed by every means all further steps taken by the Government that might enable Britain to solve the Suez problem by herself or with her allies.

CHAPTER SEVENTEEN

First Reactions

ALL Cabinets have inner cabinets. In wartime this is formalized into a War Committee, or indeed War Cabinet, from which all other Ministers normally in the Cabinet are excluded. In peacetime it is an entirely unofficial arrangement and the composition of the inner cabinet is flexible; it may vary from day to day and from topic to topic. It is an obvious convenience for the Prime Minister to meet frequently with three or four of his more powerful colleagues and hammer out the broad lines of policy which have to be discussed later in the full Cabinet. This is one of the methods by which a Prime Minister who knows what he wants to do can largely impose his will upon his colleagues, for if the four or five leading members of the Cabinet are already in agreement, though other members may make helpful suggestions it is unlikely that the conclusions already arrived at will be seriously challenged.

During the period of the Suez crisis, an inner cabinet developed of a far more formal character than is normal in time of peace. This can be justified on the grounds that Sir Anthony was planning war, and it is obvious that his intentions and plans should be confined within the smallest circle possible. The inner cabinet appears to have consisted, apart from the Prime Minister, of Mr. Selwyn Lloyd, the Foreign Secretary, Mr. R. A. Butler, Lord Privy Seal, Mr. Harold Macmillan, Chancellor of the Exchequer, and Lord Salisbury, Lord President of the Council. The Chiefs of Staff were 'frequent attenders' and it seems that Mr. Antony Head, the Secretary of State for War, was more often summoned to the deliberations of the inner cabinet than was his superior, Sir Walter Monckton, the Minister of Defence.

This was partly because Sir Walter was not in good health, and partly because, though Mr. Head was not in the Cabinet, the Prime Minister came to have a great reliance upon his judgment in this affair, since during the second world war he had been largely concerned with Combined Staff Planning. Indeed, only two weeks before the operation actually began, Sir Anthony allowed Sir Walter Monckton to go to the sinecure of Paymaster-General,* and replaced him at the Ministry of Defence with Mr. Head.

It may seem strange to insist on swapping horses when about to attack a canal, but Eden doubtless had convinced himself that he had good reasons for the change. It is important at this stage to underline the fact that, whether at the War Office or at the Ministry of Defence, Head bears an exceptional political and military responsibility for the planning and execution of the Suez operation.

As in Britain, the responsibility of leadership of the Suez operation was in Paris left to an inner cabinet of just a very few. In this case it consisted of M. Mollet, the French Prime Minister, M. Pineau, the Foreign Minister, M. Bourgès-Manoury, the Defence Minister, M. Lacoste, Minister of Resident for Algeria, and M. Chaban-Delmas, Minister without Portfolio. M. Mollet was an unusual man to have in this company, for as a Socialist he had little in common with his four other colleagues, who were all right-wing De Gaullists. As a Socialist too, M. Mollet might have been expected to be less keen on war and less eager to come to the rescue of the capitalist Suez Canal Company against the nationalization of President Nasser.

Indeed, in the months that succeeded Suez, the French officials of the Suez Canal Company, though they had frequent access to Sir Anthony Eden, Mr. Lloyd and M. Pineau, were never once received by M. Mollet. The French Premier, in fact, took much less part in the planning than did the British Prime Minister. All the French inner cabinet

---

* This doubtless provided useful training for Sir Walter, who was shortly to become Chairman of the Midland Bank.

deferred greatly throughout the planning stage to the ideas
and wishes of Sir Anthony Eden. Except for Mollet, they
were all newcomers to politics. Most of them had come to
the fore in the Resistance movement. Themselves lacking
experience of the conduct of great affairs, they naturally
held Sir Anthony Eden, who had occupied high office
throughout the war, in great esteem and had the highest
respect for his judgment.

★

The Chiefs of Staff got off to a bad start. Inquiries
immediately after the seizure of the Canal revealed that
there existed not even a plan for the reoccupation of the
Canal Zone. This is one of those seemingly incredible facts
with an increasing number of which the reader must prepare
himself to cope as the tale unfolds. Hurriedly they prepared
an inventory of what forces would be available for such an
operation.

They planned an operation known as Hamilcar, which
provided for an airborne landing on strategic points along the
Canal followed by reinforcement from seaborne troops.
However, it became quickly apparent that the airborne
troops of both Britain and France were committed to ground
duties in Cyprus and Algeria and lacked recent parachute
training and equipment. Nor was there sufficient air transport readily available in the Middle East or even in Britain
and France for such an operation. The prospects for Hamilcar were not improved by the fact that a seaborne assault
force would have to be mounted, at best from Malta, at
worst from Algiers and Marseilles, because the British
authorities had neglected to prepare Cyprus as a proper
base. This meant anything from five to nine days that must
elapse between embarkation and assault. This further meant
that the button had to be pushed ten days before results could be
obtained, an agonizing period of suspense well calculated
to put a severe strain upon Sir Anthony Eden's nerves.

So even if the paratroops had been available, the possibility of an airborne drop would have been dismissed by the strategists, who had made it a rule that airborne landings must be reinforced overland within twenty-four hours. This was a lesson that had been underlined for British soldiers at Arnhem. British planners seem, however, to have overlooked an important distinction that at Arnhem we were confronted by Germans, whereas at Suez our enemy was of a somewhat less martial character.

But even if the manpower and time had been available, there was not the shipping to convey troops to Egypt for a seaborne landing. Particularly lacking were L.S.T.s for the armour. Once again British political and strategic judgment had been found wanting. The new base in Cyprus, which was supposed to replace the bases in the Suez areas, was, as at the time of the Jordan affair five months before, still incomplete and unprepared. The air base at Akrotiri had not been completed, the harbour at Limassol had not been begun, and the mobile strategic reserve had not materialized. Without these, Cyprus could only be a hostage to fortune instead of a bastion and a springboard. Jordan and Libya, on which Eden had counted when he espoused the evacuation of the Suez Canal base in 1954, were equally useless. In Jordan a Government unfriendly to Britain was not likely to allow an increase in British forces stationed in the country. In Libya the terms of the Anglo-Libyan treaty made it quite plain that military facilities would not be extended to Britain when there was a dispute with a member of the Arab League.

This state of military unpreparedness was staggering and humiliating. With hasty improvisation, the Services tried to make good their deficiencies. The Mediterranean fleets of Britain and France began to assemble at various ports with orders to prepare to sail. Some Army units in Britain were, as early as July 31, alerted to move at twenty-four hours' notice—among them the Life Guards and the Grenadier Guards at Windsor. In Algeria similar preparations were made among the French troops. R.A.F. transport aircraft engaged on routine trooping movements were recalled or held in England. Canberra jet bomber squadrons flew from their United Kingdom bases to Malta. The troop-ship *Dunera*, outward bound for Hong Kong, was recalled to home waters on August 1.

No troops were moved from Britain until August 7, when units of five infantry battalions, a cavalry regiment, two heavy anti-aircraft and two light anti-aircraft regiments were embarked for Cyprus and Malta on ship and by air.* The three aircraft carriers *Theseus*, *Bulwark* and *Ocean*, which were lying in Portsmouth and Plymouth at the time the crisis began, had all sailed for the Mediterranean by August 7. *Theseus* had on board men and equipment of the 16th Independent Parachute Brigade. The troopship *Dilwara* sailed from Southampton with the Suffolks and Oxfordshire and Buckinghamshires On August 9. In the meantime other infantry regiments sent their stores and equipment to be loaded at Liverpool Southampton and Milford Haven and themselves marched ceremoniously from their barracks and encamped at various assembly areas. At the same time merchant shipping and civil aircraft were officially requisi-tioned by the Government for troop movement.

★

The unpreparedness of the armed forces left the Govern-ment little choice but to engage in a series of protracted diplomatic negotiations.

There were five stages in the first phase of diplomatic activity that followed Nasser's seizure of the Canal on July 26. First, at the end of July the exploratory tripartite talks in London at which Mr. Robert Murphy represented the United States. Next, at the beginning of August, the three-Power talks attended by Mr. Dulles. Thirdly, in mid-

---

* 1st Battalion Suffolk Regiment, 1st Battalion Oxfordshire and Bucking-hamshire Light Infantry, units of the Somerset Light Infantry, the Royal Berkshire Regiment and the Duke of Wellington's Regiment, the Life Guards, the 37th and 57th Heavy A.A. Regiments and the 16th and 43rd Light A.A. Regiments.

August, the conference in London of twenty-two nations interested in the Suez Canal. Fourthly, from September 3 to 9, Mr. Robert Menzies' five-member mission of explanation to Cairo. And finally, on September 11, Mr. Dulles's proposal for a Suez Canal Users' Association.

The tripartite talks opened in London on July 29, barely sixty hours after Nasser's speech in Alexandria. Sir Anthony Eden represented Britain, M. Pineau, the French Foreign Minister, France. Mr. Dulles was still in South America; and Mr. Robert Murphy, a senior official of the State Department who had served as political adviser to General Eisenhower during the North African campaign, and was consequently on terms of intimacy with Mr. Harold Macmillan, the Chancellor of the Exchequer, flew to London as the Secretary of State's representative. The first two days of the talks were concerned with the preliminary economic and financial sanctions that could be jointly imposed against Egypt. On July 28 Britain and France had already announced the freezing of Egyptian assets and forbidden the transfer of Suez Canal Company funds to Egypt. On July 30 they announced the cessation of arms exports to Egypt, and on the following day the United States froze Egyptian and Suez Canal Company funds, 'pending determination of their ownership and the existing situation'.

The British and French Governments at this time were making no great effort to keep secret the general character of the military measures that they were putting in hand— comings and goings between Paris and London, the plannings which had begun between Chiefs of Staff and the rumours buzzing round military establishments both in France and in Britain, besides the alerting of the fleets and the air forces; none of this escaped the attention of the Press or of American diplomats and advisers and military attachés in London and in Paris. Mr. Dulles, who had hastened back to Washington from South America on July 29, was well aware of these preparations. And on July 31, on the personal instructions of President Eisenhower, he flew to London to take part in the tripartite talks.

Dulles spent two days in London, and from the talks there emerged on August 2 the proposal for a conference to be held in London a fortnight later of the parties to the 1888 Convention and 'other nations largely concerned with the use of the Canal, either through ownership of tonnage or pattern of trade'. Such a conference, which envisaged the participation of twenty-four nations, recommended itself to Dulles more than a recourse to the United Nations, where at that time the balance of power was no longer very favourable to the United States in particular, and to the West in general, when it came to discussing the problems of the Middle Eastern or Asiatic nations.

Britain and France were content to acquiesce to the proposal for a conference, but they were disappointed to find that the American Government was not prepared to pursue a more active policy against Nasser. For example, Dulles refused to give orders to American ships using the Canal not to pay their dues to the new nationalized company. British and French shipowners in any case usually paid their dues straight into accounts in London and Paris, and the Egyptian Government accepted such payments, either to the old company before nationalization or to the new one after, despite the fact that these balances were now blocked. But the Americans, accustomed to paying 'on the barrel-head' in Egypt, were continuing to supply Nasser's company with much-needed ready cash.

Nor did Dulles show any enthusiasm for the military preparations that were being undertaken in Britain and France. On the very day, August 2, that invitations for the London Conference were sent out, a royal proclamation was issued in London recalling 20,000 Army reservists, and the French fleet began to concentrate in Toulon. The following day, after his return to Washington, Dulles made it plain that he did not approve of these military preparations. Though he admitted that the Canal must not be exploited

for the selfish purposes of any one country, he made it clear
that there would be 'no American involvement in the Canal
dispute even if the London Conference were to fail'.

Much later, giving evidence before the Appropriations
Sub-Committee of the House of Representatives on 29
January 1957, Dulles recalled: 'Certain elements in Britain
and France wanted to seize the Suez Canal by force immediately after it was nationalized by Egypt.' Asked whether the
United States had then prevented Anglo-French military
action, Dulles replied: 'We took the same position at that
time that we took later on when they did move—namely
that it could not be done consistently with the charter of the
United Nations and with our NATO treaty.' These observations were kept secret at the time and were not made
public until April 1957. Earlier, President Eisenhower, in a
broadcast, five days before the American Presidential election and the day after the Anglo-French ultimatum had
been rejected by Egypt, on November 1, said: 'There were
some among our allies who urged an immediate reaction to
this event [Canal nationalization] by use of force. We
insistently urged otherwise and our wish prevailed.'*

Of the twenty-four nations invited to attend the first
London Conference only two refused to come: Egypt, on
the grounds that she abided by her right to nationalize the
Canal, and in any case would not enter into discussions
while Britain and France made shows of force; and Greece,
who, apart from having a grudge against Britain because of
Cyprus, was unwilling to displease the Egyptians on account
of the large number of Greek nationals living in the Nile
delta. The conference that assembled on August 16 at
Lancaster House consisted in the main of Foreign Ministers.
Britain and France agreed that the case for the West should
be principally stated by Mr. Dulles. This was not so much
because of his forensic skill as because they were still hoping
that with full American support their grievances might be

* Yet, twelve hours before, the first British air attacks on Egypt had shown
that his views had not prevailed after all.

redressed without resorting to force. In Egypt's absence, Colonel Nasser's case was largely presented by Mr. Shepilov, Foreign Minister of the Soviet Union, and Mr. Krishna Menon of India.

Although the motives and allegiances of the participating nations were very disparate, Mr. Dulles succeeded in getting a resolution adopted (by all except Russia, Indonesia, Ceylon and India) which called for an international office that would operate the Canal, receive dues, and act as a temporary holding company. Mr. Dulles is a considerable statesman, but sometimes he reverts to his earlier role of corporation lawyer. This whole proposal smacked more of corporation law than of practical politics.

The eighteen nations agreed to dispatch to Cairo a mission composed of representatives from five countries to explain their proposal to Colonel Nasser. This was the fourth stage in the diplomatic activity. The mission, led by the Australian Prime Minister, Mr. Robert Menzies, arrived in Cairo on September 3 and was most courteously and hospitably received. But it was merely charged with explanation. It had no authority to negotiate. The support of world opinion behind the eighteen-nation resolution would have had to be extremely powerful to persuade Nasser to budge from the position that he had every right to nationalize the Canal. It was no surprise, therefore, that Menzies returned from Cairo after six days without achieving anything.

Now followed the fifth stage in this complicated international bargaining. Confronted by Nasser's repudiation of the eighteen-Power proposal, Mr. Dulles now proffered another idea—that of the Suez Canal Users' Association. As Eden understood it when Dulles told him about it on the telephone from Washington on September 11, it seemed an attractive idea. The proposed Association was to be a temporary club for those members who wished to use the Canal without giving in to Nasser's demands. The users would employ their own pilots, pay their dues to the Association, and in general stand together against any possible blackmail from Nasser. It seems that somehow there was a misunderstanding between London and Washington about the role of the Association in the event that Nasser were to show himself unwilling to acquiesce to its demands.

Undoubtedly Eden had at first assumed that Dulles's proposal envisaged that the members of S.C.U.A. would club together to force the passage of the Suez Canal if Nasser placed any impediment in the way of their operations.

For that reason Sir Anthony was cheerful and confident when he met the House of Commons on the following day, September 12, after it had been called back from its summer recess. Through many interruptions, the Prime Minister was able to say:

> I must make it clear that should the Egyptian Government interfere with the operations of the Association or refuse to extend to it the minimum co-operation, then that Government will once more be in breach of the 1888 Convention. I must remind the House that what I am saying is the result of exchanges of views between three Governments. In that event Her Majesty's Government and others concerned will be free to take such steps as seem to be required; either through the United Nations or by other means for the assertion of their rights.

Sir Anthony sat down amid tremendous cheers from the Conservative benches. Sir Robert Boothby* that night wound up the first day of a two-day debate. He expressed the relief of the Tory Members and indeed of a large section of the public:

> As I listened to the Prime Minister this afternoon, I thought of what Nasser had been saying about what he was going to do to establish an Arab Empire from Morocco to the Persian Gulf and how he was going to eliminate Israel altogether. That is all in the speeches in a horrible little book called *A Philosophy of Revolution* which is like a potted edition of *Mein Kampf*. As I heard the Prime Minister speaking, I said to myself, 'Well, thank goodness we shall not have to go through all that again', and we shall not.

* Now Lord Boothby.

Eden's triumph lasted scarcely as long as it took for his speech to reach the State Department. The following day, as the House of Commons reassembled, the first agency messages from Washington were coming through on the ticker tape in the corridor. As M.P.s eagerly crowded round the machine, they learned what Mr. Dulles had been reported as saying at a Press conference. Asked what would happen if Egypt denied transit to ships of the proposed Users' Association, Mr. Dulles had said that in such an unhappy contingency the United States would not attempt to shoot its way through the Canal, but would re-route its vessels round the Cape. The United States would be prepared to help other nations take the same course by making available for them tankers now in mothballs, and by loans. This statement very much undercut what Eden had said the day before in the House. (One possible card—the threat to force a test convoy through the Canal—had already been thrown away.) Nasser was to write his own ticket, Britain and France were to conform, and Uncle Sam as usual was to pay the bill.

In the course of that afternoon on September 14, Eden appeared to lose his nerve. A Labour back-bench M.P. who went to see him to assure him of support for firm action found the Prime Minister in a strangely hesitant and nervous mood. At 6 p.m. Eden faced a meeting of the 1922 Committee. Sir Lionel Heald and Mr. Nigel Nicolson insisted that any action against Egypt must be taken only after the question had been referred to the Security Council of the United Nations. It was known that they were prepared to abstain from the division that night, though the strength of their supporters was estimated at no more than twenty-five. The Suez Group, on the other hand, made it plain that in their view the dispute should on no account go to the United Nations. In the face of this pressure, Eden dodged the issues. He failed to give any leadership. His performance was thought by many members of the committee to have been lamentable. But what he said was enough to dismay the

Suez Group, and make some of them moan: 'Here we go again—back to appeasement.'

Their fears were confirmed when Eden wound up the debate:

> It would certainly be our intention if circumstances allowed —or, in other words, except in an emergency—to refer a matter of that kind to the Security Council. Beyond that I do not think any Government could possibly go. But I repeat, the Government must be the judge of circumstances. That is something no Government can share, no Executive can share, with anybody else, either with Parliament or otherwise.

His pledge satisfied Heald and his rebels. But it did not go far enough to persuade the Opposition to withdraw their motion. And it went much, much too far for the Suez Group.

★

Another ten days were to elapse before Britain and France actually took their case to the Security Council. But it was clear that this move could not now be long delayed, unless Nasser committed some act that would permit Britain and France to intervene on their own. At this time the military preparations of the preceding four weeks had been completed. Everything was buttoned up. It could of course be that Nasser would not be able to fulfil Egypt's obligations under the 1888 Convention in regard to keeping the Canal open and free. For on September 11 the European pilots belonging to the old Suez Canal Company had been given permission by the Company to withdraw.

For some time the Suez Canal Company had been threatening to withdraw the non-Egyptian pilots in its employ. From August 14 onwards it had assured itself that virtually all these pilots were 'loyal', indeed many of them had already expressed the wish to leave. M. Georges-Picot, the French Director-General of the company, asked them to stay, but added confidently: 'I could tomorrow end all traffic on the Canal if I chose to give the order for repatriation. The Company is now in a position to use the loyalty of its employees to paralyse the Canal at any time it chooses.' The company would have liked to have taken this action at the outset, but was dissuaded by the British and French Governments, who felt that to withdraw the pilots and thus stop traffic on the Canal might be an embarrassment to them while the first London Conference was in session.

The withdrawal of the pilots might in fact have closed the Canal at that time, but a month later, when it was decided to call out the pilots, the position had changed considerably. It had become clear that the Greek and the non-European pilots on the Canal would stay on with the nationalized company. Meanwhile, Nasser had gone out on a recruiting campaign and had succeeded in enrolling quite considerable numbers of able pilots from Russia, Greece, Germany and Yugoslavia. In any case, the Canal was accustomed to managing with something like two-thirds of its full staff on duty and one-third on leave. Obviously in this period no leave was granted, so that the position was considerably eased.

Nearly all the pilots whom M. Georges-Picot called out on September 11 were glad to be withdrawn, either through loyalty to their company or through dislike of working under the Egyptian Government. The position of the British and French Governments appeared to be that if Nasser were to stop the flow of shipping and were unable to operate the Canal efficiently international intervention would be necessary and justified. As a last resort, force would have to be used to keep the Canal free. And in order to make it harder for Nasser to keep the Canal working, they were soon prepared to authorise M. Georges-Picot to withdraw his pilots in order to 'paralyse the Canal'.

The underwriters at Lloyd's foresaw delay and even shipwreck on the Canal. They imposed a 15 per cent. surcharge on all cargoes that were to sail under the nationalized company's pilots. Some shipping lines, among them P. & O. and the Orient Line, decided not to risk their ships at all and to go round the Cape. In this way traffic through the Canal was temporarily reduced by 25 per cent., much to the relief of Nasser, who was thereby able to discharge his obligations.

On top of all this, there was the *mystique* about the intricacy of the pilots' job which had been carefully fostered by old Suez hands, but which was not borne out by the fact. As Mr. Aristotle Socrates Onassis said to the author at the time: 'An abominable snowman would have no difficulty in making a passage through the Canal.'

All this was known to the experts, and to the British and French Governments, who took the decision on September 10 to allow the Canal pilots to leave. But the leading Ministers showed a remarkable reluctance to face facts, and when an official of the Suez Canal Company pointed out to M. Pineau that in his view Nasser would be able to manage the Canal, the French Foreign Minister merely replied: 'Well, I hope you are wrong.'

For three days it was touch and go as to whether the ships could be brought through by Nasser's scratch team of pilots. These pilots worked non-stop, day and night. And on September 16 forty-two ships (against the normal daily average of thirty-nine) were brought through the Canal without mishap. With just a few extra ships to ferry through, the task might well have been beyond the capacity of the sleepless pilots. But unwittingly the shipowners who, surely not without Government advice, had diverted their vessels round the Cape had played straight into Nasser's hands, and had given his amateurs that lucky break that they so desperately needed. On that day, September 16, fifteen Russian pilots arrived, perhaps recruited from among Volga boatmen. In view of Mr. Onassis's remarks, they might just as well have been recruited from among the waiters at Shepheard's Hotel, if that historic hostelry had not been burned down by the Cairo mob four years before. On September 25 Lloyd's withdrew their Suez surcharge. Nasser had won this round. He had shown that he could run the Canal without British and French help.

Not for the first and last time in this unlucky Eden period, the British Government seems not only to have been misinformed about the facts of life, but very ready to console itself and the British public with delusive aspirations. Policy founded upon wrong information and vain hopes is always foredoomed to failure, if not disaster. It is strange that it should have fallen to Sir Anthony Eden, who had long been regarded as a specialist on the Middle East, to preside over these absurdly tragic miscalculations.

*

A second London Conference on Suez, from September 19 to 21, discussed and set out in detail the objects of the proposed S.C.U.A. and on October 1 the Association was formally inaugurated when fifteen of the eighteen governments adhered to it. The Council of the S.C.U.A. did indeed hold two meetings that month, on October 18 and 19 and again a week later. But there was an air of unreality about these meetings. Egypt had from the outset denounced the Association and had refused to have any dealings with it. And Britain and France would show no interest in the S.C.U.A. as long as the United States and other members were unwilling to withhold Canal dues from Egypt.

The five diplomatic stages which ended with the proposal for the S.C.U.A. took up the first seven weeks of the Suez crisis. At the end of this period Britain and France were no nearer obtaining a redress of their grievances than they had been at the beginning. But they were now in a military posture which would have enabled them to vindicate their rights themselves. However, they had meanwhile become involved in the international toils which Mr. Dulles had been at pains to contrive for them. Once you start talking, it is very hard to stop.

The Anglo-French case no longer looked as good as it did on July 26. Experts in international law had been laboriously explaining in the columns of *The Times* that it was really no more peccant for Nasser to nationalize the Canal than it was for Mr. Attlee to nationalize the steel industry. Now Nasser's improvised team of pilots had proved that Egypt could be relied upon to operate the Canal, and so fulfil her obligations under the 1888 Convention.

As the Presidential election approached, the Americans were showing day by day less enthusiasm for the cause of the western allies. The nearer they got to the elections, the less likely it was that the State Department would brand Nasser as an aggressor. For President Eisenhower's campaign managers were fighting for his re-election on the basis that he was the Prince of Peace. It is fantastic that the British Government failed to apprehend this elementary fact about the American domestic scene.

Indeed, there are strong grounds for supposing that they entirely misread the situation. It was certainly misread by the Suez Group. They thought that American support would be more easily obtained the closer the election came, because of the need of the Republican Party to poll the Jewish vote in New York City. What many English politicians failed to apprehend is the change that has come over the sentiments of American Jews since the establishment of the State of Israel. Since Israel became a State, American Jewry has increasingly accepted the Arthur Koestler view of the duties of Jews living outside Israel. Either they should go to Israel and become Israeli citizens or they should become wholly assimilated, except so far as their religious practices are concerned. Curiously enough, this increasing desire for assimilation, particularly when it comes to joining golf and country clubs, has led to a rather stronger social anti-Semitism than used to exist in the United States. Of course, the Jewish community has the welfare of the new State of Israel much at heart and continues to pour generous subsidies into its lap, but since the State has been achieved, Israel has largely ceased to be a political issue in America. Many of the Jews who were so stridently anti-British in the days of the late Mr. Ernest Bevin do not now wish to be associated with any agitation which could smack of being

9—RFSAE

un-American. It is more socially respectable to be a Republican than to belong to the Democratic Party, which has long been the party of protest. Mr. Harriman must have discovered this in the recent election for the Governorship of New York State. It is obvious that a large part of the Jewish community in New York City must have voted for the Republican, Mr. Rockefeller, despite Mr. Harriman's attempt to imply that Mr. Rockefeller was not a friend of the Jews.

It was in these circumstances that Sir Anthony overruled his French partners and the decision was made to take the problem to the Security Council of the United Nations. What was the Government's motive in going to the United Nations? It may be that Eden felt he ought to exhaust all possibilities before resorting to the use of force, so that going to the United Nations was merely postponing an unpleasant decision. Perhaps, realizing that he would get no support from the United States for intervention in Egypt outside United Nations approval, he hoped he would gain American support within the Security Council. But that was a considerable risk to take. Even assuming—though it was surely unlikely—that the United States would countenance in the Security Council the intervention that they had discouraged outside, was it not a gamble to expect Russia, with her power of veto, to agree? And when, as always seemed probable, Britain and France received no satisfaction from the United Nations, what conceivable pretext would be left to them to intervene in Egypt? What pretext could there be, save an attack by Israel upon Egypt? Yet despite the inherent disadvantages into which he was stumbling, Eden persuaded his French ally to join him in asking, on September 23, for a meeting of the Security Council, the date for which was later fixed for October 5.

The author has had the opportunity of talking and corresponding with those who were close to leading members of the Government at this time, and the following may fairly be taken to represent the arguments deployed by Sir Anthony Eden and his most intimate colleagues:

It would of course be desirable to settle the whole matter by negotiation. But this negotiation must be on Britain's terms. If it resulted in a settlement that strengthened Nasser's position or increased his prestige, it would be disastrous for Britain and her influence in Africa and Asia. The Government would seek to negotiate with Nasser as long as this seemed to give a chance of achieving the objects of British policy. But if that chance were to recede, and if, in the last resort, force were the only remaining alternative, the British Government would not shirk from using it. Above all, Nasser should not be allowed to give the impression that he was getting away with it.

It was becoming more and more apparent that the views of the American Government were very different from the argument condensed above. And on October 2, just three days before the opening of the Security Council meeting, Dulles held a Press conference of a singularly unhelpful character. To begin with, he admitted that there were fundamental differences between the United States and her European allies in their approach to the Suez problem. In questions of colonialism, he said, the United States must play an independent role. The fact that the official transcript of the conference was later amended to refer to the 'so-called problems' of colonialism in Asia and Africa, where, 'the United States plays a somewhat independent role', somehow only served to underline the divergence. Then, referring to the Canal Users' Association, Dulles denied that he had 'pulled the teeth' from the plan at the second London Conference held ten days earlier. But the amended version quoting Dulles as saying that 'there were never any "teeth" in it, if that means the use of force' accentuated the split which was developing between the United States and the British and French Governments.

★

The meeting of the Security Council opened on October 5. At this critical moment Eden was struck down in a most unusual way. He went to see Lady Eden, who was having a dental examination at University College Hospital. During his visit, he was smitten with a high fever of 104 degrees, and had himself to be put to bed in the hospital and remain there for the weekend. Meanwhile Mr. Selwyn Lloyd was introducing an Anglo-French resolution asking the Security Council to recommend that Egypt should join in negotiations for a new Canal agreement based on the eighteen-nation proposals adopted at the first London Conference, and that pending the outcome of these negotiations Egypt should co-operate with S.C.U.A. Most of the deliberations of the Security Council took place in secret, and there were many private discussions between delegates. But it soon became known that there was a great deal of cordiality among the delegates, though relations between Lloyd and Dulles remained strained after the latter's Press conference of October 2.

Some account of these discussions arrived in whispers on October 11 at Llandudno, where the Tory Party conference was in session. It was learned that Britain and France had accepted an amendment to their Security Council resolution which rather diluted the force of the original terms. It seemed to many of the delegates at the conference that the Government was preparing to back down and that its intentions were not in the least as resolute as had been supposed. To counter this, leading members of the Suez Group, among them Captain Charles Waterhouse, Mr. Julian Amery and Mr. Angus Maude, tabled an amendment to the motion on Suez that was to be discussed the following day. This amendment brought the Government up against the facts of life.

It took the Suez Group until two o'clock in the morning to convince the Tory authorities that they should allow the amendment to be discussed, and it was not until the Chief Whip, Mr. Edward Heath, had spoken to Sir Anthony Eden in London that it was put on the agenda for the day. The movers of the original motion were themselves crypto-

Suez Groupers, and only too readily agreed to accept the amendment, which was carried with only one vote against it, that of Mr. William Yates, M.P. In the course of the debate, Mr. Anthony Nuttin, one of the Ministers of State at the Foreign Office, who was speaking on behalf of the Government in the absence of Mr. Lloyd in New York, and from the brief of Lord Salisbury, who was ill, made a strongly worded speech.

> Britain and France . . . mean business and will stand firm. If the United Nations does not do its duty, we must do ours. . . . If that hard test should come upon us . . . I do not believe this country will flinch from it.

The following day Sir Anthony Eden echoed these strong words. Yet outside the conference chamber there were colleagues who were stating freely that they had restrained Eden from taking military action in July and again on September 13. And that if Eden were to be equally reckless in the future, they were standing by with a political strait-jacket. Mr. Butler felt that Party unity required him to go to the trouble of interpolating in his prepared speech to the conference on October 11 the statement that, having served under five Prime Ministers, there was none who could vie with Sir Anthony Eden in 'flair, courage and integrity'.

While the Tory delegates were entrained for London, the Security Council in New York met for the last time to bring its nine days of endeavour to a conclusion. Unanimously the eleven members accepted the six principles on which any Suez settlement should be based, which had been agreed upon between the Foreign Ministers of Britain, France and Egypt. They were:

(1) Free and open transit through the Canal—both politically and technically.

(2) Respect of Egyptian sovereignty.

(3) Politics not to interfere with the operation of the Canal.

(4) Canal dues should be fixed by agreement between Egypt and the users.

(5) A fair proportion of dues to be allotted to development.

(6) In case of dispute, the unresolved affairs between the Suez Canal Company and the Egyptian Government to be resolved by arbitration.

But when it came to the meat of the Anglo-French resolution, calling on Egypt to join in negotiations based on the eighteen-Power resolution, Russia and Yugoslavia voted against it. And Russia's vote acted as a veto.

It had taken the Security Council three weeks, from the time a special session was first requested, to come to this negative conclusion. Mr. Dulles 'understood the Security Council remained seized of the Suez problem'. But as far as the British and French Governments were concerned, all that remained seized was the Canal itself, and no amount of talk now seemed likely to wrest it from Nasser. The longer the delay and the talk, the argument now ran, the more difficult it would prove to dislodge Nasser.

CHAPTER EIGHTEEN

The Decision to Strike

THE abortive end to the Security Council debate was only one of the depressing events that were making October a bleak month for Sir Anthony Eden and M. Mollet. The great military enterprise that the two Premiers had built up was losing its momentum and glitter as Mr. Dulles and left-wing elements in England increasingly sought to slow it down and tarnish its morality. In Cyprus General Keightley received orders to prepare for a winter campaign. It was found that the waiting assault vessels had to be unloaded so that the vehicles and equipment that had lain on board for nearly eight weeks could be serviced— vehicles deteriorate rapidly when exposed to salt water without regular maintenance. In Britain the reservists were getting restive, and more than a hundred of them, who had been sent on leave, then refused to return to their duties. In London Sir Anthony's health gave rise to new anxiety. In Paris M. Mollet was pressed for action, and replied to the National Assembly, mysteriously: 'Wait till November.'

It was against this background that Sir Anthony Eden and Mr. Selwyn Lloyd flew to Paris on October 16. The exceptional secrecy of their discussions at the Hôtel Matignon with M. Mollet and M. Pineau was underlined by the fact that the four Ministers talked alone. It is very rare on such occasions that Ministers are not accompanied by diplomatic and military advisers, personal assistants and interpreters. The clandestine nature of this conclave, which lasted five hours, was noticed at the time and served to lend excitation to an already alarmed state of public opinion.

Meanwhile, in addition to all the military preparations that had been jointly undertaken by Britain and France, the

French Government had already been making arrangements of its own with Israel. On September 20, nearly a month before the Paris meeting described above, two representatives of the French Defence Ministry went to Israel to propose to the Israeli Government and staffs that France should aid an Israeli attack upon Egypt. This aid would not be confined to the supply of arms and to diplomatic encouragement. The French emissaries brought with them an altogether more far-reaching plan. This was that the French Air Force could give active support to such an operation, and with the French Navy protect Israel from attack by Nasser's superior bombers. It could also, they suggested, be accompanied by direct Anglo-French intervention, in the form of air attack and troop landings on Egypt. A date early in November was suggested for the enterprise.

For four or five days before this visit to Tel Aviv the French inner cabinet had had such action in mind. It had become clear during the days that followed the failure of the Menzies mission and the establishment of the Suez Canal Users' Association that the diplomatic pretexts for an attack on Egypt had been exhausted. The best remaining hope of making the long-delayed intervention lay in a war between Israel and Egypt.

The idea of joint Israeli-French action in this theatre was not new. There had been contacts and secret talks on many levels directed towards action against Egypt. It is understandable that the governing mind of France should have inclined to such action. For several years France's progressively deteriorating hold on North Africa had been loosened by arms, money and propaganda spouted out from Cairo. For some months, while Britain had shown herself increasingly reluctant to supply Israel with arms, France was ever more willing to do so. In particular, large numbers of tanks were delivered during the summer.

The military staffs of France and Israel began work on their joint project on October 1. The representatives of M. Bourgès-Manoury, the French Minister of Defence, paid several personal visits to Israel. General Moshe Dayan, Chief of Staff of the Israeli Army, came to Paris twice during October. These facts, and facts they are, will have to be borne in mind a little later, when it will be our unpleasant duty to form a view on the vexed question of 'collusion'. During this time the French were continuing to co-operate with their British allies on planning their own joint operation, Musketeer. But, suspecting that the long diplomatic delays might dishearten the English leaders, and knowing of Britain's traditional Arabist obsessions, the French kept secret their arrangements with the Israelis until October 10. Then, however, the nature of the Franco-Israeli discussions was revealed to some of the British Ministers and staff officers concerned with Operation Musketeer.

Sir Anthony has publicly and privately denied with emphasis that he had any foreknowledge of the impending Israeli attack upon Egypt. Eden is an honourable man, and his word must be accepted. But we must ask: 'Why didn't he know?'

It is the duty of a British Prime Minister who is committing his country to an act of war to know what is going on. Perhaps with his diplomatic training he preferred not to know? Perhaps some of his colleagues thought it better that he shouldn't?

The proof that there was collusion is massive and conclusive. That this collusion was ineffective may in part have been due to the fact of Sir Anthony's ignorance of it.

★

A number of border incidents between Israel and Jordan on October 4, and again the following week, resulted in offers of military assistance to Jordan from all Arab countries. In particular, Iraq offered on October 12 to move troops into Jordan at short notice, if a request for their support was received. That day, Mr. Westlake, the British Chargé d'Affaires in Tel Aviv, informed the Israeli Government that the Iraqi troops were about to enter Jordan and would be stationed there indefinitely. Furthermore, if Israel considered such troop movements a sufficient reason for attacking Jordan, the British Government would feel itself obliged to go to Jordan's assistance by virtue of the Anglo-Jordanian Treaty of 1948 and the Tripartite Declaration. The following day Mr. Lawson, the American Ambassador in Tel Aviv, also said that his Government approved of the stationing of Iraqi troops in Jordan.

A communiqué issued by the Israeli Cabinet on October 14, expressed 'anxiety and astonishment' at the British 'threat' to take action against Israel. And, in a debate in the Knesset on October 15, Mr. Ben Gurion strongly criticized the British Government's attitude. He refused, however, to accede to the demands of extremists for preventive war against the Arabs.

That day also, Major Salem, the dancing Major, who was once Nasser's Minister of National Guidance and now a Cairo newspaper proprietor, described the proposal to station Iraqi troops in Jordan as a plot between the British, Israeli and Iraqi Governments, to enable Iraqi forces to take over Jordan before the general elections which were due to take place on October 21. Within a few hours, however, the Iraqi Government, presumably on British advice, announced that they did not intend at present to station troops in Jordan.

On October 17 the Foreign Office, while reaffirming Britain's intention to come to the assistance of Jordan if it were attacked, announced: 'If we are to take action under the Treaty we would obviously have to decide what circumstances warrant the Treaty being invoked.' This piece of Foreign Office waffle was typical of the period, and seemed to indicate a piece of back-pedalling highly characteristic of the Eden era. That same day (the day after Eden and Lloyd had conferred in secrecy with Mollet and Pineau in Paris), a much more cheerful Mr. Ben Gurion replied to the debate in his Parliament with a vigorous criticism of Egypt. The threat, he said, still came from the Egyptian dictator, and it

THE DECISION TO STRIKE

was Egypt that was Israel's 'real enemy'. If attacked, Israel would carry war into the enemy's territory.

During the week before October 29, Jordan joined the Egyptian military alliance and put its army under the command of Marshal Abdul Hakim Amer, the Egyptian Commander-in-Chief. This brought all Arab armies around Israel (except for the Lebanon) under one single Egyptian command and vindicated Mr. Ben Gurion's assessment that Egypt was the main enemy.*

The elections in Jordan resulted in a victory for the National Socialists (who wanted a revision of the Anglo-Jordanian Treaty) and considerable gains for most of the pro-Nasser parties. Border tension continued, and it was in these circumstances that Israel secretly mobilized on the evening of October 25. So well briefed and so well organized was the citizen army of Israel that the mobilization by secret code words on the radio was achieved with no dislocation of daily life, without argument or debate, and in such secrecy that only the most alert foreign diplomat could gauge its scale.

The State Department in Washington received reports of this mobilization from its military attaché in Tel Aviv. President Eisenhower almost immediately began sending a series of warning notes to Ben Gurion advising him in forceful terms to refrain from taking military action against his neighbours. And on October 28, the British Chargé d'Affaires once more warned Mr. Golda Meir, the Israeli Foreign Minister, against any Israeli attack on Jordan. It was noted that the British warning was concerned only with an attack on Jordan.

It was argued at the time that either this was a signal for the Israelis to go ahead and attack Egypt, or that the British Foreign Office was so abysmally misinformed that it genuinely thought it more likely that Israel would attack

* The Command set-up did not help the Egyptians when the campaign started the next week. They tried to bring both Jordan and Syria into the war but could not succeed.

Jordan, who had a treaty with Britain, rather than Egypt, who was engaged in a quarrel not only with Britain but also with France. As the Duke of Wellington observed on a famous occasion: 'If you can believe that, you can believe anything.' It is no part of the author's intention to suggest that in this period the actions of British politicians, diplomats and generals were uniformly obtuse and asinine. Indeed, there seems reason to suppose that Sir Anthony's repeated adjurations to Mr. Ben Gurion to refrain from any attack on Jordan (which Ben Gurion certainly did not contemplate) were part of the general 'cover plan' to obviate any special precautions by Nasser.

At four o'clock on the afternoon of Monday, October 29, a battalion of Israeli parachutists was dropped forty miles to the east of the Canal, just short of the Mitla Pass.* The drop at Mitla Pass proved a useful menace for the Egyptian Forces as the track from there to Suez is the direct continuation of the shortest road to Cairo. Looking at it from the Egyptian side, it did create an impression of a menace to the Canal and beyond it to Cairo. The Egyptians reacted by immediately sending their Second Infantry Brigade to counter-attack. Fighting on the Mitla Pass between this brigade and the Israeli paratroopers continued for three days. What made this Israeli parachutist force irresistible bait was that it offered a serious strategic menace not only to the Canal but also to Cairo. The bait proved sufficiently succulent and the Egyptian armoured brigade at Fayid crossed the Canal expecting to demolish the Israeli parachutists. However, in the night of October 30-31, an Israeli armoured force which had set out from Eilat and Kuntilla had joined the Israeli parachutists.

On the morning of October 31 a considerable air battle was fought around the Mitla Pass. The Egyptians made

---

* The account which follows of these military operations is largely based on the information which the author received at the time in Tel Aviv and Jerusalem, Port Said, Nicosia and Akrotiri; and the dispatches he published thereafter in the *Evening Standard*.

forty or fifty sorties composed of an assortment of Russian MIGS and British Vampires and Meteors. The Israelis met these air operations with French Mystères, thirty-six of which had been supplied by France during October. These were manned by Israeli pilots.

The original Anglo-French plan called for immediate seizure of Alexandria. This plan when abandoned was used as the 'cover plan' for the new operation and was skilfully leaked to the Egyptians. British military planners have long been adept at selling cover plans to the enemy. In the whole Anglo-French plan for the Suez operation this successful deception plot was about the only piece of planning that seems to have worked. Nasser was misled, and sent his best tanks to Alexandria. As a result they never went into action against either the British, the French, or the Israelis. Thus by the evening of November 1 the Israelis were firmly in possession of the area around the Mitla Pass.

It was then that General Moshe Dayan, the one-eyed Chief of Staff of the Israeli Army, demonstrated his flexibility and resilience of mind to an exceptional degree. On November 2 another Israeli column struck south from Eilat at the head of the Gulf of Akaba to capture the islands at the entrance to the gulf. These two islands, Tiran and Sanafir, had been used by the Egyptians to deny entry and exit to Israeli shipping trading from Eilat to the Far East. And not only to Israelis. For it was from the mainland opposite these islands that the Egyptians two years before had shelled and hit a British ship. The 'going' down this southern route was exceptionally hard, and two small enemy posts had to be liquidated on the way. It was a minor operation but arduous in the extreme. For though there were only forty Egyptian gunners on Tiran and ten on Sanafir they were protected by two battalions on the coast. They had ample artillery and it was impossible to capture these islands until the two land garrisons had been disposed of.

In these circumstances General Dayan decided to detach a motorized force from the Mitla area and send it down the east coast to the Gulf of Suez, where there is a fine motor road, and the 'going' is far superior to that which was the lot of the force which was manhandling its vehicles down the stony, rocky route along the east coast of the Sinai Peninsula direct from Eilat.

This force which was detached from the Mitla area had to scupper a small Egyptian garrison on the way at Tur. To facilitate this, General Dayan dropped a reinforced unit of parachutists south of Tur on November 2 and the Egyptians, distracted by this, were quickly taken in the rear by the force from Mitla, which then swept on and in conjunction with the force which had come 'the hard way' scooped up the two Egyptian garrisons on the mainland which were protecting the two islands. Then it was easy for the four motor landing craft (M.L.C.s) which were already on their way from Eilat to capture these two strategic islands and evacuate their garrisons without a shot being fired.

While all this was going on in central and southern Sinai, two considerable actions were being fought in the North. General Dayan did not condescend to waste time in eliminating the 8th Egyptian Infantry Division in the Gaza strip. He by-passed the Gaza strip and after a well-contested battle for El Arish allowed his northernmost Israeli column to proceed westward along the coastal road. Twenty miles to the south the Israeli force (which had not crossed the frontier until November 2) had the bloodiest and most hard-fought action of the campaign around Abu Ageila and Kusseima. The northern column marching along the coast road included one armoured and one infantry brigade and was commanded by Brigadier Laskov (now Major-General Laskov, Israeli Chief of Staff).

Along the central road, it is true that the main battle on the road itself started in the night of November 1 but it had already been by-passed by the taking of Kusseima on October 30 by the 4th Brigade. The forces acting on that axis (Abu Ageila-Ismailia) included one armoured and two infantry brigades constituted as a divisional task force.

Co-ordination of both efforts was the responsibility of Brigadier Simchoni who was killed in an air crash two days after the end of the campaign.

However, within a few hours the Israelis broke through along the road and it was then that they achieved one of the most rewarding minor engagements of the campaign.

The Israeli column, which comprised about a hundred light tanks—American Shermans and French A.M.X.s—advanced parallel with the coast road about a mile south, shooting up, as occasion offered, the Egyptian tanks which were moving up in support of their troops at Abu Ageila.

Eventually the Egyptians realized that they were at a disadvantage on the road and ten Russian T34 tanks turned off into the desert. Not so well informed about the 'going' as the Israelis, they drove their priceless Russian tanks into soft sand; and then when they saw the Israelis they leapt out in a panic. The Israelis dismounted from their half-tracks and trucks and took possession of the Russian tanks, many of whose engines were still running. With the help of a bulldozer, which they had providently brought along, they hauled the tanks out of the sand and headed eastward with them to encounter the Egyptian column which was now fleeing westward.

A considerable share of responsibility for this rout lies with the Egyptian officers, whose quality was still, in the words of Ben Gurion, 'deplorable'. 'With the exception of a very few who fought bravely,' the Israeli Prime Minister told the author shortly afterwards, 'the officers were almost invariably the first to jump in their transport and head for home'. Their men were not generally lucky enough to have transport, and those who wanted to flee homewards had to do so on foot. To enable them to move more swiftly through the desert hundreds of them threw away their new boots which they had not yet had time to grow accustomed to. These, with much more, were carefully gathered up by the Israelis.

The Gaza strip was liquidated some days later on the

way home. The Israelis could easily have captured Ismailia and still more easily have scooped up the thirty-eight abandoned Russian T34 tanks only five miles east of Ismailia. But for reasons which will become apparent in the next chapter, they left them there as an easy spoil for the English, the French or the Egyptians. I wonder who's driving them now?

By reason of its swiftness and the totality of its success, this operation ranks with the highest military exploits. The code name for the invasion of Sinai was 'Kadesh', which invoked symbolical, nostalgic and Biblical memories. For it was at Kadesh that Moses and the children of Israel when on the very borders of the promised land were turned back by the King of Edom because they had 'rebelled against God's word at the Water of Meribah'. Thus it was that the children of Israel wandered for further years in the Sinai Peninsula and, in the words of the Biblical mnemonic,

> Joshua, the son of Nun,
> And Caleb, the son of Jephunneh,
> Were the only two
> Who ever got through
> To the land of milk and honey.

It seems worthy of note that though Moses and the children of Israel took forty years to reach what is now the State of Israel, General Moshe Dayan made the return trip in a campaign which, including mobilization, lasted no more than seven days. It looks as if the children have grown up in the last four thousand years.

★

During the last week in October two squadrons of the *Escadron Dijon* were flown to Israel and stationed at Lydda airport, thirteen miles from Tel Aviv. These two squadrons, comprising thirty-six aircraft, were manned by French pilots, and were additional to the thirty-six Mystères which had earlier been supplied to the Israeli Air Force.

The French-manned fighters played an important part

in the war. During the first two days of the Israeli offensive they did not themselves attack Egyptian ground forces, but they did supply the air cover above the ground forces; and more important still they provided the protection that was necessary for the Israeli towns left open against Egyptian air attack.

Mr. Robert Henriques, in his excellent account of the Israeli campaign,* written at the request of the Israeli authorities and passed for publication by the Israeli censor, is at great pains to prove that there was no collusion between Israel and France. But he makes an interesting comment on the task allotted to the Israeli Air Force when they received their orders for the campaign early in the hours of Thursday, October 25. On this occasion, it was 'to support the ground forces, and to be prepared to counter enemy interference'. Mr. Henriques comments: 'This was a role for which [the Israeli Air Force] had never planned. All previous planning had been based upon the appreciation that it would take six days to reduce the Egyptian Air Force, of which the first three days would be critical.'

Colonel Henriques correctly assesses the situation. But from an excessive discretion he fails to explain that the reason that the Israeli-manned Mystères were able to dedicate themselves to the front-line battle was that the two French-manned 'Dijon' squadrons had been detailed for this collusive task. Indeed, when it seemed that there was no likelihood of Israeli towns being attacked by Egyptian bombers, the French-manned Mystères themselves joined in the main land battle, and with considerable effect.

The author arrived in Tel Aviv on the evening of Monday, November 5, hot-wing from New York and London to find an uproarious party proceeding in the Dan Hotel, at which some twenty French pilots were being fêted by all the pretty girls in Tel Aviv for the aid which they had given to Israel with their Mystère fighters. Everyone seemed highly collusive. And why not? It looked like a splendid victory.

*100 Hours to Suez. Collins, 1957.

CHAPTER NINETEEN

The Ultimatum

AT four-fifteen on the afternoon of October 30 the Egyptian Ambassador in London, M. Samy Abdoul-Fetouh, and the Israeli Ambassador, Mr. Eliahu Elath, answered a summons to the Foreign Office. First the Egyptian Ambassador, then the Israeli, was seen by Sir Ivone Kirkpatrick, the Permanent Under-Secretary at the Foreign Office, and M. Pineau, the French Foreign Minister. Each envoy was handed the following joint ultimatum from the British and French Governments:

The Governments of the United Kingdom and France have taken note of the outbreak of hostilities between Israel and Egypt. This event threatens to disrupt the freedom of navigation through the Suez Canal on which the economic life of many nations depends.

The Governments of the United Kingdom and France are resolved to do all in their power to bring about the early cessation of hostilities and to safeguard the free passage of the Canal.

They accordingly request the Government of Israel:

(a) to stop all warlike action on land, sea and air forthwith;

(b) to withdraw all Israeli military forces to a distance of ten miles east of the Canal.

A communication has been addressed to the Government of Egypt, requesting them to cease hostilities and to withdraw their forces from the neighbourhood of the Canal, and to accept the temporary occupation by Anglo-French forces of key positions at Port Said, Ismailia and Suez.

The United Kingdom and French Governments request an answer to this communication within twelve hours. If at the expiration of that time one or both Governments have not undertaken to comply with the above requirements, United Kingdom and French forces will intervene in whatever strength may be necessary to secure compliance.

Earlier that afternoon, at the end of questions at three-thirty, Mr. Butler had announced in the House of Commons that the Prime Minister wished to make a statement, but that he was still in conference. The House of Commons had, therefore, to busy itself as best it could for an hour with the problems of Scottish schools. As 4.30 p.m. approached, members began to file into the Chamber in such numbers that the debate on schools became inaudible, and Mr. J. Henderson Stewart, the Government spokesman, thanked 'the Honourable Members who have now filled the House, for the great interest they have shown in what we are doing. I hope I may take this as an example of the faith they have in the Scottish Ministers'.

When the Prime Minister addressed the House, he referred to the invasion of the Sinai Desert by Israel and gave news of the ultimatum which had just been handed over to the Egyptian and Israeli Ambassadors. Egypt was asked to agree 'that Anglo-French forces should move temporarily—I repeat, temporarily—into key positions at Port Said, Ismailia and Suez' so that the belligerents could be separated and the passage of the Canal safeguarded.

The ultimatum ordered Israeli forces to withdraw to a line ten miles from the Canal. Sir Anthony himself said that spearheads of the Israeli advance were not far from the banks of the Suez Canal and that 'in all likelihood there is air and other fighting in the very close vicinity of the Canal, perhaps over the Canal'. Later that evening, Mr. Lloyd added: 'The facts as known to us at the present time are that Israeli forces are within a very few miles of Suez. They are moving towards Suez.' Yet, as is now known, the nearest Israeli forces were the paratroops dropped east of the Mitla Pass, who were at that moment digging themselves in nearly forty miles from the banks of the Suez Canal. Either through ignorance, or on the grounds of security, the Government continued to give contradictory and misleading information to the country. On November 1 Mr. Antony Head told the House of Commons: 'We have no direct information about Israeli-Egyptian operations. Reports indicate that paratroops are holding high ground about twenty miles east of Suez.' Yet the previous day Eden had again told Parliament: 'Israeli troops are continuing to advance towards the Canal . . . some troops may already be on it.' And on November 3, Selwyn Lloyd said: 'Israeli forces are now advancing on the Canal.'

It is known that the British and French military attachés were being kept informed of the progress of the Israeli advance throughout the operation. But somehow British intelligence reports tended to pay greater attention to the reports of Cairo Radio than to the information gathered in Tel Aviv.

This may of course have been the result of their experience in the preceding months. British intelligence had discovered that they were being fed with deliberately misleading information by the Israelis, because the Israeli staff believed that British sources had been passing Israeli information to the Arab Legion in Jordan.

Both the Americans and the French were much better informed about Israel's actions than the British. The British military attaché in Israel was not popular with the intelligence section of the Israeli army and they made sport of misleading and misinforming the British representatives. It is of interest that Israeli intelligence knew that Glubb was going to be dismissed at least three weeks before the event. They failed to inform the British because British intelligence had previously passed on some of their information to Jordan. Israeli agents penetrated the war-room of the British-commanded Arab Legion in Amman and photographed a document which Israeli intelligence had supplied to the British.

In almost every respect, British intelligence at the time of Suez was hopelessly wrong, not only about Israel—her strength and intentions—but also about Egyptian strength—their mine-fields and even their equipment.

Israeli forces did reach the Canal (or were rather within ten miles of the Canal as set by the ultimatum) on the evening of November 2.

The Western military attachés in Tel Aviv, including the

British (once the fighting started), were kept informed all the time of all Israeli moves and advances. But somehow it seems that the War Office did not rely very much on that information. It was said that at General Keightley's Head-quarters in Cyprus British Intelligence reports relied on Cairo Radio announcements, refusing to pay attention to the items sent by the British and French attachés in Israel.

All this made the ultimatum look a pretty maladroit and misleading piece of work. But it gives the appearance of being positively hypocritical when viewed in the light of later knowledge. The British and French Governments had issued the ultimatum to 'do all in their power to bring about the early cessation of hostilities'. Their declared object was to separate the combatants. Yet at the very moment that these words were made public, French transport aircraft based on Cyprus were preparing to drop petrol, ammunition and supplies to the advancing Israeli Army. Did Sir Anthony Eden really not know what was going on in Cyprus, a British Crown Colony? If he did not know, he ought to have known. And if he did, he was not telling the truth when he denied that Britain and France had colluded with Israel.

It was at a two-hour Cabinet meeting in the morning that Sir Anthony had informed his colleagues of what he planned to do. Until then only the inner cabinet (Mr. Lloyd, Mr. Butler, Mr. Macmillan, Lord Salisbury and Mr. Head) had been in the picture. Now when the Prime Minister read out to the assembled Cabinet the terms of the ultimatum which was shortly to be handed over to the Egyptian and Israeli Ambassadors, some of his colleagues were taken aback. They had not realized that war was barely sixteen hours away. They felt that it was impossible for them at such short notice to discharge their constitutional responsibilities.

When one of the Ministers complained about the short notice at which they had to make their decision, the Prime Minister rather grandly said: 'A lot of my present colleagues

never served in a War Cabinet.' Upon which another
Cabinet Minister said: 'Well, Prime Minister, we didn't
know we were at war.' There was a ghastly hush. But it was
too late to do anything about it. To resign when British
troops, ships and aircraft were already committed to the
battle was not a thing that any patriotic man could do. And
those who disliked what had been done had only four hours
or so before the ultimatum became public in which to dis-
sociate themselves, if they so wished, from what was being
done in their name.

★

It took the Israelis four hours to accept the ultimatum and
Nasser only nine hours to reject it. The French escort vessel
Kersaint, lying off Haifa, fired on the Egyptian destroyer
Ibrahim El Awal as the ultimatum expired at four-thirty on
the morning of Wednesday, October 31. But it was not
until seven-thirty that evening, fifteen hours after the ultimatum had expired, that Britain went into action.

The reason for the delay was valid. About the time the
ultimatum was expiring it became known that some fifteen
American transport aircraft were passing during the day
through Cairo West, evacuating American civilians from
Israel. Canberra squadrons from both Malta and Cyprus
were already airborne when this news became known in
London. Urgent signals were sent both from Malta and from
Cyprus to recall the bombers. Malta was unable to contact
her squadrons, but fortunately for what was left by this time
of Anglo-American relations R.A.F. Headquarters in
Akrotiri made contact with their squadrons, who were able
to pass the message on to the squadrons converging from
Malta. The pilots who had been standing by for many weeks
for this operation and who did not know the cause of their
recall were naturally 'browned off' and attributed, unjustly
on this occasion, the recall to further vacillations by the
politicians in London.

The R.A.F. planners had, however, already contributed

to the delay in mounting the operation. With plantigrade folly they had insisted on a six-day bombardment as an essential precursor to any invasion. Although hampered in their operations by the political decision which had reduced the size of their bombs from first 1,000 lb. to 500 and later to 250, the R.A.F. easily destroyed the Egyptian Air Force in thirty-six hours.

The R.A.F. requirement carried with it a further delay upon an operation that had already been over-delayed. But this was not all. The Cabinet was encouraged to believe that Nasser might be destroyed by the bombing alone, and that, in a favourite phrase of the R.A.F., it would not be necessary to 'land the pongos'.* This delectable carrot excited the political appetite of some members of the Cabinet, and made them think that they might achieve their objective without becoming involved in any land operations.

There was a pressing strategic reason for making a landing —the safety of the Suez Canal itself. It was known that the Egyptians were prepared to block the Canal if an attack was made upon Egypt. Speed and surprise might well have prevented the Egyptian scuttlers from doing too much damage. On November 1, for instance, Allied aircraft spotted and attacked a blockship that was being towed to the southern end of Lake Timsah, well clear of the Canal. An official communiqué that day reported the blockship as sunk. But on the following day aerial reconnaissance found the blockship in a position across the Canal itself. Now it was about to be sunk—but by the Egyptians themselves. It was not until November 2, four days after the ultimatum, that aerial reconnaissance revealed for the first time that extensive blocking of the Canal had begun. And on that day it became known that the pipelines had been cut in Syria, and that oil-pumping installations had been heavily damaged. The two things that Sir Anthony had said he wanted to preserve—free passage through the Canal and

* Pongo is Navy and Air Force slang for soldier. In standard English, it is a species of ape.

continuous oil supplies—had been destroyed before any British or French soldier had set foot in Egypt.

★

Meanwhile, as time went by without any action, the diplomatic battle for world opinion seemed to be going against Britain and France. As soon as news of the Israeli attack against Egypt became known on October 29, President Eisenhower instructed Mr. Cabot Lodge, the American representative at the United Nations, to ask for an immediate meeting of the Security Council. This was fixed for 11 a.m. Eastern Standard Time (4 p.m. in Britain) on October 30. On their arrival at the United Nations Headquarters in New York, Sir Pierson Dixon, the British representative, and M. Cornut-Gentille, of France, asked for a short adjournment because they were expecting statements from their own Prime Ministers. The delegates hung around for a while with Mr. Cabot Lodge becoming increasingly impatient, and after a delay of about twenty-five minutes the proceedings began. About a quarter of an hour later, though neither the British nor the French delegates was yet in a position to make a statement, the Russian representative, Mr. Sobolev, was able to read out to the Council the contents of the Anglo-French ultimatum which had just been cabled from London by news agencies. As usual in this period, the British had to rely on information services other than their own.

Mr. Cabot Lodge had tabled a resolution calling on Israel to withdraw behind the 1950 armistice lines immediately, and on all members of the United Nations to refrain from the use of force and from giving military, economic or financial assistance to Israel as long as she persisted in her aggression. After an adjournment between 1.10 p.m. and 4 p.m. the Security Council debated this resolution and Sir Pierson Dixon begged Mr. Lodge not to press it to a vote. Both he and M. Cornut-Gentille had been instructed during the adjournment if necessary to veto the resolution, and when Mr. Lodge insisted on putting it to a vote Britain and France

for the first time in the history of the United Nations
exercised their right of veto.

Australia did not vote with Britain on this resolution;
she abstained. And on a subsequent resolution proposed by
Russia, the Australian delegate actually voted against
Britain. It was extraordinary that Sir Anthony Eden was
not able to carry with him the vote of Australia, even after
Australia's Prime Minister, Mr. Menzies, had spent a great
deal of time in London, and in the service of the Suez Canal
users in Cairo, at the time of the crisis in August. But as
the British Government had not informed Mr. Menzies in
time, the Australian Premier had no opportunity to instruct
the Australian delegate at the Security Council. Considerable
culpability seems to attach to the Secretary of State for
Commonwealth Relations, Lord Home. It appears that he
was wholly unaware of the marvels of the modern telephone
which enable London and the capital cities of the Empire to
communicate. Certainly he did not make use of them on the
day of the ultimatum, with the result that not one Commonwealth country was forewarned of the British Government's
decisions.

At the outset of the General Assembly's emergency session,
the British and French delegates challenged the legality of
the session, but their argument was rejected by the Assembly
by sixty-two votes to two. And rightly so. It was not a hopeful
start to the week of continuous debating that was to follow.
Thereafter Mr. Dulles introduced a resolution based on the
American proposal put forward to the Security Council two
days before, calling for an immediate cease-fire, and this time
addressed his appeal to 'all parties'. After a nine-hour
debate, the resolution was carried by sixty-four votes to five
at 2.30 a.m. on Friday, November 2. In addition to
France and Britain, it was only found possible to rally
Australia and New Zealand and, of course, Israel.

By the evening of November 2 Egypt had accepted the
cease-fire resolution. The Israeli Cabinet considered it the
following day, asked for clarification of some of the points

affecting the future, but, conditional on those points being cleared up, gave their acceptance. That was on Saturday night, November 3.

At the same time Mr. Antony Head, the Minister of Defence, was dispatched to Cyprus on a seventeen-hour round trip. His object was to assure himself, and so the Cabinet, that the Anglo-French plans had been perfectly concerted. On the air-strip at Akrotiri early on Sunday morning, Head spoke to General Keightley, the Allied C.-in-C., and Vice-Admiral Barjot, his deputy. He accepted the final plan for a paratroop descent on Port Said the following day, and returned home.

When Mr. Head arrived at 10 Downing Street later that afternoon, he found there M. Pineau, who had flown over from Paris that morning, bringing with him, for the first time, M. Bourgès-Manoury, the French Defence Minister. To them and to the assembled Cabinet Mr. Head reported in reassuring terms what he had seen and heard in Cyprus.

Then at 8.15 p.m. British time, just twelve hours before H-hour, General Sir Charles Keightley received a message from London asking him to state what was the latest time by which a decision would have to be made should a postponement of the airborne landing prove necessary. Keightley records his reply in his dispatch, published in September 1957: 'I gave the hour as 2300 hours G.M.T. and added that any such postponement would have most serious consequences and must be avoided at all costs.' This was typical of the fidgety points with which the Prime Minister was always confronting his commanders and which made their lives so difficult. Though Sir Anthony still had his doubts about the operation, even he could at this stage vacillate no longer. For better or for worse, whatever may have been his doubts, Britain was now committed.

★

At dawn on the morning of November 5, shortly after six o'clock, the airborne assault on Port Said and Port

Fuad was launched. Six hundred men of the British 3rd Parachute Battalion and 16th Parachute Brigade, under the command of Brigadier M. A. H. Butler, descended on Gamil Airport, west of Port Said. Near the waterworks, to the south of the town, five hundred men of the 2ème Régiment Parachutistes Coloniaux were dropped. Both landings were successful. The paratroops met with only light, though accurate, opposition. The French quickly secured intact one of their chief objectives, the waterworks, and went on to advance into Port Fuad. The British had taken Gamil airfield by 9 a.m., and were heading eastwards towards Port Said.

At three o'clock in the afternoon the local Egyptian commander in Port Fuad contacted the commanding officer of the French parachutists to discuss surrender terms on behalf of the Governor and military commander of Port Said. He was referred to Brigadier Butler, who at 3.30 p.m. ordered a cease-fire while negotiations were in progress. Surrender terms were agreed, and in some parts of the town the Egyptian forces began to lay down their arms.

It was 3.30 p.m. in London. Mr. Selwyn Lloyd was answering questions in the House of Commons, which was in an uproar. He had been confronted by evidence supplied to the Opposition by the Foreign Office that morning of broadcasts from Cyprus Radio addressing the Egyptian people in a bellicose and threatening manner.

> Imagine your villages being bombed. Imagine your wives, children, mothers, fathers and grandfathers escaping from their houses and leaving their property behind. This will happen to you if you hide behind your women in the villages. . . . If they do not evacuate, there is no doubt that your villages and homes will be destroyed. You have committed a sin . . . you placed your confidence in Abdul Nasser.

Whatever may be thought of the efficacy of this message as psychological propaganda, there was certainly nothing to be gained by the Foreign Office in gratuitously handing over the text of these broadcasts to the Opposition. The Foreign

Secretary had to fall back on such explanations as 'I was not aware', 'I have no knowledge', 'I will certainly look into the matter'. Mr. Aneurin Bevan demanded: 'Will the Government stop lying to the House of Commons?'

It was into this atmosphere that a flushed and excited Sir Anthony Eden entered the House of Commons to read the text of a signal he had just received from Headquarters in Cyprus: 'Governor and Military Commander, Port Said, now discussing terms with Brigadier Butler. Cease-fire ordered.'

Brief though it was, this message was substantially an accurate summing-up of what had happened in Port Said. But thrown into the hectic atmosphere of the House of Commons, it had a remarkable effect. We do not know whether the Prime Minister was misled by this laconic message into believing that it implied a general cease-fire in Egypt. But that was the sense in which the House took it. The Opposition ceased to press its attack against the Foreign Secretary. The Tories, in one of the greatest Parliamentary demonstrations since Munich, rose to their feet, shouting and waving order papers. Everyone assumed that 'our side had won', and that Nasser, and not just the Governor of Port Said, had surrendered. These sanguine expectations were bankrupt. The cease-fire was only local, and even that did not last long.

What had gone wrong in Port Said? As soon as the Governor of the city had approached the Anglo-French commanders, Colonel Rouchti, the chief of police, a tougher character who was more conversant with the convenience of the telephone than Lord Home, called Cairo. He was told that the battle was to be continued, if necessary until all Port Said lay in ruins. The Governor, fortified by the police chief, proceeded to execute these orders to the best of his abilities, which did not extend to 'laying Port Said in ruins'. At 8.30 p.m. operations were resumed, and the fighting for the first time became fierce and bitter. For touring the streets of Port Said were loudspeaker vans declaiming: 'Soviet MIGs will be here soon. London and Paris have been bombed by atomic rockets. The third world war has begun.' At the same time, arms were distributed to civilians from lorries and from arms dumps in the streets.

It became clear that street-fighting in the narrow alleyways of Port Said would take many hours, and that the landings planned for the following morning would be opposed. Especially dangerous to British troops were the Russian recoilless SU100 anti-tank guns. The French meanwhile had fulfilled their part of the plan by capturing Port Fuad during the night, and they were now heading south along the causeway to Ismailia.

On November 6, at 4.40 a.m., the main Anglo-French force landed at Port Said. The assault was preceded by no aerial bombardment, and by only forty-five minutes' fire from destroyers. Despite the tough fighting which many troops encountered in the centre of the city, most of Port Said was in Allied hands by mid-afternoon. An air attack on Navy House just before dusk served to destroy one of the last centres of resistance. But by that time the Allied commanders had received new orders—to cease fire at midnight.

CHAPTER TWENTY

Why?

THE news that Britain and France had agreed to the
cease-fire called for by the General Assembly of the
United Nations was greeted with incredulity both by
the Allied troops in Egypt and by the general public in
Britain and France. It seemed grotesque that after such
lengthy and elaborate preparations and with the invasion
proceeding so swiftly and so bloodlessly it should suddenly be
abandoned when total victory was not only in sight of the
troops but within their grasp.

The cease-fire resolution which also called upon all parties
concerned to halt their troop movements in the area, was
carried sixty hours before the cease-fire was accepted by the
British and French and twenty-four hours before the first
Allied airborne landings were made. The resolution was
carried by fifty-nine votes to five with twelve abstentions, the
five opponents of the resolution being Britain, France,
Australia, New Zealand and Israel. Despite this massive
vote, the British and French Governments decided to persevere in their enterprise, though it is plain that the United
Nations resolution had given qualms at least to some
members of the British Cabinet. Egypt promptly, and
very sensibly, accepted the cease-fire order, and it was this
fact coupled with the rising hostility of the General Assembly
in New York which prompted Sir Anthony Eden to send his
telegram to General Keightley (already referred to in the
previous chapter) in which he asked how much notice he
would require if the operation were to be postponed for
twenty-four hours. As we have seen, General Keightley replied
that he must know within three hours. The Cabinet remained
in session pending his answer and then decided to 'let it rip'.

This background to the Anglo-French acceptance of the cease-fire forty-eight hours later must be carefully borne in mind if comprehension is to be achieved of why we gave in. The Cabinet was far from united in the matter. As is plainly shown by the telegram to General Keightley, there were some who wished to gain time for further thought and negotiation. There was at least one member of the Cabinet (Mr. Iain Macleod) who seriously considered resignation on the Sunday. There were three or four other important and influential Ministers outside the Cabinet who cogitated and discussed the same course. These doubts about Britain's moral position had already been actively ventilated before the final decision was taken.

Britain and France, however, ostensibly went to war with no division within their two Governments. The British and French Cabinets each contained at the time a number of hard-headed, resolute men, who having cold-bloodedly drawn the sword after so many months of deliberation were unlikely to sheathe it in mid-action without compulsive reason. Three reasons have been advanced as to what decided the issue—the Russian threat of intervention, the apparent hostility of sections of the British Parliament and public, and the run on the pound which started on the Monday and which became increasingly serious throughout Tuesday. All these three factors weighed to a greater or smaller degree with the British Cabinet. Few were worried by the Russian threat, which was rightly treated as a bluff. Some may have been swayed in their judgment by the ugly scenes in Parliament and the strident clamour of the left-wing Press. If so, they miscalculated, for it very quickly became apparent that a very large majority of the British people endorsed Sir Anthony Eden's action. But it was certainly the third factor which counted most with the Cabinet as a whole.

On the morning of Tuesday, November 6 before going to the Cabinet the Chancellor of the Exchequer, Mr. Macmillan, looked in at the Treasury. There he was faced with ugly facts and figures. He was told that the run on the pound, which had begun at the end of October, had accelerated to such an extent since the attack on Egypt that the pound was now dangerously near its minimum level of 2·78 dollars. This was attributed to the nervousness of holders of sterling balances throughout the world which usually accompanies the threat of war; and since sterling finances half the world's trade and therefore virtually represents half the world's money, it can be seen that there were a lot of nervous people about.

In New York sterling was being offered in blocks of 5,000,000 dollars, and the Bank of England was supporting the market by buying blocks of £1,000,000 at a time, a much higher level of support than normal. And on the day before Macmillan called in at the Treasury even the Federal Reserve Bank in New York began to release for sale some of its own comparatively small holdings of sterling. The Treasury made it clear that the Bank of England would be unable to continue its support of the pound at such a high level, and that only a decisive £1,000 million intervention could prevent the devaluation of sterling.

The Treasury also made it clear that the bank would be unable to maintain the level of the pound that day, unless the Bank of England stepped in, through its exchange equalization account. Otherwise sterling would have to be immediately devalued. This must have been a rude shock to anyone who had read the inspired optimistic report on sterling and the encouraging first leader that went with it in that morning's *Times*.

But, to take this decisive step, the Bank needed the hard currency of gold and dollars—at least 300 million dollars would be needed for that day's rescue operations alone. Unfortunately, during the preceding three months, the drain on Britain's gold and dollar reserves had been unusually heavy and the balance sheet since August showed a loss of 328 million dollars. The reserves were down to less than 2,000 million dollars. The rescue operation could not be performed unless there was a guarantee of more money coming into the kitty. The International Monetary Fund was an obvious source, but could the Government secure an immediate loan?

The Americans were being most unhelpful. Not only was the State Department allowing the Federal Reserve Bank to sell sterling, it was also raising tiresome difficulties as to whether Britain could withdraw capital from the International Monetary Fund. Mr. Macmillan had been among the most resolute of the members of the Cabinet in seeking ways to counter Nasser's theft of the Canal. More accustomed to modern methods of communication than Lord Home, he got through on the telephone to Washington and said that Britain must have an immediate loan of 1,000 million dollars if the pound was not to be devalued. Mr. John Foster Dulles was at that time in hospital, having been operated on a few days before for cancer of the large intestine. It was, moreover, about three or four in the morning in Washington, so it took a little while to get an answer. Meanwhile Mr. Macmillan had informed the Cabinet of Britain's dire financial straits, and a little later, while the Cabinet was still in session, the answer arrived from Washington that the loan could only be made if Britain accepted the cease-fire by midnight. There seems little doubt that this bleak intelligence, which it was Mr. Macmillan's hard duty to convey to the Cabinet, almost instantaneously convinced everyone that the cease-fire must be accepted.

That afternoon when the pound had slipped to 2·78 dollars and 9/32 of a cent, the Bank of England stepped in and sterling remained steady at that rate for the rest of the crisis. The Americans had agreed to back the Government's request for a loan from the International Monetary Fund (it amounted to 561,500,000 dollars), to waive interest on the American loan to Britain which was due on December 31 (amounting, with the Canadian loan, to over 100 million dollars), and to support borrowing from the United States on the strength of the Government's 1,000 million dollars worth of United States and Canadian securities.

The cease-fire became effective at midnight on Tuesday.

The full consequences of this decision only gradually dawned upon the British and French troops. They had, perhaps somewhat naïvely, assumed that no more shooting would take place, but that they could move easily forward to Sir Anthony's proclaimed objectives, Ismailia and Suez. But as it became apparent to the commanders and the troops of the leading detachments in the course of Wednesday that this was no temporary halt but a final resting-place, bewilderment and incredulity turned to rage. And the staff of the higher commands in Port Said, Port Fuad and Episcopi in Cyprus became seriously concerned for the safety of the 8,500 troops which they had dropped and landed.

The causeway across the marshes from Port Said to Kantara is twenty-six miles long. When the cease-fire became effective, leading elements of the British and French troops were eight miles from Kantara. Compelled to halt, they would have been in a tactical situation of extreme danger if Nasser should have decided to employ unofficial guerrilla warfare against them. They had a mass of vehicles which could not deploy off the causeway and which because of the congestion could hardly turn round and retreat. Five determined Egyptians could have blown one of the culverts under the causeway and several thousand men would have been like cut flowers in a vase.

The situation confronting General Keightley at Episcopi was still worse. A mass of men and material was tied up in a tiny area around Port Said without any form of effective air defence. There was the airstrip of Gamil, five miles to the west of Port Said. The runways at Gamil were not long enough to accommodate fighters and the only possible defence of all British and French shipping crowded into Port Said and Port Fuad and all the vehicles, tanks and troops in the area around was from two aircraft carriers, *Ocean* and *Theseus*, which between them could put into the air seventy aircraft of Wyvern and Sea Hawk type. The Egyptian air force, it is true, had been destroyed, but what of the twenty-five Russian Ilyushin bombers which had flown away from Egypt via

Saudi Arabia and were now in Syria? The speed of the Royal Navy fighters was 383 m.p.h., the speed of the Ilyushins was 580 m.p.h.; and no one could tell what the Russians would do. Seldom in history have the forces of two great Powers been left in so feckless and perilous a situation.

The soldiers did not trouble to hide their anger and disappointment. Only four days later Brigadier Butler, now back in Cyprus, made what was for a serving soldier a remarkably forthright statement: 'I felt frustrated about the midnight cease-fire, because I knew we could have gone a long, long, long way. We believed we could have raced through Kantara to Ismailia at the latest by lunch-time.' And more than eighteen months later General Massu, who was in command of the French airborne forces, spoke to the author in Algiers with a bitterness untempered by the passing of time. 'If I had known,' he said 'what my superior officers had intended at Suez, I would have disobeyed their orders and would have marched to Cairo or at least to Ismailia. This is the one great remorse of my life, and you may be quite sure I shall not make a mistake like that again.'

Ironically, the Israelis had done their best to prevent their allies, or enemies as they were pretending to be, from blundering into such a dangerously exposed strategic and political position. By November 3, a full five days after their attack had begun, the Israelis were less than three miles from the Canal, and the Anglo-French land operations had still not taken place. So, in view of the speed and success of their land operation, the Israeli High Command made three successive suggestions which provided new alternatives to the original plan. First they proposed that the Israeli troops should be supplied with French uniforms. Thus when their troops had seized the Canal, the French could say that their advance parties had in fact already reached one of the objectives of the campaign. The Anglo-French military leaders repudiated this ingenious suggestion. That, they were instructed, would be collusion.

So then the Israelis suggested that British and French

paratroops could be dropped immediately behind the Israeli front-line troops and advance towards the Canal through the Israeli lines while the Israeli troops withdrew. This obviously had the merit of saving five or six days of campaigning which might have been required for the Anglo-French forces to reach these areas. Again the reply was 'No'—that would be collusion. So then finally the Israeli High Command made its simplest and most logical suggestion. As Israeli troops were in such a good position, let them capture the Anglo-French objectives along the Canal —Port Said, Ismailia, and so on. The Anglo-French troops could intervene and the Israelis would hand these objectives over to them. But again the reply was 'No'.

Of course the reason that Britain and France were unable to take advantage of any of these three attractive suggestions was that they were the prisoners of their own hypocritical and disingenuous ultimatum. Having made a mock show of anger and disapprobation of the Israeli attack, and having issued the ultimatum to them to desist, how could we logically connive at these imaginative proposals? It may be argued, of course, that we had already committed a comparable act of collusion when we had allowed French transport aircraft operating from Cyprus to drop supplies on the Israeli army at the time when we were calling upon them to abandon their aggression. Perhaps it was hoped that this earlier, long-planned act of collusion would never be discovered, and feared that a sudden improvised act of collusion, now that the whole world was watching, might be detected. We do not know, and must suspend judgment until writers with direct knowledge of the motives which animated the Allies, such as Sir Anthony Eden, tell us the whole story.

We must now consider the part played by the United States in the Suez story. Among the most serious consequences of the Suez débâcle was that it nearly destroyed the Anglo-American alliance. It was one of Mr. Harold Macmillan's greatest acts of statesmanship that he was able to heal the breach so very soon after he became Prime Minister in

January 1957. Though relations between the British and American Governments are now as intimate as they have ever been in time of peace, considerable differences of opinion still remain on both sides of the Atlantic. Without any wish to revive old animosities, it is right that the facts should be put in their true perspective so that the reader may form an objective view. In brief, the British complaint is that the Americans let us down, while the American answer is that the British have no right to complain since the Americans were not only not informed of what we intended to do, but were actively deceived.

From the very day that Nasser grabbed the Canal, America made it plain that she would not countenance any military action taken by France and Britain outside the context of the United Nations. It was to discourage any violent action that all through the months of August, September and October Mr. John Foster Dulles laboured unceasingly to involve Britain and France in a series of abortive discussions. With an ingenuity which one cannot but admire, he produced an endless series of proposals for discussions on different levels and at different venues. Whatever may have been the wrong-headedness of American policy now and heretofore about the Middle East, neither the British nor French Cabinets could possibly pretend that they were unaware of the American attitude, which had been consistently unhelpful from start to finish. Yet in mid-November, Mr. Selwyn Lloyd, at a small gathering of American journalists in New York, revealed that the calamity of Suez was due to a 'series of glaring miscalculations'. The greatest had been in completely underestimating the reaction of the American Government. The British Government had thought that American opinion would vary from 'benevolent neutrality' to 'hostile neutrality'. What they had never expected was that America 'would lead the pack against us'.

By a curious aberration of judgment Sir Anthony Eden contrived that there should be no British Ambassador in Washington during the critical month before he struck at

Suez. The retiring Ambassador, Sir Roger Makins, left the United States on October 11. The new Ambassador, Sir Harold Caccia, did not take up his duties in Washington till November 8, two days after the cease-fire and two days after the American presidential election. This can hardly have been an accident. With the crisis mounting from hour to hour, it might have been supposed that the new Ambassador might have availed himself of modern means of communication and have flown to Washington so that when the crunch came there would be someone who could authoritatively explain Britain's position to the President. Instead, Sir Harold Caccia crossed the Atlantic by sea. The Foreign Office may, of course, have wished to spare the new Ambassador the possibility of being asked embarrassing questions which he could not answer, and thereby seeming stultified at the outset of his mission; and in view of what happened to the French Ambassador, M. Hervé Alphand, one can see that there may have been some force in this consideration.

On October 30, the day after the Israeli attack, President Eisenhower summoned the French Ambassador first thing in the morning and called upon him to explain the rumours that had been pouring into Washington about French intentions in the Middle East. He demanded to know what France's plans were. M. Alphand, who had only taken up his appointment as French Ambassador to the United States on September 7, earnestly replied that he knew of no plans for war and assured him of France's most honourable intentions. M. Alphand returned from the White House to his Embassy where he was handed a copy of the Anglo-French ultimatum. When Mr. Dulles saw M. Alphand shortly after the cease-fire, the American Secretary of State told him, 'I will never again trust the word of a French Ambassador'.

★

By the middle of October some members of the British Cabinet who had been getting wind of what was planned for the end of the month and the beginning of November began to express concern as to whether any proposed action on our part would carry with it the support or at least the goodwill of the United States. Eden let it be discreetly known that he had had a letter from the President of a reassuring character. Simultaneously in Paris the President of the Republic, M. René Coty, who evidently had some doubts about the proposed Israeli invasion of Sinai and the Anglo-French synchronized intervention, consulted a number of important officials and military leaders who were not directly concerned in the proposed operations. In the course of these consultations M. Coty showed a copy of the letter which President Eisenhower had written to Sir Anthony. It was dated October 16. This was doubtless the communication on which Sir Anthony was relying when he reassured his colleagues about the likely American reaction to the proposed Franco-British intervention. The letter of October 16 indicated that while there was some divergence of opinion between the United States and Britain as to how the Suez situation should be handled, it would be possible after the elections to come to some agreement acceptable to both Britain and the United States.

The true interpretation of the force and meaning of this letter has been the cause of much misunderstanding on either side of the Atlantic. Some of Sir Anthony's friends seemed to have gained the impression that President Eisenhower had in effect given Sir Anthony the green light to go ahead. Others, who had seen the text of the letter, considered that at most it was an orange light that flickered from the White House; but one that unmistakably carried the message: 'Keep quiet till after the election.'

Ten days later on October 26 when the Americans began to get their first reports of the Israeli mobilization, the American Ambassador in France, Mr. Douglas Dillon, had a conversation with M. Chaban-Delmas, Minister without Portfolio in M. Mollet's Government. During this talk, Chaban-Delmas let fall something which made Dillon feel that the French knew a good deal more than they were prepared to say. Accordingly, speaking in the terms of Eisenhower's letter to Eden of October 16 (of whose contents he had doubtless been informed), Dillon suggested that agreement between Britain and France and the United States might well be possible following a meeting of Heads of Governments immediately after the elections. It is clear that Dillon's suspicions were aroused by Chaban-Delmas's remarks, for the following day he called formally at the Quai d'Orsay on M. Louis Joxe, permanent head of the French Foreign Office, and asked him specifically whether France had any warlike intentions against Egypt. M. Joxe assured him that there were no such intentions. No doubt M. Joxe in Paris, like M. Hervé Alphand three days later in Washington, was speaking the truth, so far as it had been vouchsafed to him. But neither episode contributed to Franco-American cordiality and trust.

★

We have seen earlier in this book (page 257) how some English politicians thought that it would be more likely for the President to take an indulgent view of what Britain and France contemplated before the election rather than after it. This conception was based on the outmoded assumption that the Jews in New York could exercise a decisive influence on the President's reaction; for the reasons already set down this was wide of the mark. But on any calculation it seems fantastic that Eden and Mollet and their colleagues in the British and French Cabinets should have disregarded the naked implications of the President's letter. Three months had already passed since Nasser's grab. It would have cost little to have waited another week. Such postponement, ordered around October 18, would not greatly have interfered with the military preparations. This is one of the key episodes on which history will turn a remorseless scrutiny; but until the text of President Eisenhower's letter is made public it is impossible to divide with exactitude the culpability for a tragic misunderstanding and miscalculation.

Against this background it is hardly surprising that the President, already overtired by a strenuous election campaign now in its last few days, was outraged by the Anglo-French ultimatum. The head of the *New York Times* Bureau in Washington, Mr. James Reston, the best-informed and most accurate political reporter in the United States, wrote on October 31: 'When Eisenhower first heard of the ultimatum the White House crackled with barrack-room language the like of which had not been heard since the days of General Grant.'

CHAPTER TWENTY-ONE

Some Answers

THE other day the poor Egyptians were very near effecting a successful revolution . . . but, unfortunately for us . . . the Prime Minister of Great Britain . . . came upon them with his armies and his fleets, destroyed their towns, devastated their country, slaughtered their thousands, and flung back these struggling wretches into the morass of oppression. Without a moment's hesitation, and for the wretched motive of concluding a commercial treaty with France, he joined hands with that country, and cast the whole weight and power of Britain against the struggling people. A greater crime was never committed, a greater departure from our modern foreign policy cannot be conceived. But I may be told, 'In thus accusing . . . you are in reality accusing me, the people of this great country, who allowed, and who may even be said to have approved his policy'. I am not sure that the people have approved his policy. As far as by-elections can be said to go, they disapprove it. The people of this country have not yet had an opportunity of giving judgment. Parliament may be said to have approved the Government policy, if you consider only the . . . majority of the House of Commons. But is the approval of the . . . majority of the House of Commons so very valuable or so very conclusive? But even if the British people had sanctioned the entire Egyptian policy . . . the British people could not be held to be responsible if they were in error. For from first to last you have been systematically furnished with false information. You were told that . . . his movement was a military rebellion. This was the first fabrication: no one will now deny that he was the leader of a nation, the exponent of a nation's woes, and that the military rebellion was the desperate struggle of a race. You were told that the British fleet was in danger from . . . Alexandria: this was the second fabrication. . . . All the money-lending blood-suckers and harpies, with their hordes of hangers-on, had fled panic-stricken before the wrath of an awakened and an aroused people. You were told that the Suez Canal was in danger; this was fabrication No. 3. The Suez Canal was never in danger at any time. During the whole Egyptian difficulty commerce traversed the Suez Canal, with the exception of a period of forty-eight hours.

This is my object—to show you, the people, so that if you believe me you may intervene, that Great Britain . . . has gone astray, has commenced a hopeless task, and has entered upon a fatal course.

And this brings me to the last and greatest of all the fabrications which have been diligently crammed into your minds. The Prime Minister has stated over and over again that we went to Egypt with no selfish aim or object, but only in the interests of Europe and for the benefit of the Egyptian people. He first struck a desperate blow at the commerce between Europe and the East by laying the city . . . in ashes. He struck a second desperate blow at the same interests when he laid violent hands on the Suez Canal, which, since its construction, had been preserved sacred from the operations of war. He struck a third desperate blow at Eastern commerce when, for a period of three months and more, he put a stop to all commercial transactions over the whole land of Egypt: and the result of these three blows is that he has created a hatred of Europeans in general and of the British in particular among the Egyptians so bitter, so unappeasable, that for years to come the commercial interests of Europe in Egypt will hang upon a thread.

You will be told that Egypt is the high road to India, and that Britain must hold it at all costs. This is a terrible and widespread delusion. Similar delusions have before now led astray the foreign policy of this country. At one time it was the balance of power: that has passed away. . . . Now we have the high road to India will-o'-the-wisp, which in time will vanish too. Egypt is not the high road to India. The Suez Canal is a commercial route to India, and a good route too in time of peace; but it never was, and never could be, a military route for Great Britain in time of war. In time of war there are no well-marked high roads to and fro across the British Empire. The path of Britain is upon the ocean, her ways lie upon the

deep, and you should avoid as your greatest danger any reliance
on transcontinental communication, where, at any time,
you may have to encounter gigantic military hosts. But if you
wanted to make Egypt the high road to India, so that you
might traverse it at any time with your armies and your
fleets, how can you do so better, how can you do so at all,
except by gaining the confidence, the gratitude, and the love
of the Egyptian people, by giving them that freedom for
which they have made such a struggle—a struggle which,
mind you, would have been successful if the first germs of
popular rights had not been trampled upon and crushed
down by the heavy tread of the British grenadier? /

Who said all that? Mr. Aneurin Bevan on 4 November
1956 in Trafalgar Square? No. These words were spoken by
Lord Randolph Churchill on 18 December 1883 in Edinburgh shortly after that great Liberal, Mr. Gladstone, had
bombarded Alexandria and invaded Egypt. Though none of
the Government's critics found themselves able to marshal
against Sir Anthony so powerful a case as Lord Randolph
contrived against Mr. Gladstone, the above speech may
perhaps be thought to crystallize the gravamen of the case
against what Britain did seventy-three years later.

*

In attempting a final assessment of the rights and wrongs
of the Suez operation, the author finds himself confronted
with some difficulties. In common with many other people
he feels compelled to revise the judgment and opinions
which he held in October 1956. There are today many
politicians and publicists who openly supported the Suez
operation at the time, who feel very differently about it
today. If we had known with what ineptitude the campaign had been planned, if we had detected the inherent
fraudulence of the Anglo-French ultimatum, if we had
known of the Government's miscalculations about American
reactions, if we had perceived that because of these miscalculations the enterprise would have to be abandoned in

thirty-six hours, many of those who, like the author, applauded the action on the day might have adopted a very
different line. Though we might not have been as bitter in
our attacks on Sir Anthony Eden as Lord Randolph was on
Mr. Gladstone, we could not, if we had known in November
1956 what we know now, two years later, have spoken and
written in the way we did. The author, for one, is prepared
to stand in a white sheet and admit that he was wrong. And
the assessment which follows is made from a clean table
from which all earlier misconceptions and judgments have
been swept.

To this day, friend and foe alike, in all parts of the world,
express mystification that the British Government should
not have found it possible to go on just a little while longer
at Suez and so ensure that we were not cheated of the fruits
of our victory. How much longer? It has been seen how
Brigadier Butler said that his paratroops could have reached
Ismailia at the latest by lunch-time on November 7.* Most
of the military commanders on the spot—not only Brigadier
Butler but also the two French generals, Beaufre and Massu
—believed that Suez could have been reached and captured
in forty-eight hours. This judgment received confirmation
barely a week later from Mr. Selwyn Lloyd, the Foreign
Secretary, who when asked at the private talk with American
newspapermen already referred to in New York† how long
it would have taken British and French troops to finish the
job replied 'Forty-eight hours'. If this was also the advice
given to the Cabinet, it would hardly have been possible
that they should have stopped the operation embarked on so
many months before with such care and diligence when it
was so near the final objective. But there is good reason to
believe that this was not the advice tendered to Sir Anthony
Eden and his colleagues.

On December 5 Mr. Antony Head, the Minister of
Defence, in reply to a question in the House of Commons,
said that it would have taken 'about seven days' to get to

* See page 291   † See page 293

Suez.* This, and not forty-eight hours, seems to have been the military advice given to the Cabinet at the crucial moment. This, and not the knowledge of the British and French front-line commanders, seems to have determined the acceptance of the cease-fire. The estimate of the warlike character of the conscripted *fellaheen* that led to these demoralized assumptions was preposterous in the light of what even the British general staff must have absorbed in the previous ten years, and what every soldier who served in Egypt during the second world war had had in his bones for even longer.

The British general staff had for many years entertained an exaggerated notion of the fighting potential of the Egyptian soldier. When the Egyptian-Israeli war broke out in 1948 one soldier alone, the late Field-Marshal Lord Wavell, advised that the Jews would win. The rest were blinded by the overwhelming numbers of the Egyptian Army, deceived by the quality of the British arms which had been supplied to it, and falsely believed in the training that many British officers had given to the Egyptians in the use of their arms. Though the British Intelligence had been stultified in its prognosis in 1948, it failed to gain new wisdom thereafter. It continued to underestimate the battle-worthiness of the Jews and to overestimate that of the Egyptians and of the Arab States.

The intelligence reports of the general staff tended to make much of the training given to the Egyptian Army by ex-Afrika-Korps officers, and in the improvement in morale with which Colonel Nasser was believed to have infected his troops. The intelligence reports from the Foreign Office, which were disfigured by their traditional Arabist slant, neglected to take account of the mental and moral degradation of a people born and nurtured in the enervating atmosphere of a lush delta. They deluded the military staffs into the error of overestimating their enemy, and mounting

* Two years later in the House of Commons he was less precise; he said 'a few days'. See page 314.

an operation almost on a scale appropriate for war against a major European Power.

The planning of the operation was as elephantine in its scale as in its speed. The staff work was a monument to diligence, a memorial to patient endeavour. The meticulous character of timings, loading tables and strategic appreciations could have served as a model for future operations, had it not been for the constant political interferences from above, and the wholly erroneous premisses on which this devoted work was based.

The plan always demanded ten days of warning before the land operation could be effectively begun. This remained the firm rule throughout all the planning from August onwards. Through all the chopping and changing dictated by the vacillations of the Allied statesmen one factor was common and constant in all the seventeen different plans which were successively devised. The failure to build a harbour or even an adequate number of 'hards' in Cyprus involved the operation being mounted in the main from Algiers, Marseilles and Malta, and that meant that ten days must pass from the time when the decisive order was given before the first seaborne troops could land.

This difficulty could only have been surmounted if the planners had been content with a plan of a lighter, speedier, more daring and more flexible character. As one French critic of the ultimate plan remarked to the author: '*Il faut arriver vite à la guerre.*' The failure to adopt such a strategy was more the fault of the generals than of the politicians. Unfortunately Sir Anthony Eden was misled by Sir Walter Monckton and Mr. Antony Head into the classical error of falling into the hands of his generals, a fate almost as dreadful as being in the hands of lawyers, almost as ghastly as being 'under doctor's orders'. But the politicians must bear part of the blame since instead of goading the generals into swift ruthless action, they kept impeding and rattling them with every artful contrivance of indecision. Here the nervous hand of Sir Anthony Eden could often be detected.

When Nasser first nationalized the Canal Sir Anthony Eden, Mr. Selwyn Lloyd and Mr. Harold Watkinson, the Minister of Transport, all made the same point in their broadcasts to the nation: the supply of oil, and thus the economy of the whole country, were threatened if the Canal did not remain open. And yet no attempt was made to restrict the consumption of oil and petrol until November 7, after the cease-fire, when a 10 per cent cut in oil supplies was ordered. Rationing did not come into operation until December 8, and then only after a month's warning which gave everyone a chance to 'top up' and 'tank up'. Other European countries, like Ireland and Poland, who were not directly involved in the Suez affair had been forced to introduce rationing some time before that. Switzerland had had to ban pleasure motoring on Sundays and public holidays.

Under more resolute leadership rationing in Britain would have been imposed on the day that Nasser nationalized the Canal. This would have enabled Britain to face the ultimate emergency with ample stocks, with less depleted dollar reserves. And it would also, from a psychological point of view, have brought home to the British people what was at stake, and would have been a striking manifestation to our friends in America of the seriousness of our situation. It might also have made Colonel Nasser realize, while time remained, how deadly a blow he had struck at Britain, and have warned him that an outraged and united nation was clearing the decks for action. Petrol rationing would have been a card of high and pervasive value if it had been played at the outset. It is one of the cardinal indictments of the British Government that it went to bed with this card in its hand, and that it was only produced when the game had already been lost. If Sir Anthony Eden had ever read his colleague Mr. Iain Macleod's book, *Bridge is an Easy Game*, he would have produced this trump card much earlier in the game. This is only another example of the lack of finesse which characterized this unhappy period.

One of the extraordinary features of this period was the

way in which Sir Anthony swapped his most important service and defence Ministers around. On September 2, just when the initial military preparations were nearly complete, the Prime Minister allowed Lord Cilcennin to retire from the Admiralty and become Chairman of Welsh commercial television. He was replaced by Lord Hailsham. Certainly Lord Cilcennin had for a long time expressed his desire to leave the Administration. Certainly Lord Hailsham was able to introduce a new, invigorating spirit into the direction of the Navy. But why make this change at this particular time?

Even more extraordinary was the replacement of Sir Walter Monckton at the Ministry of Defence on October 18, less than a fortnight before the Suez enterprise was launched. It is true that his successor, Mr. Antony Head, had, as Secretary of State for War, been entrusted with the major share of the planning. As a former Combined Operations planner, with the rank of brigadier, Mr. Head was regarded as an expert in these matters, and he certainly enjoyed a greater degree of intimacy with and access to the Prime Minister than did Sir Walter Monckton in this period. It is true also that Sir Walter had for long expressed a desire to leave the Government and go into business. But why at this particular moment? In fact, Sir Walter was not allowed to leave the Government, but was retained in the Cabinet with the sinecure of Paymaster-General. And on November 1 he was charged with the co-ordination of Government information services during the operations in Egypt. But it can hardly have been with this in view that Sir Walter was replaced by Mr. Head on the eve of the operations for which he bore at least a considerable nominal responsibility. Mr. Head, though in every way the strategic and intellectual superior of Sir Walter, was not perfectly cast for his new role. He was an expert in combined operations; but that was not what was required. The military commanders needed firm and statesmanlike control, not expertise overlaid upon experts.

This chopping and changing of key Ministers during the vital period of planning did little to improve either military or civilian morale. It began to be said of Sir Anthony that he was a fidget, a fusspot who could not leave well alone. As someone wrote at the time: 'He was slow to make up his mind, and quick to change it.'

It has already been recorded in this story how several Ministers, both inside and outside the Cabinet, had expressed misgivings at various stages of the crisis. In the event, there were only two resignations—that of Mr. Anthony Nutting, Minister of State at the Foreign Office, and that of Sir Edward Boyle, Financial Secretary to the Treasury. Mr. Nutting resigned on October 31 and Sir Edward Boyle on November 5, though the letters of resignation were not published until November 3 and November 8 respectively. Mr. Nutting wrote: 'I have advised most strongly against the decisions and actions of the Government. I do not honestly feel it is possible for me to defend the Government's decision.' This was a curious declaration in view of what he had said at the Tory Conference at Llandudno less than three weeks before: 'If the United Nations does not do its duty, we must do ours . . . if that hard test should come upon us . . . I do not believe this country will flinch from it.'

Sir Edward Boyle, on the other hand, wrote in more moderate terms:

> I fully realize the very great difficulty of the problem which the Government have had to face in the Middle East. But I do not honestly feel that I can defend, as a Minister, the recent policy of the Government, and I feel bound to associate myself with that body of opinion which deeply deplores what has been done.

He was, shortly after Mr. Macmillan became Prime Minister, readmitted to the Government.

The state of Mr. Butler's conscience is hard to fathom. We know how he felt at the time of the Llandudno Conference; but rightly or wrongly, he did not succeed. It is known, however, that at a dinner party a few weeks after Suez was dead and buried he said to two total strangers in his naïve and engaging way: 'Do you think I ought to have resigned over Suez?' His interlocutors were taken aback since they were wholly unaware of any differences between him and the Prime Minister.

There was a third resignation, on a lower level. It was that of Mr. William Clark, the Prime Minister's adviser on public relations. Some people doubted whether the Prime Minister had been wise from his own point of view when he made this appointment on his arrival at 10 Downing Street. Mr. Clark is an able and vigorous journalist who had also worked for many years as a broadcaster and as an information officer, and for the previous four years as Foreign Editor of the *Observer*. He had long held markedly left-wing views, and though the job at No. 10 was concerned with Government and not with party propaganda, some of Sir Anthony's friends thought that the appointment was ill-judged. Politicians of both parties when they come to office inherit civil servants who have been long trained in the suppression and indeed the oblivion of their own partisan opinions. They have schooled themselves to do their duty faithfully by politicians of either party. For a Minister to introduce into the Civil Service someone from outside its ranks who had long held opinions directly opposed to himself seemed to present an unnecessary risk and to impose an almost superhuman act of self-discipline on the appointee.

No assessment of the rights and wrongs of the Suez story can even be tentatively formed without bearing in mind the fact that Sir Anthony was a sick man throughout the crisis. We have already seen how less than a month before the attack on Suez he was suddenly and mysteriously seized by a chill and high fever while visiting Lady Eden at University College Hospital. In 1953 he had suffered from a renewed attack of the persistent jaundice which had often troubled him. In the same year he was three times operated upon, twice in England and once in Boston, Massachusetts, for disorders arising from the gall bladder. The Boston operation was a great deal more successfully carried out than the two previous ones in England, and for the next year he was in much better health than he had been for some time. But at the end of 1954 he was temporarily laid aside with a chill, in 1955 had two attacks of influenza, and at the end of the year another chill.

Courage, both physical and moral, is something which Sir Anthony has never lacked in peace or war, and even those who feel most strongly that he must bear the main responsibility for the mismanagement of British policy at this time cannot withhold an honourable salute to a man who, in the grip of recurrent pain, worked himself unsparingly to the verge of the grave doing his duty as he saw it with selfless devotion. Sir Anthony's ill health must nevertheless be reckoned as a national, no less than a personal, tragedy. Some may doubt whether he possessed the qualities and fibre necessary for the handling of this crisis, even if he had been in good health. But with these bodily infirmities, he was certainly incapable of discharging the role which he had chosen to play. His colleagues in the Cabinet were much more aware of how the strain was affecting him than were his colleagues in the House of Commons, and all bear testimony that he could not have maintained the brave front he did without the passionate loyalty and devotion of his wife.

As has been made clear on several occasions in this narrative no pretence is made that this is the last word on the Suez story. It has not been without many poignant emotions that the facts so far as they can presently be known have been set out with all the fidelity and objectivity of which the author is capable. No one can study the career of Sir Anthony Eden—his careful, well-ordered rise, his sudden catastrophic fall—without sympathy and sorrow. But it would be wrong to allow emotional sympathy for the spectacle of a blasted career to outweigh the incomparably greater damage done to the nation. Britain's misfortunes were bound up with the personal tragedy. And the main justification of the writing of contemporary history is that folly may be exposed, that the lesson may be learned and that wiser counsels may prevail in the future.

We have referred above to the ill health which dogged Sir Anthony and which certainly affected his judgment and conduct during the Suez crisis. But there are grounds for thinking that even if there had been no Suez crisis and even if Sir Anthony had been granted better health, he would not long have endured as Prime Minister. Well before the Suez crisis many of his colleagues were beginning to doubt whether he had the firmness of mind, the moral stamina, the breadth of vision essential to a British Prime Minister in these contracting years; but this is all in the world of surmise. Sir Anthony was soon to pass from the political scene. The British people have extended to him in his misfortunes, in which they have largely shared, a generous and forgiving comprehension and can console themselves with the reflection that Sir Anthony's friend Mr. Macmillan was standing by to take over; and that the consequences of the ineptitude and maladress of the Suez operation have not in the end proved as costly and disastrous as seemed almost inevitable on the morrow of that ill-starred venture.

★

The British Government had capitulated over Suez on November 6. It was announced from 10 Downing Street on November 22 that the Prime Minister, on the advice of his doctors, would spend a three weeks' holiday in Jamaica. He returned from Jamaica on December 14. On January 8 he went down to Sandringham and, on the following day, tendered his resignation to the Queen, who had travelled up to London in his wake so as to be at Buckingham Palace to receive it. The next day the Queen, contrary to what most people had expected, sent for Mr. Harold Macmillan rather than Mr. R. A. Butler and invited him to form an Administration. He accepted.

Mr. Antony Head and the Author

I N November and December 1958 the six concluding
chapters of this book were published in a necessarily
abbreviated form in the *Daily Express*. They led to some
factious and factitious controversy. At this time it is not
necessary to revive these disputations save for the purpose of
putting on record a speech made in the House of Commons
by Mr. Antony Head, who had been Secretary of State for
War and subsequently Minister of Defence during the Suez
crisis, and of the reply which the author made in the *Daily
Express* of December 18:

Consider the problem of seizing the Canal by military force
at very short notice. It could be done either from Suez or
Port Said, or both, or perhaps a landing from either side of
these areas. It is not worth my going into possibilities of doing
it from Suez, which is on the Cape route and outside the area
of our bases. That leads inevitably to Port Said and to those
who think that we might have landed round the port. I would
say that that country is singularly ill-adapted for doing so.
An operation plan was prepared for a frontal assault on Port
Said which, for all we knew, was a defended port. What does
one do if one mounts an operation to assault Port Said and
debouch from Port Said? I suggest to hon. Members that one of
the first things one does is to see what is opposed to one. To
the west of the Canal there was one armoured group and on
the other side of the Canal three armoured groups.

Many people have said categorically how slow this operation was and how it should have been done much more
quickly, but I have not yet heard a single suggestion as to how
it could have been done more quickly, except by an all-airborne operation to seize the Canal. I should like hon. Members
to consider for a moment whether, given almost unlimited

aircraft, they would have dropped airborne troops along the Canal and left them for six days—which I will explain in a moment—without support and with a large number of Egyptian tanks in the area.

There may be hon. Members who would accept that. All I can say is that after a great deal of consideration and all the responsible military advice, both British and French, that course was unanimously rejected. There may be those who say that they would have carried out an all-airborne operation. Very well. But it would have been a bold man whose ultimate responsibility it would have been to undertake an airborne operation against all military advice and probably with the resignation of those military advisers who had been overruled. There may be arguments the other way, but, personally, I am absolutely convinced that to have done that would have been a most risky and unwise measure which would have risked a very large number of lives.

I remind hon. Members of one further fact. At the very start, when we pushed the button and decided on the operation, there was in existence a well-manned Egyptian Air Force —and when I say 'well-manned' I do not necessarily mean by Egyptians—which might have inflicted very serious damage on the slow-flying aircraft which bring in airborne troops.

If hon. Members have followed as far as this, I would now point out that in this plan we were tied down to doing it with land forces—that is to say, with the necessary infantry and tanks to occupy the Canal Zone. Again, the critics, who, perhaps, have not thought this matter out very carefully, will ask why it did not happen more quickly. Any hon. Member who has made a study of the war, or operations of this kind, knows one thing for certain—that it is quite impossible to mount an operation comprising very large numbers of tanks and vehicles without a deep-water port. I do not believe that a single hon. Member would disagree with that.

The Suez operation was placed, so to speak, in a strait-jacket so far as how it was to be executed by the fact of our getting out of Egypt. Hon. Members opposite—I remember, because I had to make a speech on that occasion—were very much in favour of that move, but from the day we got out of Egypt the nearest deep-water port in the Eastern Mediterranean was Malta. Hon. Members may ask, 'Why not make one in Cyprus?' But, financially and from an engineering point of view, it was impracticable, and on that day the nearest deep-water port to Port Said was Malta.

The steaming distance for a ship from Malta is six days. If hon. Members follow me, therefore, this operation which has been so heavily criticized as being slow and a classic example of military ineptitude, was, unless we did an all-airborne operation, in a straitjacket in respect of its form. That strait-jacket was this. Push the button, give the order for it to take place and six days elapse before the order and the assault on Port Said (Hon. Members: 'Hear, hear.') I am talking about the criticism of ineptitude which has been made against our armed forces.

The operation has been compared with that of the Israelis. People said, 'Look at the Israeli operation, which was so fast, and then look at ours, which was so slow and so laborious.' The comparison between a seaborne operation and a land operation, with vehicles and tanks on a contiguous land frontier, is utterly irrelevant. The problems are in no way related. If one has a force ready on a contiguous land frontier one can motor through with great speed, but if one has the appalling problem of funnelling a force through the bottle-neck of a port, it is an utterly different matter, both in speed and in nature. Whatever hon. Members may think of this operation, therefore, its form was dictated by geography and ports——

MR. BEVAN: What the right hon. Member is saying apparently is that in a push-button operation of this sort it should have been realized that it would take six days for the bell to ring. Was not that known to the Government at the time?

MR. HEAD: Of course it was well known. Nobody could have planned any operation to take place without being aware of that fact. It should have been apparent to anybody who either studied or thought about the operation. As far as I know nobody has made any attempt to conceal that this was so. The right hon. Gentleman is looking for things which do not exist. In fact, very great pressure was, naturally, brought to bear to shorten that interval but no Government, no planner, and not even the right hon. Gentleman, can escape from the physical fact that that if you mount an operation from a deep-water port that interval of steaming time is inevitable.

I am saying that this almost unacceptable fact—and I am coming to the justification of the operation in a minute—had to be accepted because there was no alternative. The operation was planned and the air operation started and eliminated the Egyptian Air Force. That was a brilliant exploit by the Royal Air Force, and I should like the House to be aware of it and to recognize how well they did it.

It is true that the second target of the Royal Air Force was dictated by the inevitable delay of the arrival of the seaborne assault, and it was to beat up the Egyptian Army. The way in which they did that was exemplified by the fact that anybody in a military vehicle in Egypt got out and ran and anybody in a civilian vehicle motored on and was fairly sure he would not be hurt. That is another great tribute to the Royal Air Force, and that, too, was done by the Fleet Air Arm.

What was the next aspect of the plan? It was said that there should be an assault on Port Said, with minimum damage. An assault on a defended port is not an entirely easy matter, and everybody felt and said that this must be an example of what the Air Force could do towards the capture of the place with the minimum damage. I went to see General Keightley, not for the reasons reported by that very fine imaginative writer Mr. Randolph Churchill—who can be bracketed with Edgar Allan Poe for imagination—but to see whether the airborne drop could be made earlier to overcome the beach defences and eliminate the naval bombardment, which would inevitably cause more destruction at Port Said. That was done and the airborne drop went absolutely without a hitch, and was 100 per cent successful. The landing went in exactly on time and the objective was seized as planned. The follow-up went as planned. The debouching from the bottleneck of Port Said was going according to plan when the operation was stopped.

Let us pause there for a moment. The hon. Member for Dudley (Mr. Wigg) and many others have said 'There was a shortage of L.S.T.s and of supply aircraft', and both are mentioned in General Keightley's report. I admit that. If any blame falls on me I am willing to accept it, although there was a necessity to work quickly on the part of those responsible.

I would say to anybody who is critical of this operation that if we had had half as many supply aircraft again, it would not have altered the basic plan of this operation by one iota.

Mr. Strachey: Does the right hon. Gentleman not see that what he is proving by dilating on the 'military strait-jacket', as he called it, of this operation is that it was bound to produce the terrible disaster which it did produce, and that he is just proving that, and proving up to the hilt our case against the folly of the Government.'

Mr. Head: The Right hon. Gentleman is anticipating what I am about to say.

By explaining the problem of this operation, for which the forces and the chiefs of staff are being so much condemned, I am not condemning the Government, but going on to explain later the reasons for this decision. What I am at pains to do is to say something to explain that those military authorities who were responsible, the chiefs of staff and the planners, are not the half-witted, infatuated fools that they have been made out to be. I believe that to be an unnecessary slur on our military prowess and our military advisers. I say that this particular operation was extremely well planned and executed, within its limits, which, I have tried to explain, were fixed ones.

The assault succeeded 100 per cent, and the unloading of vehicles proceeded rather better than anticipated. When the report of surrender, not true, was announced in this House, I can remember to this day all the Order Papers that were waved. Supposing that surrender report had been correct, supposing that Nasser had surrendered, I do not think that we would have heard so much about the faults of the Suez operation, but one thing happened. It stopped. A few days would have been necessary to complete the occupation of the Canal Zone, but the operation was not completed.

It is not my business to go into that in this debate, but I would say that my right hon. Friend, Sir Anthony Eden, was a man who saw that the gradual infiltration and erosion by Communism into backward countries and elsewhere was a menace. He saw that if, at some time or another, this country did not make a stand, we should go down the slippery slope of infiltration. He saw the disadvantages of this operation, that it was in the 'straitjacket' to which the right hon. Gentleman referred; but he accepted those deficiencies and he saw them through during that period.

The operation was circumscribed by geography and the operational confines in which it had to be carried out. The Government knew of those problems and accepted them. The operation is now regarded as a failure. Why? (Hon. Members: 'Because it failed.') Because of its execution? Because of its planning? No—because it stopped. When we ask why it stopped, hon. and right hon. Gentlemen opposite have not, I think, an entirely clean sheet.

In my view, the tragedy is that the operation stopped. I would say that those responsible for military advice, for planning and for execution, did nothing wrong. In my view, Sir Anthony Eden was absolutely right in his decision.

This biography, or whatever it is called, which has been written about Sir Anthony Eden is a very peculiar document. I do not know what was the purpose behind Mr. Randolph Churchill's writing it. Mr. Churchill bears what is perhaps the most illustrious name in England today, and the very fact of his bearing that name gives a certain authority to his book. I would say that this life of Sir Anthony Eden, particularly those parts which have been published, is a smear not on Sir Anthony, but on Mr. Randolph Churchill as the son of our greatest statesman.

I believe that history, looking back, will regard this episode in Mr. Randolph Churchill's journalistic career as a disgrace to the proud name that he bears. I believe that what he has said about our forces and the incompetence and incapacity of the British power to act—which is the only matter I have dealt with tonight—will be condemned, but I know, also, that nothing will be condemned more than his attack on Sir Anthony Eden himself.

★

In the course of a graceless and unconvincing intervention in the House of Commons on Monday night, Mr. Antony Head, successively Secretary of State for War and Minister of Defence during the Suez crisis, is reported to have said:

'I went to see General Keightley (in Cyprus), not for the reason reported by that very fine imaginative writer Mr.

Randolph Churchill—he can be bracketed with Edgar Allan Poe for imagination—but to see whether the airborne drop could be made earlier, to overcome the beach defences and eliminate the naval bombardment, which would inevitably cause more destruction at Port Said. That was done and the airborne drop went absolutely without a hitch and was 100 per cent successful.'

The reason which I ascribed in the *Daily Express* of December 4 to Mr. Head's visit to Cyprus was to 'assure himself, and also the Cabinet, that the Anglo-French plans had been perfectly concerted. He accepted the final plan for a parachute descent on Port Said the following morning and returned home'.

It is strange that Mr. Head should accuse me of imagination. I had the good fortune to see him in London when I was *en route* from New York to Tel Aviv on the night of Sunday, November 4. He had returned earlier in the day from his seventeen-hour round trip by a Canberra aircraft to Cyprus. I find it difficult to believe that I imagined what Mr. Head told me that Sunday evening.

Of course it is possible that Mr. Head may not have given me the true or full explanation of his flight, but I find it impossible to accept the explanation he gives us now. I feel sure that his recollection is at fault.

The Anglo-French paratroop landings were made on Monday, November 5, shortly after 10 a.m. Egyptian time.

It is hard to see how Mr. Head, as he now claims, could have accelerated on Saturday night an airborne drop that was due in thirty-six hours.

Indeed (as is shown in General Keightley's dispatches) on the Sunday night, just twelve hours before H-hour, the Allied C.-in-C. in Cyprus received a message from London asking him to state the latest time which a decision would have to be made should a *postponement* of the airborne landings prove necessary.

Thus, if Mr. Head is correct in claiming that he accelerated the airborne landings, we are driven to the conclusion that under his original planning the paratroops would have landed after, instead of before, the seaborne troops—which seems a tactical absurdity unless he had been prepared to keep the troops who were already five days waterborne from Malta wallowing around indefinitely in the sea.

I have read Mr. Head's speech in *Hansard* with fascination. According to him the plan was perfectly executed. But was it the right plan? Mr. Head casts no light on this important point. It is here that history will linger, and ultimately pronounce.

The other fascinating argument in Mr. Head's speech is that he tells us the only thing that went wrong was that the operation was 'stopped'. But Mr. Head was a member of the Cabinet which (against the advice of the soldiers on the spot) 'stopped it'.

He casts no light whatever on the political imbroglio, to which he was a party, and which led to this stultification. His speech goes to show the dangers inherent in putting a military man in charge of generals, admirals and air marshals. Perilous enterprises such as Suez are best left in the hands of experienced, competent politicians. No one could possibly judge from Mr. Head's speech that he was a politician and would-be statesman; and that he was a consenting party to the abandonment of the Suez enterprise, for the planning of which he was so largely responsible.

Mr. Head was one of the numerous Ministers of the Suez period who had an opportunity of reading my articles before they came out. Unlike most of his erstwhile colleagues he availed himself of it. He made only one detailed complaint of inaccuracy. I sought to meet his point. He could, of course, on grounds of principle, have refused, as many others did, to comment at all.

I had supposed that Mr. Head was a friend of mine, and I am naturally taken aback that he should prefer to correct me publicly rather than privately.

What distresses me most, however, is that behind the privilege of Parliament he should think it proper to drag my family name into this controversy. Even if I had the protection of parliamentary privilege, I should not seek to animadvert on whether Mr. Head had added to or detracted from the lustre of the name he bears.

I do not like this sort of personal family smear. I shall content myself with saying that Mr. Head, as a Cabinet

Minister, had a political responsibility, of which he seems vacuously unaware, for deciding that several thousand British troops were landed in what proved to be a dead-end enterprise half-way down a causeway. I will only add this: Mr. Head, like all my other critics from the Foreign Office downwards, refuses to say in detail where I am wrong.

Letter to a Lady*

THANK you for your letter and for all the trouble you have taken in reading my Suez chapters. I was as grateful to you for your compliments as I was for your criticisms; though I doubt whether either are well judged.

You say you think it 'brutal' that the book should be published while Anthony is still alive; but he might easily live for many more years. Is it your view that in that event total silence should be observed on these grave matters?

If that is so, surely Anthony ought not to be writing about them himself? Did you think it 'brutal' of Lord Alanbrooke and General Kennedy to criticize my father while he is still alive? And in general do you think it honourable to wait till people are dead and cannot reply before you criticize their public conduct?

If all criticism is, at your behest, to be stifled until the grave, then one would encounter a set of critics who would say: '*De mortuis nil nisi bonum*' (or '*bunkum*' as someone wittily added)? Of course, I fully understand that the general view of the propertied classes is that practically nothing should be written about public events at all, at any time, lest it should have a disturbing effect on somebody or other.

You refer to what you call 'a more serious aspect'—collusion, but add that 'the British public . . . will comfort themselves by thinking it is only speculation on my part'. I am not sure whether the British public are quite as stupid as some politicians in both parties suppose. I was brought up on my grandfather's slogan: 'Trust the people'.

Of course, if the public are as stupid as you seem to think they are, there is all the greater need for enlightening them. Alternatively, you seem to make out a strong case for abolishing the very expensive system of compulsory free education which we have had for fifty years and which you think renders them incapable of discerning truth from falsehood.

* The 'Letter to a Lady' was published in the *Daily Express* of 6 December 1958.

Since you predict that on second thoughts no one will 'beleave [sic] it', I do not follow your subsidiary point that no harm 'will be done here (except to the Tory Party)'. If no one believes that I have written the truth how can it be harmful to anyone except myself?

You continue by opining that abroad 'it will be a different story . . . and that it will do considerable damage'. Why is this? Because foreigners are cleverer than our own fellow countrymen? Because they are more gullible, or because my credibility stands higher abroad than at home? The long and the short of it is that the truth will out, sooner or later. The trouble is that most people prefer lies to the truth. I consider truth the buckler of all other virtues, and that without it all other virtues are dross.

I would not have written at such length if I had not appreciated the trouble you had taken in reading the book, and if I did not think that you possessed a mind capable of reflecting on the foregoing and profiting from it.

Postscript

In January 1957 shortly after the Suez fiasco Mr. Paul Johnson of the *New Statesman* published a book entitled *The Suez War* (MacGibbon & Kee). I read Mr. Johnson's book at the time, but only in a cursory way. He made all sorts of statements which I thought implausible, without giving any authority for them.

Two years have passed since Mr. Johnson's book was published. I have just re-read it and I find that in almost every respect I have reached, after two laborious years, the same conclusions which he arrived at immediately after the event.

I think it is only right to salute him and recommend all my readers to read his book as well as mine.

R. S. C.

15 April 1959

Index

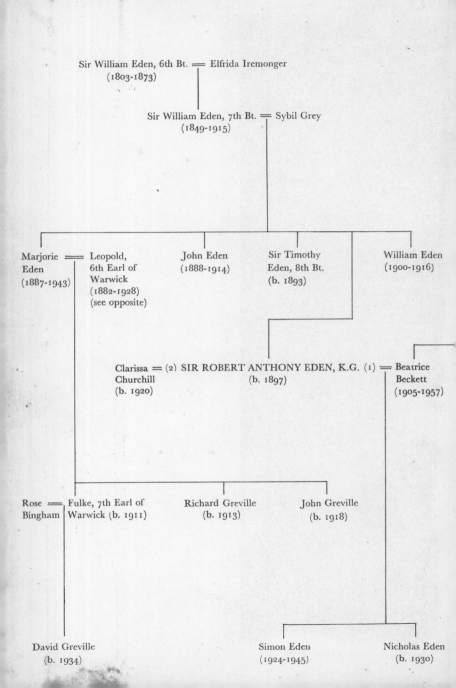